family **fh** **handyman**

WHOLE HOUSE
REPAIR
GUIDE

Whole House Repair Guide

Chief Content Officer, Home & Garden: Jeanne Sidner
Content Director: Mark Hagen
Creative Director: Raeann Thompson
Senior Art Director: Kristen Stecklein
Senior Designer: Anna Jo Beck
Deputy Editor, Copy Desk: Dulcie Shoener
Copy Editor: Sara Strauss
Associate Assigning Editor: Mary Flanagan
Contributing Editor: Kathy Childers

Text, photography and illustrations for *Whole House Repair Guide* are based on articles previously published in *Family Handyman* magazine (*familyhandyman.com*). For more information on advertising in *Family Handyman* magazine, call (646) 518-4215.

ISBN: 979-8-88977-026-8

We are committed to both the quality of our products and the service we provide to our customers. We value your comments, so please feel free to contact us at *TMBBookTeam@TrustedMediaBrands.com*.

For more *Family Handyman* products and information, visit our website *www.familyhandyman.com*.

A NOTE TO OUR READERS: All do-it-yourself activities involve a degree of risk. Skills, materials, tools and site conditions vary widely. Although the editors have made every effort to ensure accuracy, the reader remains responsible for the selection and use of tools, materials and methods. Always obey local codes and laws, follow manufacturers' operating instructions and observe safety precautions.

Printed in China
10 9 8 7 6 5 4 3 2 1

SAFETY FIRST–ALWAYS!

Tackling home improvement projects and repairs can be endlessly rewarding. But as most of us know, with the rewards come risks. DIYers use chain saws, climb ladders and tear into walls that can contain big, hazardous surprises.

The good news is that armed with the right knowledge, tools and procedures, homeowners can minimize risk. As you go about your projects and repairs, stay alert for these hazards:

Aluminum wiring
Aluminum wiring, installed in millions of homes between 1965 and 1973, requires special techniques and materials to make safe connections. This wiring is dull gray, not the dull orange characteristic of copper. Hire a licensed electrician certified to work with it. For more information, go to *cpsc.gov* and search for "aluminum wiring."

Spontaneous combustion
Rags saturated with oil finishes, such as Danish oil and linseed oil, as well as oil-based paints and stains, can spontaneously combust if left bunched up. Always dry the rags outdoors, spread out loosely. When the oil has thoroughly dried, you can safely throw the rags in the trash.

Vision and hearing protection
Safety glasses or goggles should be worn whenever you're working on DIY projects that involve chemicals, dust or anything that could shatter or chip off and hit your eye. Also, sounds louder than 80 decibels (dB) are considered potentially dangerous. For instance, sound levels from a lawn mower can be 90 dB, and levels from shop tools and chain saws can be 90 to 100 dB.

Lead paint
If your home was built before 1979, it may contain lead paint, which is a serious health hazard, especially for children 6 years old or under. Take precautions when you scrape or remove it. Contact your public health department for detailed safety information or call 800-424-LEAD (5323) to receive an information pamphlet. Or visit *epa.gov/lead*.

Buried utilities
A few days before you dig in your yard, have your underground water, gas and electrical lines marked. Just call 811 or go to *call811.com*.

Smoke and carbon monoxide (CO) alarms
The risk of dying in a reported home-structure fire is cut in half in homes with working smoke alarms. Test your smoke alarms every month, replace batteries as necessary and replace units that are more than 10 years old. As you make your home more energy efficient and airtight, existing ducts and chimneys can't always successfully vent combustion gases, including potentially deadly carbon monoxide (CO). Install a UL-listed CO detector, and test your CO and smoke alarms at the same time.

Five-gallon buckets and window-covering cords
Anywhere from 10 to 40 children a year drown in 5-gallon buckets, according to the U.S. Consumer Products Safety Commission. Always store empty buckets upside down and ones containing liquid with the covers securely snapped.

According to Parents for Window Blind Safety, hundreds of children in the United States are injured every year after becoming entangled in looped window-treatment cords. For more information, visit *pfwbs.org*.

Working up high
If you have to get up on your roof to do a repair or installation, always install roof brackets and wear a roof harness.

Asbestos
Texture sprayed on ceilings before 1978, adhesives and tiles for vinyl and asphalt floors before 1980, and vermiculite insulation (with gray granules) all may contain asbestos. Other building materials made between 1940 and 1980 could also contain asbestos. If you suspect that the materials you're removing or working around contain asbestos, contact your health department or visit *epa.gov/asbestos* for information.

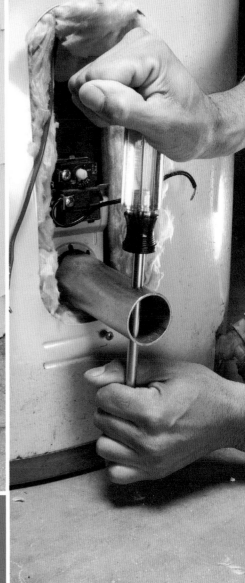

CONTENTS

Chapter One
DECKS & ROOFS

Chapter Two
ASPHALT & CONCRETE

Chapter **Three**
LANDSCAPE

Chapter **Four**
ELECTRICAL & PLUMBING

Chapter **Five**
HVAC

Chapter Six
TOOLS, APPLIANCES & EQUIPMENT

Chapter Seven
WALLS, CEILINGS & FLOORS

Chapter Eight
DOORS & WINDOWS

Chapter **Nine**
FURNITURE, CABINETS & COUNTERTOPS

Chapter **Ten**
PESTS

Special **Section**
PREVENTIVE MEASURES

CHAPTER **ONE**

DECKS & ROOFS

Deck Revival

Upgrade your decking and railings with manufactured boards to make an old deck better than ever.

Are you tired of looking at your worn-out deck? If the framing is in good shape, leave it in place and just replace the old decking and railing. Not only will your deck look better than the original but it will virtually last forever with no maintenance except an occasional cleaning. Our deck was just nine years old, but the railing was warped, and the decking was weathered and cracked. We decided to scrap the treated lumber and upgrade both the decking and the railing to maintenance-free products available at home centers. This is a project a DIYer with intermediate skills can easily tackle.

1. BE PREPARED FOR STRIPPED SCREWS

If the old decking is held down by screws, you're bound to strip a few of them trying to remove them, so buy a screw extractor before you get started. The one shown here is a Grabit, but there are other brands.

Just bore out the inside of the screw head with the burnishing end of the bit, then flip the bit around and back out the screw. As the bit turns counterclockwise, it digs down into the screw head, creating a very strong connection.

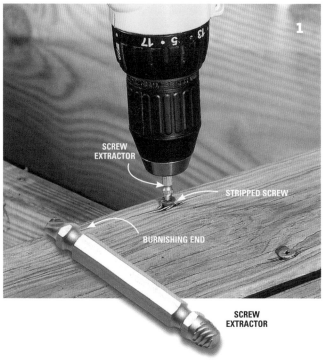

SCREW EXTRACTOR

STRIPPED SCREW

BURNISHING END

SCREW EXTRACTOR

CHALK LINE

2A   TOP OF JOIST

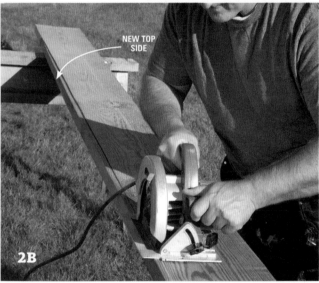

NEW TOP SIDE

2B

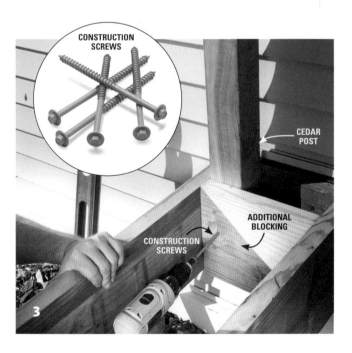

CONSTRUCTION SCREWS

CEDAR POST

ADDITIONAL BLOCKING

CONSTRUCTION SCREWS

3

2. STRAIGHTEN BOWED JOISTS

Wood decking is stiff and tends to flatten out the deck, even if joists are bowed. Manufactured decking isn't nearly as rigid as wood, so before you lay down the new decking, check the joists for flatness. Stretch a string or chalk line across the joists at the middle of the deck. You may need to put a spacer under each end of the string to raise it above the joists. Measure the distance between the string and each joist.

If some joists are bowed way up (more than 1/4 in.), snap a chalk line from the top of one end of the joist to the top of the other, then either plane down to the line or grab your circular saw and cut along it. If a joist is bowed down in the middle, you'll have to pull some nails and remove it from the deck. Straighten the edge and reinstall it with the straightened edge up. Some of the joists on this project were bowed more than 1 in.

3. BRACE YOUR RAILING POSTS

If you want super sturdy posts, install additional blocking. This is especially important if your balusters aren't going to be attached to the deck framing. The 5-in. construction screws we chose (the brand is LedgerLOK) are made for treated lumber and don't require predrilling. We suggest buying cedar posts. Posts made from treated lumber can warp as they dry and wreck your new composite railings.

4. ADD JOIST BLOCKING

If your joists span more than 8 ft., install blocking between the joists. Blocking holds joists straight and adds stiffness to a bouncy deck. It also allows each joist to share the impact of footsteps with neighboring joists and reduces "deflection," or flexing. Snap a chalk line at the center of the longest span of the deck framing perpendicular to the joists, and install blocks made from the same size material. Stagger the blocks along the chalk line so you'll be able to drive the nails or screws straight in from the other side of the joist.

5. TAPE THE JOISTS

Install flashing tape to cover the old joists. If you don't cover them, water will get trapped in the nail/screw holes and rot the wood from the inside out. You can use tape designed for doors and windows or one for decks. Avoid buying white or shiny silver tape—it may be noticeable in between the deck boards. Flashing tape isn't cheap. We used a product called Barricade from a local lumberyard. To save money, you could cut the tape in half to double the coverage.

6. BEEF UP THE STAIRS

When replacing wood decking with maintenance-free decking, you may have to add a stringer to the stair framing (check your manufacturer's specifications). The distance a deck board can span is less on stairs. That's because the force from stepping down onto a stair tread is much greater than the force from just walking around on the deck. Carefully dismantle the stairs, and use one of the old stringers as a pattern for the new one. Space the stringers at equal intervals and reassemble.

7. TRIM OFF THE DECKING AFTER INSTALLATION

Cut the first and the last deck boards to length before you install them, but run the rest of them long. Snap a line between the two trimmed end boards and cut along the line with a circular saw. The fascia board will fit nice and snug against the decking if you let the deck boards run about 1/16 in. past the joist.

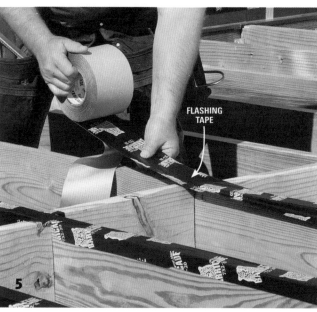

8. REPLACE THE FLASHING

We removed the existing flashing on this deck because it was aluminum, which corrodes when it comes into direct contact with treated lumber. We replaced it with a galvanized steel product designed specifically for deck ledger boards.

You'll need to remove a couple of courses of siding to make this happen, but it's a small price to pay to keep water out of your house. Tape the top of the new steel flashing with a flashing tape designed to seal windows and doors or a tape designed for decks. If your house wrap ends at the ledger board and isn't installed behind it, install the flashing under the house wrap and tape the house wrap to the flashing.

9. USE PLENTY OF SCREWS ON THE FASCIA

Wide PVC and composite fascia boards expand and contract more than regular wood, so they need a lot of fasteners to keep them from becoming distorted. We held the fascia board on with three colored deck screws at the ends and two every 12 in. in the field.

10. USE HIDDEN FASTENERS FOR A CLEAN LOOK

We ordered boards with a groove on each side so we could use the Hideaway Universal Hidden Fasteners from Trex. A pack of 90 clips will finish 50 sq. ft. of decking. This system requires you to partially install clips on both sides of the board before permanently tightening the side that butts the installed boards. These clips are self-gapping, and installation is quick and easy.

NEW FLASHING

FLASHING TAPE

LEDGER

8

FASCIA BOARD

9

FASTENING CLIPS

GROOVE

FASTENING CLIPS

10

Prep Your Deck for New Stain

Spend the time needed to properly remove old stain to ensure the new finish looks great and lasts.

If the stain on your deck is weathered and peeling, you can renew the finish with a few simple steps, starting with removing all the old stain. Solid-color stains protect wood decks and look great when new, but even the best begin to flake and wear away eventually. At that point they need to be completely removed before the deck can be recoated.

First, scrape off as much of the old finish as you can with a paint scraper. As you scrape the wood, reset any nails or screws that stick out from the wood surface.

Next, strip the deck with deck stain remover (1 gallon covers 100 sq. ft.). Tape plastic over nearby siding, and cover or wet down bushes and grass around the deck. Then spread a heavy coat of stain remover over the stained boards. Coat 20 to 30 sq. ft. at a time, keeping the wood wet until the finish is soft enough to be scrubbed off with a stiff brush **(Photo 1)**. Rinse the residue off with a hose and allow the deck to dry. Use a stripping disc on areas that are heavily discolored or covered with traces of residual stain **(Photo 2)**. The rough discs work much faster than belt or orbital sanders. They're available for both angle grinders (the fastest option) and drills (much slower).

Finally, apply a deck brightener/conditioner **(Photo 3)** to neutralize the stain remover and to clean and restore the wood to something close to its original color. One gallon covers roughly 200 sq. ft.

After the wood dries, restain or apply a clear penetrating finish. Clear finishes show more of the wood's natural color but must be reapplied every year. Solid stains protect the wood longer but can be a pain to scrape off. Penetrating stains also need to be reapplied more frequently, but unlike solid stains, they don't need to be stripped off before renewal.

STIFF BRUSH

WET FINISH REMOVER

1 GET THE OLD STAIN OFF. Give the finish remover 15 to 30 minutes to soften the old stain, then scrub off the old stain using a stiff brush.

COARSE STRIPPING PAD

ANGLE GRINDER

2 GRIND THE TOUGH SPOTS. Sand off rough spots on the deck or in small areas with a coarse stripping pad on a grinder or drill.

CONDITIONER DILUTED WITH WATER

3 CONDITION THE DECK. Brush on a brightener/ conditioner diluted with water. Scrub the deck and rinse it thoroughly to restore the original wood color.

Tips for Maintaining Your Chimney

Take steps today to preserve the integrity of your chimney and avoid costly repairs later.

Most homeowners never think about masonry chimney maintenance beyond the occasional flue cleaning. But ignoring your chimney can cost you big time. A cracked crown or spalling bricks can be expensive to repair.

It doesn't have to be that way. By simply sealing the bricks and the crown and adding a chimney cap, you'll greatly extend your chimney's life. And you can complete all three procedures in just a few hours. You'll have to climb up on your roof a couple of times, and you must be able to safely reach the chimney crown from your roof. If you can't reach the chimney crown, have a very steep roof pitch or aren't comfortable working on a roof, call a pro. If you decide you can handle the heights, make sure you wear a safety harness.

START AT THE CHIMNEY CROWN

Masonry chimneys are capped with a mortar "crown" to prevent water from getting behind the bricks, alongside the flue and into the house. Over time, normal expansion and contraction cycles can cause cracks to form. Sealing the chimney crown with crown sealer, a flexible elastomeric coating, is the best way to stop existing cracks from spreading and to prevent new ones.

Choose a clear or overcast day for the project (no rain in the forecast for at least four hours). Prepare the crown by cleaning it with a stiff poly or nylon brush. Fill any large cracks with patching cement or 100% silicone caulk (either will cure even after you apply the crown sealer).

Next, wrap duct tape all around the crown about 1/4 in. below the edge of the crown-to-brick seam. Press the tape into the vertical brick joints. Then tape around each flue liner 1 in. above the crown. Lay canvas (not plastic) tarps around the base of the chimney to protect the shingles from crown sealer drips.

Apply crown sealer by hand so you can force it into cracks and get the first coat done quickly. Slip on a disposable glove and apply the sealer (one brand is Chimney RX Brushable Crown Repair; see **Photo 1**). Cover the entire crown and then smooth it with a paintbrush **(Photo 2)**. Wait until the sealer dries tacky to the touch, then apply a second coat with a brush. Clean up with water.

SEAL THE BRICKS

Once the crown sealer feels dry to the touch (30 to 60 minutes), remove the duct tape but leave the roof tarps in place. Then mask off any painted chimney flashings before applying water repellent to the bricks (one brand is Chimney RX Masonry Chimney Water Repellent). Use a low-pressure garden pump sprayer **(Photo 3)**.

FINISH IT OFF WITH A CHIMNEY CAP

A chimney cap keeps water and critters out of your flue and extends flue life. Many codes require a mesh cap, so check before buying. Chimney expert Jim Smart recommends spending extra to get a stainless steel cap because it will last much longer than the galvanized type. One source for stainless steel caps is efireplacestore.com.

You'll need the outside dimensions of the flue liner to get the right size cap for your chimney. Then install it on the flue liner **(Photo 4)**.

2 EVEN OUT THE FIRST COAT. Stroke the wet sealant with a brush to level the high and low spots and create a smooth surface.

3 SEAL THE BRICKS WITH WATER REPELLENT. Start at the bottom of the chimney and spray the brick until the excess repellent runs down about 8 in. below the spray line. Work your way up to the top. Apply a second coat within five minutes using the same technique.

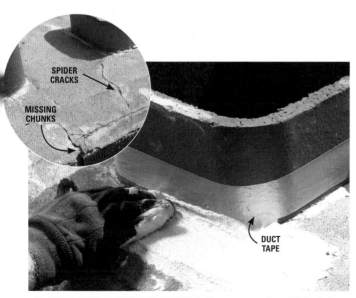

1 SEAL THE CHIMNEY CROWN. Scoop up a handful of the sealer and wipe it onto the crown. Force the sealant into the cracks and into the crown-to-brick seam.

4 INSTALL A CHIMNEY CAP. Set the cap over the flue liner and secure it with screws. Tighten until snug, but no more. Excessive pressure can crack the clay liner.

1 SOAK THE SHINGLES. Saturate a large area of shingles with the cleaner. Start at the bottom row and work up to the peak. Spray until you see runoff. Respray any areas that dry out.

Wash Off Ugly Roof Stains

If your roof isn't too steep and you're comfortable working on it, you can clean it yourself and save the cost of hiring a pro.

Black streaks on the north- and west-facing parts or on the shaded areas of your asphalt-shingled roof can really wreck the appearance of your home. The streaks look like mold, but they're actually algae colonies that form and feed on moisture and limestone filler agents in the shingles.

Using shingles that have been treated with algicide keeps the growth at bay for about 10 years (thus the 10-year algae warranty found with some shingles). But once the algicide wears off, your roof hosts an all-you-can-eat buffet for the neighborhood algae spores. As the algae eat away at the limestone, they dig into the asphalt and dislodge the light-reflecting granules. That's the beginning of the end of your roof, so it pays to clean your shingles as soon as you spot algae growth.

You'll need a full-body harness, a garden sprayer, a garden hose and a nontoxic, noncorrosive roof-cleaning chemical. Some manufacturers sell a special rinsing tool, but if the staining on your roof isn't too severe, you may not need it.

CHOOSE THE RIGHT CHEMICALS

If you search online, you'll see hundreds of posts on roof-cleaning methods. In less than 10 minutes, you'll sign off convinced that all you need is a few gallons of household bleach and a power washer on its lowest setting.

We don't recommend that approach. Even at low pressure, a power washer can seriously damage shingles. Plus, chlorine bleach is a corrosive agent that can damage metal roof flashings, gutters and downspouts. It can lighten the color of your roof and "bleach" anything the overspray contacts. Also, the runoff harms plants. But here's the kicker: Bleach may kill the top layer of algae and lighten the stains, but it doesn't kill the underlying algae. So the algae colony gets right back to work, growing and damaging your roof.

Sodium hydroxide (lye) products, on the other hand, work better than bleach and are less harmful to vegetation. But they're also corrosive, and using them requires you to don full protective gear.

Look for a roof-cleaning product that's noncorrosive and safe for the environment. We used Defy roof cleaner, but there are other brands.

CHOOSE THE RIGHT DAY AND PREP THE WORK AREA

Check the weather forecast and choose a cool or overcast day with little to no wind so the spray hits your shingles, not the neighbors' houses. Those conditions are also ideal to allow the cleaning solution to soak deep into the algae colonies without it evaporating too quickly.

Next, repair any loose shingles or flashings, and clean the gutters and downspouts so they can drain freely.

Then prepare the area by moving lawn furniture and covering vegetation, because you're going to have overspray. Even though the product we chose isn't toxic, the runoff can be pretty ugly. A little prep work saves cleanup later.

THE CLEANING PROCESS

Mix the product with water for a 1:7 dilution ratio (a gallon covers about 700 to 900 sq. ft.). Pour it into a pump sprayer, strap yourself into a full-body harness, tie it down and climb up on the roof.

Before applying the cleaner, spray the roof with water to cool it down. That'll prevent the cleaner from drying out too quickly. Then spray the cleaner onto the shingles (**Photo 1**). Wait about 20 minutes, then rinse.

If the staining is fairly light, you can rinse off the cleaning solution with just a garden hose sprayer. But go slowly and

HARNESS

TIE-DOWN

SPECIALIZED
RINSING TOOL

2 BLAST OFF THE CRUD. For severely stained roofs, a garden nozzle may not be effective. Instead, you can use a specialized rinsing tool. These tools have enough power to blast off the dead algae colonies.

use even strokes. If you don't, you'll wind up with clean patches that were rinsed properly alongside dirty patches that were skipped over too quickly. For severely stained roofs, a garden nozzle won't exert enough pressure to dislodge the stains. In that case, you'll want to invest in a specialized rinsing tool **(Photo 2)**.

PREVENT REGROWTH

Depending on weather conditions, you can expect algae regrowth in as little as one year. There are two ways to slow the regrowth process. One is to install zinc or copper strips along the entire ridge of the roof. Theoretically, rainwater picks up algae-killing ions from the strips and spreads them over the roof. But, in reality, the protection falls short

because algae can still feed off humidity when it's not raining. Still, you don't have a lot to lose by trying it and, depending on your situation, it may work.

The second method is to spray on a coating of stain-blocking solution (Defy Stain Blocker for Roofs is one product, but there are other brands). A stain-blocking product can buy you up to three years of protection from algae. If you decide to try it, make sure you apply it shortly after you've cleaned the roof.

Whether you install the metallic strips or apply a stain-blocking solution, you're still going to experience algae regrowth sometime down the road. Plan to get back up on your roof and clean it when you notice the algae so the stains don't set in permanently.

Replace a Rain Cap

It's an easy repair that takes very little time.

High winds, sleet and plain old corrosion can cause a rain cap on a flue pipe to break apart, rattle and leak water into your home. If you feel comfortable climbing up on your roof and can access the flue, you can replace the old one yourself. Make sure you wear a safety harness.

You can buy a new rain cap and a sheet metal crimping tool at any home center. Flues are usually 5 or 6 in. in diameter, so buy both size caps and return the unused one. You'll also need three hex-head or Phillips self-drilling 1-in. sheet metal screws and a drill and bit.

Remove the old rain cap and toss it. Select the correct cap and check the fit **(Photo 1)**. Then use the screws to secure the new cap **(Photo 2)**.

1 CHECK AND ADJUST THE RAIN CAP'S FIT. Slide the new cap into the flue. If the stub section on the cap is too large, crimp it with a crimping tool.

2 LEVEL AND SECURE THE CAP. Plumb the cap so it fits squarely in the flue. Secure it with one sheet metal screw. Recheck the cap for plumb; install two more screws.

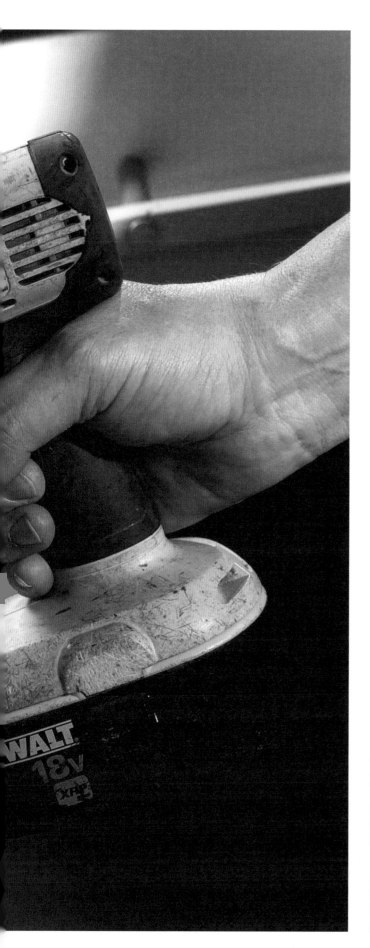

Nine Easy Gutter Fixes

With basic tools and some accessories, you can repair most gutter problems yourself, preserving your home and saving money.

Gutters can help keep a basement dry, prevent landscaping from washing away and add decades to the life of a foundation. But if they're not working correctly, they can be a major headache. Here are DIY solutions to the most common gutter problems.

1. LOOSE GUTTERS

THE FIX: BETTER BRACKETS

Years ago, spikes and ferrules were a common method for hanging gutters. They do the job all right, but eventually the spikes work themselves loose. Pounding them back in is a temporary fix at best.

One way to make sure your gutter doesn't fall off the house is to install fascia hanger brackets. Installation is simple: Just hook the bracket under the front lip of the gutter, and then screw the other side of the bracket to the fascia. Leave the old spikes in place—a spike head looks better than a hole in the gutter.

If your shingles overhang your fascia by a few inches or you have steel roofing, buy the brackets with the screws built in (the type shown here). They cost more, but the head of the screw remains a couple of inches away from the fascia, making the brackets a lot easier to install.

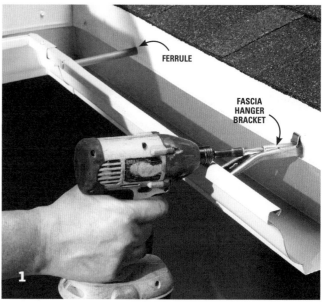

FERRULE

FASCIA
HANGER
BRACKET

2. SIDEWALK IN THE WAY
THE FIX: A ROLLOUT SPOUT

There is no perfect way to get water from one side of a sidewalk to the other, but consider installing a retractable downspout. It rolls out when it rains and then rolls back up when the water stops flowing. Products such as these do leak when the water flow is too light to extend the plastic downspout, but they should keep your landscaping from washing away during moderate to heavy rains.

Retractable downspouts are super easy to hook up, and for very little money, they might be just the solution you're looking for. Pick one up at a home center or order online.

3. GUTTERS OVERFLOW
THE FIX: A LARGER DOWNSPOUT

If you have a 50-ft. gutter with one 2 x 3-in. downspout, your gutter probably overflows during heavier rainfalls. When installing an additional downspout isn't an option, install a 3 x 4-in. downspout in place of the smaller one.

Start by removing the old downspout. Use the new 3 x 4-in. drop outlet that you buy with your new downspout as a template to trace an outline for the larger hole. You can cut out the larger hole with a tin snips, or you could use an oscillating multitool equipped with a metal-cutting blade. Insert the drop outlet in the hole and fasten the new downspout with sheet metal screws. Make sure to seal the drop outlet to the gutter with seam sealer. If you need a color other than white or brown, you should be able to special order it.

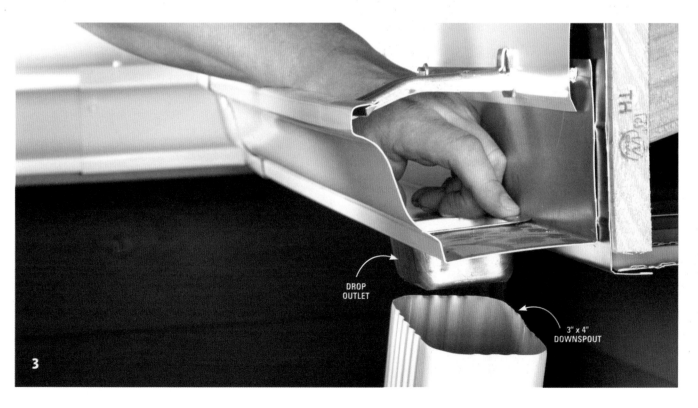

DROP
OUTLET

3" x 4"
DOWNSPOUT

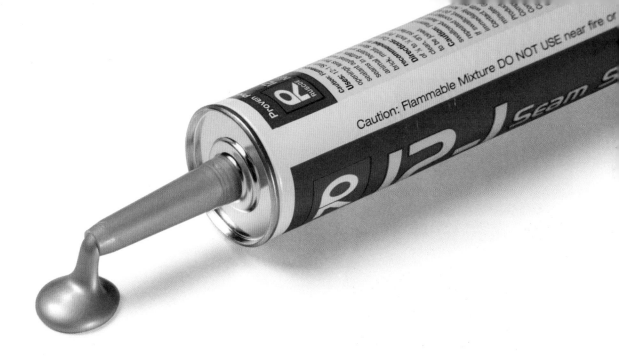

4

4. LEAKY GUTTERS

THE FIX: SEAL THE SEAMS

Every connection on a metal gutter needs to be sealed: end caps, splices, drop outlets and miters. Buy a product that's specifically formulated to seal gutter seams. Seam sealer can handle submersion for long periods of time. It's also resistant to light, of which it will get plenty.

Most important, high-quality seam sealer is runny so it can penetrate down into the seam for a durable, long-lasting connection. Most products refer to this property as "self-leveling." And the runnier the better, so if you're applying it on a cold day, keep the seam sealer somewhere warm so it stays fluid.

Try to remove as much of the old sealer as you can, and make sure the area you're sealing is completely dry. Home centers usually stock seam sealer near the gutter parts.

5. WATER GETS BEHIND THE GUTTERS

THE FIX: INSTALL NEW FLASHING

If water is dripping behind your gutter, it's probably because the gutter was installed without any flashing over the back. Gutter apron will prevent the dripping.

Gutter apron is a bent piece of flashing that tucks up under the shingles and over the gutter. Home centers sell 10-ft. sections of it. You may have to temporarily remove your hangers as you go, or you can notch out the apron around them. Once the apron's in place, fasten it securely with sheet metal screws.

If there's a drip edge installed where the fascia meets your shingles and the gutter is hung below the drip edge, get some roll flashing and tuck it up under the drip edge and over the top of the gutter. Home centers sell rolls of 6-in. x 10-ft. aluminum flashing. Use tin snips to cut the roll in two 3-in. strips. If your gutters are steel, buy steel roll flashing because galvanized steel corrodes aluminum.

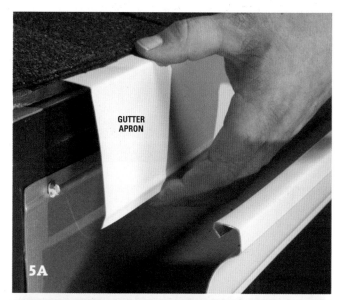

GUTTER APRON

5A

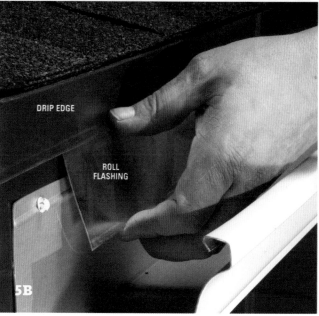

DRIP EDGE

ROLL FLASHING

5B

HINGE

6

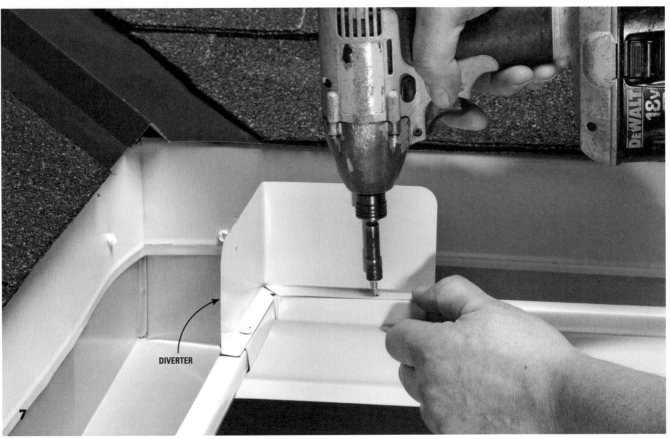

DIVERTER

7

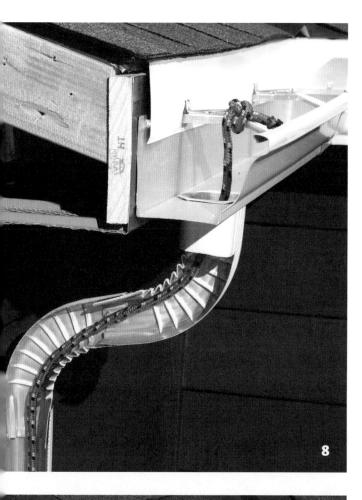

6. DOWNSPOUTS IN THE WAY

THE FIX: ADD SOME HINGES

Are you tired of removing your downspouts every time you mow? Consider installing a hinge where the lowest elbow meets the section of downspout that runs into your yard.

We used a brand called Zip Hinge. Installation is simple: Just cut the downspout at a 45-degree angle with tin snips or a metal-cutting blade and fasten the two-piece hinge with eight sheet metal screws. The hinges, sold online, come in white only, so you might have to spray-paint them to match.

7. WATER SPILLS OVER GUTTER

THE FIX: ADD A DIVERTER

Some roofs have long sections of valley that carry a lot of rainwater at high velocity. When that water comes blasting out the end of the valley, it can shoot right over the gutter. A diverter will help direct the water back into the gutter where it belongs. Fasten a diverter to the top of the outside edge of the gutter with a couple of sheet metal screws. We used a brand called Gusher Guard, sold at home centers and online.

8. ANNOYING DRIPS

THE FIX: DROP IN A ROPE

Is the sound of dripping in your downspouts driving you mad? Eliminate the problem by tying a rope onto one of the gutter hangers and running it into the downspout. Drops of water will cling to the rope instead of plummeting the whole length of the downspout and causing that loud dripping noise.

Adding a rope does restrict water flow, so this may not be the best option if your gutter is prone to overflowing or if your downspout is easily clogged with twigs and leaves. Buy a rope made of a synthetic such as nylon—a rope made from natural fibers will rot away.

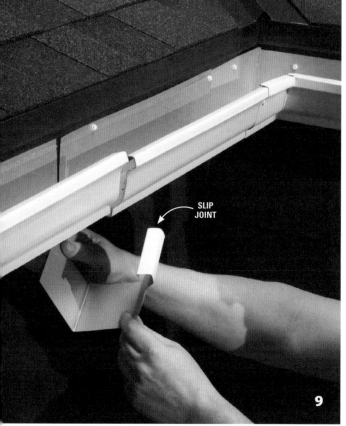

SLIP JOINT

9. NO SLIP JOINT

THE FIX: MAKE YOUR OWN!

If a tree branch falls on the last 4 ft. of your 60-ft. seamless gutter, you don't need to replace the whole thing—just replace the damaged section. If your gutters are white or brown, adding a section of gutter to an existing section is easy. Most home centers sell white and brown sections of gutters as well as slip joints to tie them together.

If your gutters are a custom color, a home center can special-order your color but not the slip joint to match. Don't worry though. You can make your own from a box miter, and box miters are available in every color gutters are made.

When you buy your new gutter section, make sure you order either an inside or outside box miter at the same time. Cut a 3-in. section from the box miter with tin snips, and you've got yourself a custom slip joint. Hang the new gutter next to the old one, and then slide the patch under the seam.

CHAPTER TWO

ASPHALT & CONCRETE

How to Seal a Driveway

With the right materials on hand and these tips for preparation and application, you can restore asphalt and lengthen its life.

An asphalt driveway can last almost 30 years. But you can't achieve that long life span unless the driveway was installed properly and you perform regular maintenance, such as filling cracks annually and applying sealer when needed. We'll show you how to clean and prepare the driveway so you get the longest life and best protection from driveway sealer.

Preparation can take a full day (including drying time), and it's tedious. The application phase is much faster, taking only a few hours per coat for a typical driveway. Most sealer manufacturers recommend two coats with a minimum drying time of eight hours between coats, so this project will fill an entire weekend.

Using a power washer speeds the process, but you can do the job without it. You'll also need a squeegee or application brush, a broom, a drill, a mixing paddle, duct tape, a dashing brush and poly sheeting to protect painted surfaces.

BUYING THE RIGHT MATERIALS
Driveway sealer is available in various grades and price ranges. Some bargain products contain almost 50% water and have lower coverage rates and a correspondingly shorter guarantee, so they're not the most cost-effective solution over the long term. Use one of them if you're trying to spiff up the driveway before selling your home. Premium products, on the other hand, are made with higher-quality resins and UV stabilizers, and they contain filler and elastomeric material, so they'll last longer and carry a longer guarantee. Use them when you want to extend the life of your driveway.

Manufacturers also make different formulas for different driveway conditions: one formula for newer driveways in good condition and another formula for older driveways that haven't been well maintained. The two formulas also vary in their coverage, so read the labels carefully and choose the correct sealer and quantity for your particular driveway. Follow the manufacturer's directions for the type of applicator to use (brush or squeegee). Using the wrong one can cause premature failure.

You will also need liquid driveway cleaner/degreaser to remove oil and tree sap. If your driveway has visible oil stains, pick up a bottle of oil spot primer.

Driveway Sealers: Real Protection or Just Black Paint?

Some asphalt driveway companies tell their customers that driveway sealer is a waste of money, that it's cosmetic and doesn't do anything to extend the life of the asphalt.

It's true that driveway sealer can't replace the liquid asphalt (oil/tar) that oxidizes and bakes out of the mixture from heat and sun exposure. But a high-quality sealer can dramatically reduce future heat and UV damage. Plus, it seals the pores to prevent aggregate breakup damage caused by water penetration, freeze/thaw cycles and chemicals. So it really does extend the life of your driveway.

CHECK THE WEATHER BEFORE YOU START

You'll need at least two days of dry weather to seal your driveway. Temperatures must be above 50 degrees F during application and throughout the night. And it's best to avoid scorching-hot sunny days (the sealer may dry too fast). If you ignore the weather forecast, you may see hundreds of dollars worth of sealer wash away in a heavy rain.

START WITH CLEANING AND PRIMING

Even if you think your driveway is clean, trust us, it isn't. Exhaust gas contains combustion byproducts that deposit a light, sometimes oily film on your driveway. That film, along with dirt and tree sap, must come off if you want the sealer to stick. So clean the driveway first **(Photo 1)**.

Next, rinse the driveway with clear water **(Photo 2)**. Let the driveway dry completely before applying the sealer. Then perform a final sweep with a push broom. Treat any oil stains with an oil spot primer **(Photo 3)**.

MASK, STIR AND TRIM

Driveway sealer will splash onto your garage door and sidewalks as you pour it—and it'll get all over your shoes and clothes. It's very difficult (often impossible) to remove later, so wear old work clothes and shoes. Mask the garage door with poly sheeting and apply strips of duct tape to concrete walks where they butt up to the asphalt.

Choose an area on the driveway for mixing and cover it with poly sheeting to protect against spills (dried spills will show through the sealer). Remove the pail lids and cut a small hole in the center of one lid. Use that lid to prevent splashing during mixing. Stir until the mixture is smooth **(Photo 4)**.

Next, cut in all four edges of the driveway with a large dashing brush **(Photo 5)**. Clean the brush with soap and water as soon as you're done cutting in the edges—you'll need it again the following day. Then stage the pails equally down the driveway **(Photo 6)**.

1 **SOAP AND SCRUB. Use the soap nozzle on your power washer or a garden hose applicator to apply the driveway cleaner.** Then scrub the entire driveway with a stiff-bristle push broom.

2 **RINSE WITH A STRONG STREAM. Flush the soap and dirt residue with a 40-degree power washer nozzle or a strong stream of water from your garden hose.**

3 **PRETREAT THE OIL STAINS. Pour the oil spot primer on the damaged areas and brush it into the pores with a disposable chip brush.** Apply a second coat to heavier stains. Let the primer dry fully before applying the driveway sealer.

POUR AND SPREAD

Pour the sealer onto the driveway **(Photo 7)**. Then spread the puddle with a squeegee or broom, depending on the manufacturer's directions **(Photo 8)**. Pour enough sealer to maintain a puddle in front of the applicator tool.

When you reach the bottom of the driveway, cap the remaining pails and clean the squeegee or brush. Set the empty pails along the curb to prevent cars from ruining the job. Then let the sealer dry overnight.

Repeat the sealer application the next day. Let the sealer dry for 48 hours before driving on it (better safe than sorry). Don't ask how we learned that lesson.

4 MIX THE SEALER. Start the mixing paddle near the top of the pail and slowly lower it into the contents settled at the bottom. Cycle the mixing paddle up and down while it spins to combine the water and solids into a smooth consistency.

5 CUT IN THE EDGES. Dip the dashing brush into the sealer and apply a liberal coating of the sealer to all four edges of the driveway. Don't spread it too thin; you want it to fill in all the pores.

POLY SHEETING TO MASK DOOR

STAGED PAILS

6 STAGE THE PAILS. Guesstimate the coverage of each pail and stage each additional pail along the driveway. That saves time and reduces the need to walk through wet sealer to get the next pail.

Avoid These Common Driveway-Sealing Mistakes

- Depending on the sealer to fill cracks—it won't. Fill them properly before applying sealer.
- Failure to clean and prep the driveway before applying the sealer. If you don't want to spend time cleaning the driveway, you may as well skip the sealer too because it won't stick to a dirty driveway.
- Failure to stir properly. Do not depend on a stir stick. It simply won't blend the water and solids enough to get a consistent mixture.
- Use of the wrong applicator. Using a brush when the manufacturer specifies a squeegee (or vice versa) will cause premature failure.
- Applying sealer too often. Too much sealer will flake off. Wait until you begin to see asphalt aggregate before you apply a new coat of sealer.

7 POUR ONTO THE DRIVEWAY. Start at the top left or right edge of the driveway and pour the sealer in an upside-down U-shape pattern.

8 SPREAD THE SEALER. Start at one leg of the upside-down U. Apply even pressure to spread the puddle across the driveway and down along the opposite leg. Then pick up the excess sealer on the down leg and start the next row.

Patch Pitted Asphalt

Make this easy repair to keep a driveway in top condition.

Asphalt driveways can develop pitted areas from motor oil and coolant contamination and from repeated freeze/thaw cycles. If the pits are 1/2 in. or less, you can fill them with a spreadable filler product. (Latex-ite Trowel Patch is one choice available at home centers.)

Clean oil stains and prime with oil stain primer. Then coat entire pitted area with patch material and let it dry overnight **(Photo 1)**. Apply a second coat to top off any partially filled pits **(Photo 2)** and smooth the surface. Let dry.

1 FILL THE PITS. Force the filler material into the cracks and pits with a trowel. Then smooth the streaks with an old broom.

2 ENLARGE THE AREA AND SMOOTH. Pour more filler material onto the pitted area and spread it with a floor squeegee to smooth the surface.

Fix a Driveway Apron

Repair a sunken driveway yourself, saving you money and extending the life of the asphalt.

It's normal for asphalt driveways to sink a bit over time. But when your driveway has sunk to the point where it's 4 or 5 in. lower than your garage floor, it's time to fix it. If you don't, water will pool in the depression, seep into the soil below and eventually destroy the driveway.

Asphalt companies will charge a lot of money to dig out the old portion and install a new apron. Concrete contractors will charge even more. Or you can rebuild your asphalt driveway apron yourself. The entire job takes a full day and it's not much fun, but the materials and tools are affordable so the savings are worth it.

You'll need a diamond blade for your circular saw, a tamper, a pry bar and a short square-blade shovel. Plus, you'll need enough cold patch material to fill in the trench you make (one choice is Quikrete Asphalt Cold Patch, No. 1701-58). To figure out how many bags you'll need, refer to the depth and width tables on the bag. Finally, you'll need mineral spirits and rags for cleanup. Take the following steps to make the repair.

FIRST CHECK THE WEATHER

Cold patch cures by solvent evaporation, and it takes about 30 days to reach a full cure. The best time to do the project is during an extended warm, dry spell. You can do it in spring or fall, but cold weather and rain will greatly extend the time needed for it to cure.

WEAR OLD CLOTHES AND PROTECT YOUR CARPET

This is a messy job, and no matter how careful you are, you're going to get tar on your clothes and shoes. You can't wash off the tar with soap and water, so wear old clothes and

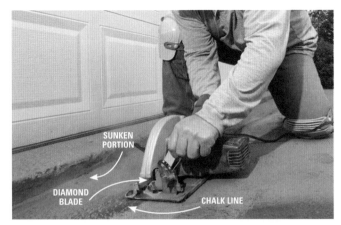

1 CUT OUT THE SUNKEN ASPHALT. Slap a diamond blade into your circular saw and set it to its maximum cutting depth. Then snap a chalk line out from the garage floor to a maximum distance of 24 in. Wear an N95 respirator and safety glasses; cut out the old asphalt.

2 PUT IN THE BOTTOM LAYER. Pour in a small amount of cold patch material and level it with a square-blade shovel. Tamp down a test section and measure the depth. The bottom layer should only be 1/2 in. thick when compacted. Add or remove cold patch material and then tamp down the entire starter row.

3 BUILD ADDITIONAL LAYERS. Add and compact the cold patch in 1-in. layers until you reach the garage floor. Then overfill with an additional 1/2 in. of material and tamp to get a smooth surface.

4 DRIVE OVER IT TO COMPACT. Cut a piece of plywood slightly wider than the trench. Lay it over the patch material and cover it with 2x4s. Then drive over it several times with your vehicle until the patch is level with the garage floor.

shoes that you can toss into the trash when you're done. If you have to go into the house during the project, leave your shoes outside so you don't track tar into the house.

CUT OUT THE SUNKEN AREA

Cold patch works only when it's compacted and "keyed" into at least two vertical surfaces, so don't think you can build up the driveway height by pouring cold patch on top of the old sunken asphalt—the patching material will just break off in chunks. Instead, cut out the sunken asphalt **(Photo 1)**.

After it's cut, lay a block of wood on the soil at the edge of the driveway, shove a pry bar under the old asphalt and pry against the wood block. The old asphalt will lift up and break off in sections. Remove all the cut asphalt and scrape off any caulking material sticking to the edge of the garage floor. Next, build a starter row of patch material **(Photo 2)**. Once

the starter row is in place and tamped, apply additional patch material in 1-in. layers **(Photo 3)**. Resist the temptation to completely fill the area and compact it in one fell swoop. You simply can't exert enough compaction force with a tamper to properly key it into the vertical surfaces—the patch material will just creep out the sides when you drive on it.

Once your tamped layers are level with the garage floor, add a final topping layer. Then lay down wood scraps and use your vehicle to do a final compaction **(Photo 4)**. Clean all your tools with mineral spirits and dispose of the rags properly to prevent spontaneous combustion.

The instructions on the patching material say you can drive over the patch immediately. But tires may still make slight depressions in the asphalt until it's fully cured, which takes 30 days. It's wise to leave the plywood in place for a few weeks at least.

Sidewalk Surgery

Replace crumbling concrete yourself and save money.

Concrete work is hard labor. But for small jobs, you can do it yourself—and for about one-third a contractor's cost.

Experience working with concrete isn't necessary, but you'll need tool know-how and a strong back. Follow the steps shown here. For more information on working with concrete and repairing sidewalks, search for "concrete" and "sidewalk repair" at familyhandyman.com.

What Happened?

This sidewalk is more than 80 years old and still in good shape—mostly. So what went wrong with this section? Most likely, it was excess water: The builders added too much water to the mix or misted the surface to make troweling easier. Or maybe rain came before the concrete cured. Any of these circumstances will make concrete weak, porous and destined to disintegrate.

1 DIG DITCHES. Dig trenches at least 6 in. wide and 6 in. deep along both sides of the sidewalk that's being repaired. These trenches will allow you to set up forms later for the new concrete.

WARNING
Use the blade guard. It was removed here for the purposes of photography.

2 CUT A CRACK STOP. When you break up the bad section, a cut that's at least 1-1/4 in. deep will prevent cracks from spreading to the good section. An existing groove in the concrete is usually the best place to cut. Cut with a diamond blade in a circular saw or an angle grinder.

MATTOCK

3 BUST UP THE BAD SECTION. A small section of sidewalk usually doesn't require a jackhammer rental; try a sledgehammer first. A mattock is perfect for prying up broken concrete. Remove the chunks.

FORM

4 PLACE THE FORMS. Select straight 2x4s for the forms and drive stakes every 24 in. Position the forms even with the adjoining sections of sidewalk, then drive screws through the stakes into the forms. The forms should feel rock-solid. If not, add more stakes.

5 TRIM OFF THE STAKES. Cut the stakes flush with the forms with a handsaw or recip saw. Then span the forms with a 2x4 and slide it along the length of the forms. It should slide smoothly without hitting obstructions.

TAMPER

6 PREPARE THE BASE. Set a 2x4 across the forms and measure to the soil or gravel below in several spots. Your goal is to achieve a 4-in.-deep space for concrete. You may need to add or remove material. Then compact the base with a hand tamper.

EXPANSION JOINT

7 ADD EXPANSION JOINTS. Tack expansion joint material (sold at home centers) to the existing concrete with 1-in. masonry nails.

SPRAY LUBRICANT

8 OIL THE FORMS. A "release agent" allows for easy form removal after the concrete has cured. Spray lubricant is fast, but you could also use a rag to wipe on any oil.

REBAR

CHAIR

9 **ADD REBAR.** Rebar isn't essential for sidewalks, but it adds strength and longevity. The 3/8-in. rebar and support "chairs" shown are inexpensive. Pin the new concrete to the old by drilling 3-in.-deep holes into the old concrete, inserting 16-in. sections of rebar and tying the rebar frame to the pins (Photo 10).

REBAR TIED TO PIN

10 **WET THE BASE.** Dry soil or gravel can absorb water and cause concrete to dry out quickly, before it has time to fully cure. Give the base a good dousing, but do not use enough water to create puddles.

WATER LEVEL

11 **MAKE A MEASURING BUCKET.** A strong, workable concrete mix contains just the right amount of water; follow the instructions on the bag. Measure the water into a bucket and mark that level on the bucket.

12 **MIX AND DUMP.** Consider renting a small concrete mixer. Aside from saving you some hard labor, it lets you mix faster so all your concrete is at the same stage in the curing process. That allows for a more consistent finish.

13 SCREED IT FLAT. Drag a 2x4 screed board over the forms as you add concrete and fill in any low spots. When the form is evenly filled, round up a helper for the final screed. With each of you holding one side of the screed board and making a sawing motion, screed off the entire length of fresh concrete.

14 FLOAT THE CONCRETE. Immediately after completing the final screed, smooth the concrete with a wood or magnesium float. Don't worry about small ridges left by the float; brooming the surface will erase them.

15 **BROOM THE SURFACE.** Drag a broom lightly across the concrete to create a nonslip surface. The time to do this is typically 30 minutes after floating, but that will vary a little depending on the temperature and humidity.

EDGER

16 **EDGE THE PERIMETER.** An edger forms a rounded edge, which looks good and is less likely to chip off. This can be done before or after you broom the surface.

GROOVER

17 **GROOVE THE SURFACE.** A groover cuts a "control joint," which encourages any cracking to occur in the joint, rather than at random. Typically, control joints are spaced 5 to 8 ft. apart.

Tips for a Smooth Project

- Once you add water to the cement mix, the clock starts ticking, so the most important step in any concrete work is preparation. Mentally run through the entire job, make a list, and be absolutely certain you have all your tools and materials ready to go.
- To determine how many bags of cement mix you need, search online for "bagged concrete calculator." Buy a couple of extra bags. Running out can lead to disaster.
- Consider renting a mixer or calling in a ready-mix truck. Here is a general rule: If you need more than 15 bags, rent a mixer. If you need more than 30 bags, order ready-mix.
- Whether you're mixing by hand or using a mixer, it's best to have a helper so you can get the final batch mixed before the first batch becomes too stiff to work with.
- A couple of hours after finishing the concrete, cover it with painter's plastic for a few days. Concrete that stays wet longer grows stronger.
- Wait overnight (or even longer) before you remove the forms.

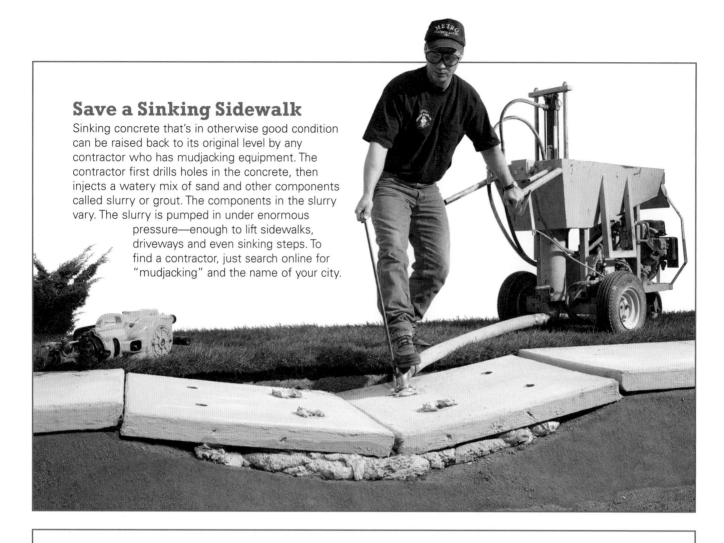

Save a Sinking Sidewalk

Sinking concrete that's in otherwise good condition can be raised back to its original level by any contractor who has mudjacking equipment. The contractor first drills holes in the concrete, then injects a watery mix of sand and other components called slurry or grout. The components in the slurry vary. The slurry is pumped in under enormous pressure—enough to lift sidewalks, driveways and even sinking steps. To find a contractor, just search online for "mudjacking" and the name of your city.

Patch Hairline Cracks in Concrete

It's easy to ignore hairline cracks in your sidewalk or concrete patio, but patching them early is the key to preventing them from growing into larger and uglier cracks. The type of sealant you use is critical to a long-lasting repair. Don't use a traditional vinyl or latex concrete patching product—it will dislodge as soon as the slab moves. Instead, use a self-leveling flexible urethane sealer (two choices are Quikrete Polyurethane Self-Leveling Sealant and DAP Concrete & Mortar Filler & Sealant).

Blow loose sand and debris out of the crack with compressed air. Cut the tube nozzle slightly smaller than the crack width and inject the sealer **(Photo 1)**. Allow a few minutes for the surface bead to self-level. Clean up the excess with a rag and mineral spirits **(Photo 2)**.

URETHANE SEALANT

1 USE URETHANE SEALANT. Hold the tube upright and force the sealant deep into the crack until it oozes up around the nozzle tip.

MINERAL SPIRITS

2 WIPE OFF THE EXCESS. Wet a clean rag with mineral spirits, and wipe the rag across the crack to remove excess sealer.

Replace a Small Concrete Pad

With the right tools and these tips, you can replace a pad in a single day.

A sagging, cracked concrete pad at an entryway says anything but "welcome." And it can go from eyesore to disaster if it slopes toward your home's foundation and directs rainwater right into your nicely finished basement! If your old pad needs replacing, you'll be happy to know it's a fairly easy task. Here are some tips for building a new home for your welcome mat.

1 START WITH A SLEDGEHAMMER. Usually a 10-lb. sledgehammer is all you need to bust up that nasty old pad (and get a good workout in the process). To protect the house from flying chips, cover any nearby glass with a sheet of 1/2-in. plywood (shown above). And be sure to wear goggles to protect your eyes.

A few swings with a sledgehammer will let you know right away if you need to call in some heavier equipment. A rental jackhammer will break up a slab much faster than a sledgehammer, with fewer blisters and less sweat. For a small slab, rent an electric rather than a pneumatic hammer.

LEVEL

CORNER-
TO-CORNER
MEASUREMENTS
SHOULD BE
EQUAL

WOODEN
STAKES

2x4 FORM
SLOPED
AWAY
FROM
HOUSE

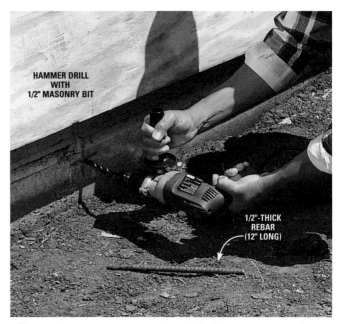

HAMMER DRILL
WITH
1/2" MASONRY BIT

1/2"-THICK
REBAR
(12" LONG)

2 BUILD THE FORM. Using straight 2x4s, lay out the form's three sides and screw them together. Take diagonal measurements to check for square (if they're equal, the form is square). Drive stakes—one every 3 ft.—along the outside of the form, being careful not to bend the 2x4s. Level the 2x4 that runs parallel to the house, then drive screws through the stakes and into the 2x4 to hold it in place. Next, be sure the form's sides slope away from the house 1/4 in. for every foot. Screw through side stakes to secure them.

3 PIN THE PAD TO THE FOUNDATION. Using a hammer drill and masonry bit, drill 1/2-in. holes 4 in. deep in your home's concrete foundation, spacing them about a foot apart. Then, using a hammer, tap 12-in.-long pieces of 1/2-in. rebar into the holes to connect the new pad to the foundation. The rebar will ensure that your new pad maintains its slope away from the house. Note: Not all municipalities allow this practice, so check with your local building inspector.

Reinforcement Isn't Required, But ...

For a small concrete pad—less than 40 sq. ft.—you normally don't have to bother installing steel reinforcing bar (rebar). However, laying out the rebar in a grid pattern 2 ft. on center adds strength and crack resistance to the pad.

You'll find 10-ft. lengths of rebar at home centers, and you can cut them to size with a hacksaw or an angle grinder. You'll also need tie wires and a wire-twisting tool to connect the pieces of rebar to create a grid pattern.

For more information about reinforcing concrete with rebar, visit familyhandyman.com and search for "concrete slab."

2x4
SCREED

2x4 PERCH
TO EXTEND
REACH

4 **LEVEL THE WET CONCRETE.** To get a nice, flat surface that's perfectly sloped, find a straight 2x4 that's a foot longer than the width of the form and set it on top of the form as you start pouring the concrete. Use the 2x4 to level the wet concrete by pulling it from the house toward you while working the board side to side—a process called screeding.

The mix should be slightly higher than the top of the form when you start. Poke the mix with a shovel to work out any air pockets, especially near edges and corners. For a smoother finish on the pad's edges, tap the sides of the form with a hammer.

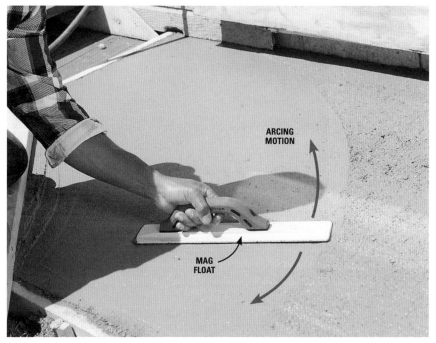

ARCING
MOTION

MAG
FLOAT

5 **FLOAT THE CONCRETE.** Start smoothing the concrete—also called floating—with a magnesium (mag) float. They're sold at home centers. Do this when the concrete has started to set up and you can push your finger into it only about 1/4 in. To float hard-to-reach areas, kneel on a 2x4 laid across the form **(Photo 4)**. Make long, sweeping strokes in an arc with the leading edge of the mag float lifted slightly. Try to finish this step within an hour of starting to pour the concrete. If it's hot and dry outside, you'll have to work even faster.

Four Things to Know About Concrete

1. **Too much water weakens concrete**
   If you mix too much water with cement, the crystals form farther apart, leaving concrete weak and porous. That can cause trouble later as pores and pockets fill with water, freeze and break up the concrete's surface. With the right amount of water, cement crystals grow tightly together and interweave to form strong, watertight concrete.

2. **Floating concrete too soon leads to trouble**
   As concrete sets, water rises to the surface. Left alone, this "bleed water" is reabsorbed into the concrete. But if you float the watery surface, you'll force the aggregate and cement down, leaving a watery mix of sand and too little cement on top. Wait for the bleed to disappear before floating. Also, don't overwork this step. Too much floating (or troweling) will lead to a less durable surface.

3. **The longer concrete stays damp, the better**
   Concrete doesn't harden because it's drying; it hardens because it's wet. The longer concrete stays damp, the harder and stronger it gets. The hardening or "curing" process can continue for weeks if the concrete dries slowly. Covering it with a sheet of plastic slows the curing process **(Photo 8)**.

4. **It can burn your skin**
   Some people get concrete on their skin and don't have any problems, but others are more sensitive to it. Until they cure, all cement-based products have the potential to leave minor burns on your skin. Play it safe and wear a long-sleeved shirt, long pants, boots and waterproof gloves when working with concrete.

6 ROUND OVER THE EDGES. Fifteen to 30 minutes after screeding, use a steel edging tool—sold at home centers—to smooth and round over the edges of the pad. This gives a nice-looking shape to the edges and forces the aggregate away from the corners. Do this a few times during and after floating **(Photo 5).**

EDGING TOOL

Order the Right Cement Mix

Bagged cement vs. ready-mix

Most small pads require less than a yard—27 cu. ft.—of concrete. You can buy several bags (sold at home centers) that you'll have to lug home, mix with water and pour yourself. It's a lot of work, but it might make more sense financially for a small pad at the bottom of your deck stairs. For bigger pads, have ready-mix concrete delivered. It comes mixed with water and the delivery person will pour it right into your forms. Prices vary by region. Order it a few days ahead. If rain threatens, you can usually cancel up to two hours before a scheduled delivery.

Order the right concrete mix

■ Plan to pour a pad at least 4 in. thick and calculate the right volume. Concrete is ordered in cubic yards. Many suppliers have calculators on their website, but it's fairly easy to figure out how much you need. First figure out the cubic footage, then convert to yards by dividing by 27. Here's how: Multiply the length of your pad by the width by the depth (4 in. = .33 ft.) and divide the total by 27. Order a little bit more than you need. A good rule of thumb is to order an extra 5% rounded up to the next 1/4 yd. to handle spillage and uneven bases.

■ Order from the nearest supplier. Get fresh concrete mixed near the site, not across town by some company with a lower price.

■ Ask for 5% "air entrainment" in the mix. Suppliers add a chemical that traps microscopic air bubbles to help the concrete accommodate the expansion and shrinkage caused by climatic changes such as freezing.

■ Get the right strength. Explain that you're pouring a pad and the concrete supplier will recommend the correct "bag mix" (the ratio of cement to aggregate and sand). In cold climates, they'll probably suggest at least a 3,000-lb. mix. That means the concrete

will be able to support a 3,000-lb. load per square inch without failing.

■ Typically, you'll have to pay for the concrete after it's been unloaded.

The truck will arrive with the concrete premixed with the correct water content, but the driver may send a little concrete down the chute and ask if you'd like more water added. Unless the mix is too dry to get down the chute, forget it. It should be thick—not runny. Wetter mud may be easier to place (pour into the forms), but the wetter the mix, the weaker the concrete.

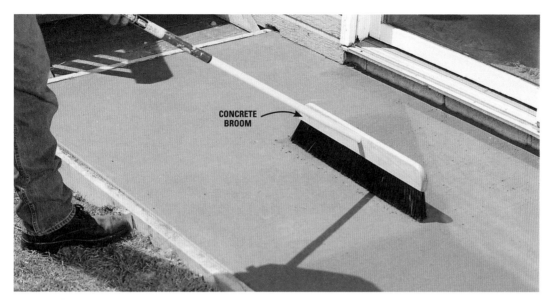

7 **ADD TEXTURE WITH A BROOM.** Use a special concrete broom or any stiff-bristle broom about 15 minutes after floating to add a slip-resistant texture to the top of the pad. The coarser you want the texture, the earlier you should broom. The grooves created by the broom should follow the direction of the slope so water runs off easily. Brooming also hides imperfections in float work.

CONCRETE BROOM

2x4 TO HOLD BACK EDGE OF PLASTIC

8 **COVER THE PAD.** To prevent the concrete from cracking while it's curing (hardening), cover it with a plastic sheet to slow the process. Wetting the pad with a fine spray of water every two to three hours for the first day helps too. Higher temperatures require more frequent wetting. The more time concrete has to cure, the stronger it will be.

WALK-BEHIND FLOOR GRINDER

1A

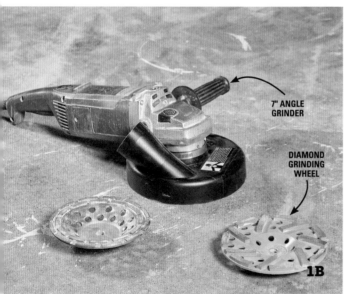

7" ANGLE GRINDER

DIAMOND GRINDING WHEEL

1B

Save That Slab!

Repair heaves and ridges, and prep for resealing, using equipment you can rent.

If you have an uneven concrete slab, you could replace it or cover it with leveling compound. But consider grinding it instead. Powerful grinding equipment is available at rental centers that cater to contractors. Here are a few of the most common uses for this equipment:

- Tapering cracks or heaves to reduce tripping hazards.
- Flattening high spots or ridges before you install flooring.
- Grinding down leftover thin-set or other hard coatings.
- Removing a sealed surface to prepare it to accept adhesive, thin-set or epoxy.

1. DIFFERENT SIZES FOR DIFFERENT JOBS

A. If you have a large floor that needs to be ground down, plan to rent a walk-behind floor grinder. Depending on the store and the machines it carries, a diamond grinding wheel may be included in the rental or you may have to buy diamond grinding inserts.

B. For a small job, rent an angle grinder equipped with a diamond grinding wheel. It's the perfect tool for taking down just a few high spots or tough-to-reach areas near walls. Be sure the one you rent comes with a means of attaching a vacuum to suck up the dust. If you plan to grind right up to a wall, make sure you rent a grinder with a convertible dust shroud that will flip up to expose the wheel enough to get into the corner.

Find a Rental Store

Call around to find a rental store that carries a few floor-grinding options. Grinding down high spots in concrete requires removing lots of material; be sure to rent a high-speed grinder that rotates 1,500 rpm or faster. Once you explain your task, the rental store staff should be able to set you up with the right equipment for your project.

How Long Will the Job Take?

If you have a 3/4-in. difference in height between sidewalk slabs, you should be able to knock that down in a few hours, but it depends on how hard the concrete is and the grinding wheel you use.

2. CHOOSE YOUR DUST CONTROL

There are two great ways to keep the dust from going wild. But remember to wear your respirator either way!

A. You can use a hand-pump sprayer to soak the floor with water as you grind to keep the dust down. But you'll have a messy slurry that will need to be hosed away or sucked up with a wet vacuum.

B. You can rent a heavy-duty vacuum (regular shop vacuums won't be able to keep up) to hook up to the grinder. The vac will also do a very good job of dust removal, but you'll need to put up walls of plastic sheeting and cover nearby vents.

3. WEAR SAFETY GEAR!

Plan to wear safety gear, including hearing protection, safety glasses and a respirator. The high-speed machines are loud and can send concrete rubble flying from the grinding wheel.

Grinding concrete also releases fine silica dust, which can cause health problems. Always wear a NIOSH-certified N95-rated respirator. Disposable masks are inexpensive, but for a little more money you can get a half-mask respirator that has a better seal. Check the seal with this easy test: If you can exhale and inhale sharply without air escaping, you're good to grind. Our model has facial hair, but if you have even a bit of stubble, it will ruin the seal.

4. KEEP THE MACHINE IN MOTION

While you're grinding, keep the cutter head moving, especially with a large floor grinder. Pivot the machine on its wheels, moving the cutter head in an arcing motion. If the cutting surface is riding on only one edge, work the machine in small circles to flatten out the surface.

5. DIAMOND GRAINS DO THE CUTTING

The cutting surfaces of these grinders are diamond grains held by "segments," the raised metal parts of the wheel. An aggressive wheel, which can take down 1/4 in. of concrete or more, grinds away material faster but leaves a rougher surface. A less aggressive wheel removes smaller amounts of concrete and leaves a smoother surface.

Here's the rule of thumb for choosing a wheel: The more surface area, the less aggressive the wheel. Choose an aggressive one to remove high, long ridges or large, rough areas of concrete, and choose a less aggressive one for tasks such as prepping for an epoxy coating.

6. NIBBLE AT A HEAVE

For a heaved sidewalk or cracked slab, tilt the grinder slightly, remove the meat of the concrete and then feather back the high spot. You may never get toe-stubbing heaves completely flat, but you can lessen the hazard. When tilted, the dust shroud can't catch all the dust, so you'll need a second hose and a helper.

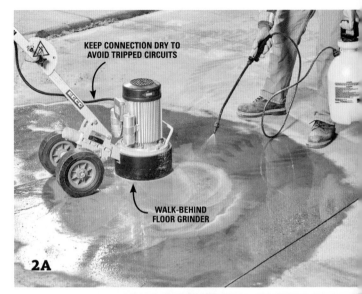

KEEP CONNECTION DRY TO AVOID TRIPPED CIRCUITS

WALK-BEHIND FLOOR GRINDER

2A

HEAVY-DUTY VAC

PLASTIC SHEETING

2B

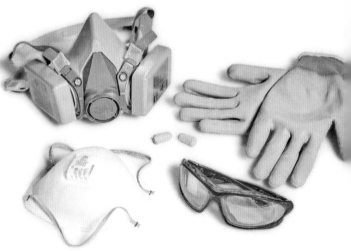

3

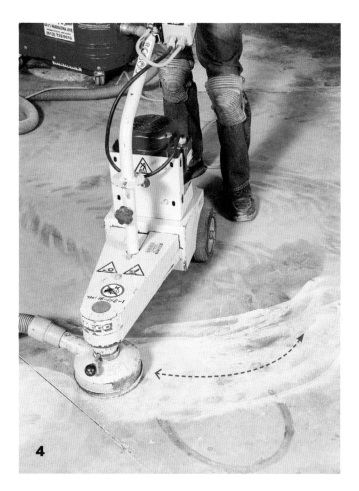

4

5

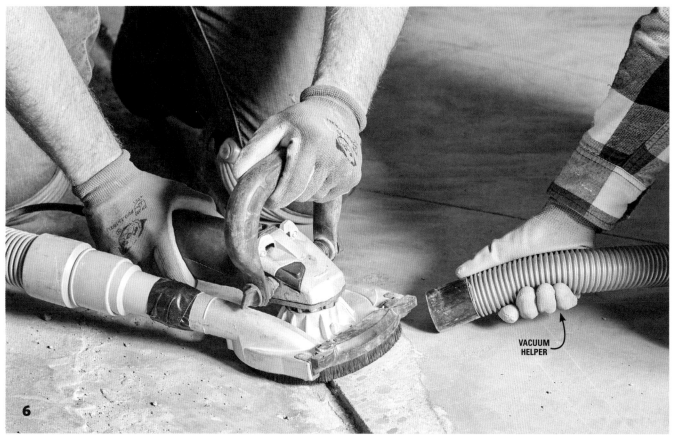

VACUUM
HELPER

6

7A

7. MARK WHERE TO GRIND

A. Outline the space that needs to be ground. Using a level or other straightedge, find where the high spot meets the flat surface. Balance the straightedge on the high spot, mark where the ends of the level are equidistant from the ground and trace around the high spot. This can be done by eye; it won't be perfect, but it will be a good start.

B. Start grinding on the crown of the high spot and work your way toward your marks. When you feel you've made progress, use the straightedge again to check for flatness. Retrace the high spots and grind them down. Repeat this grind-and-check process until the high spot is gone.

8. GRIND EDGES WITH A DUST SHROUD

Never remove a dust shroud to get close to a wall. You'll increase your exposure to nasty silica and remove a safety barrier. To grind near walls with a convertible dust shroud attached, push the open end of the dust shroud against the wall and make steady, shallow passes. Be sure you don't dig the edge of the wheel into the concrete as you move it back and forth.

7B

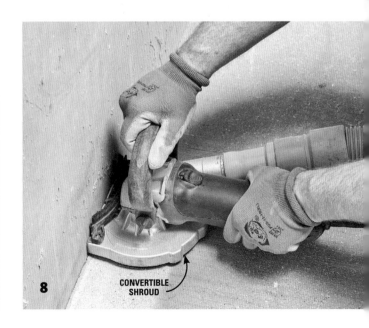

8   CONVERTIBLE SHROUD

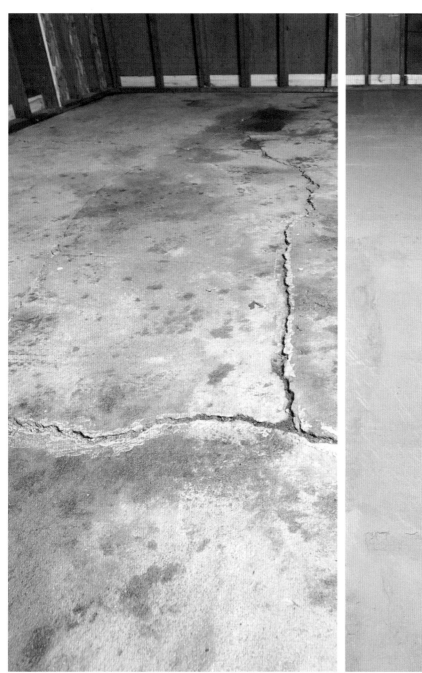

Restore a Garage Floor

Cover flaws in just a day using a resurfacing material that coats the existing concrete.

If your slab is suffering from low self-esteem because of pits, craters or cracks, you can cover up those scars. Concrete resurfacer is a cement-based coating that forms a smooth new surface right over the old concrete.

Cleaning and resurfacing the floor usually takes one day (even though clearing out your garage so you can work

may take weeks!). Spreading the resurfacer smoothly is the trickiest part of the project, so it helps to have some experience with concrete or drywall finishing. Cool weather, with temps in the 60s, also helps. Warmer weather makes resurfacer harden faster, reducing the time you have to finish the surface. You'll also need to buy or rent some special tools.

Gather your materials

Everything you'll need for this project is available at home centers. Aside from basic tools such as a hammer, a chisel, buckets and a steel trowel, you'll need:

Resurfacer
We used Quikrete Concrete Resurfacer. Similar products, such as Sakrete Flo-Coat, are also available. To estimate the amount you'll need, check the label and then buy two or three extra containers. Better to have to return some than to run out before the job is done.

Plastic sheeting
Protect walls with a band at least 3 ft. high. We used 6-mil plastic, but lighter stuff will work too.

Concrete cleaner
We used Quikrete Concrete & Asphalt Cleaner. Other brands are available.

Brush
A stiff version designed for stripping decks and mounted on a handle will keep you off your knees.

Pressure washer
For thorough cleaning, you'll need a model with 3,000 psi and a 15-degree spray tip. You can rent one.

Squeegee
Get a beefy version designed for floors, not a lightweight window-cleaning tool. A quality squeegee will give you better results and is worth the price.

Mixing equipment
A powerful 1/2-in. drill and a mixing attachment are the only way to go. Mixing by hand is too slow.

Protective gear
Rubber boots and gloves protect your skin against the degreaser and resurfacer (which can burn skin). You'll also need eye and hearing protection.

PREP THE SLAB

The cleaner the concrete, the better the resurfacer will stick. Start with a thorough sweeping. If you have oil spots to clean, scrub them with a deck brush and concrete cleaner. Once you've removed the stains, apply cleaner to the whole slab with the brush. Then fire up the pressure washer **(Photo 1)**. Start in the back of the garage and work your way to the front, forcing the excess water out the overhead doorway.

Important: If you find that the cleaner doesn't soak into the concrete but just beads up into droplets on the surface, you have a sealer over the concrete that you'll need to remove. In that case, apply a stripper first to remove the sealer, then clean.

When the slab is clean, look for any pieces of concrete that the sprayer

1 START WITH A CLEAN FLOOR. Scrub the slab with a concrete degreaser and a stiff brush, and then follow up with a pressure washer. Rinse the floor twice to remove all residue.

Results to Expect

As a first-timer, you might achieve a perfectly smooth, flat finish. Or you might end up with a few rough spots and small ridges. But even if your work is far from flawless, you'll still make a bad floor look much better. And remember this: If you make some major mistakes, you can add a second coat—this time with the benefit of experience.

Resurfacer is tough stuff that will withstand decades of traffic. It will permanently fill craters, but with cracks, long-term success is hard to predict. Tight, stable cracks may reappear. Cracks that have shifted slightly with the seasons or gradually widened over the years probably will reappear. That doesn't mean you shouldn't resurface the floor—even a crack that reappears and gradually grows will look a lot better than one that's left alone.

2 REMOVE THE LOOSE STUFF. Chisel away any loose fragments along cracks or craters; there's no need to bust away concrete that's firmly attached.

3 FILL CRACKS AND CRATERS. Mix up a stiff batch of resurfacer, using just enough water for a workable consistency. Scrape off the excess so repairs are flush with the surrounding floor.

GARAGE DOOR WEATHERSTRIP

4 CREATE A DAM. Glue weatherstrip to the floor exactly where the garage door rests. This will stop resurfacer from flowing onto the driveway.

may have loosened. Chip these away **(Photo 2)** and collect the debris as you go, sweeping it into a dustpan with an old paintbrush.

Now's the time to fill these cracks or divots. Mix some resurfacer to a mashed potato–like consistency and push the mix into the cracks. Smooth it flush with the surrounding surface with a cement trowel **(Photo 3)**.

If you have expansion joints cut into the existing slab, push a weatherstrip into the joint. This will maintain the joint and give you a convenient time to stop and take a break. Apply and smooth no more than 150 sq. ft. of resurfacer at a time for the best results. You can glue a length of weatherstrip to the slab to define a stopping point if you don't have a control joint and then continue from that edge once you've smoothed the first section.

For a nice-looking finished edge under the overhead door, apply a heavy-duty vinyl weatherstrip **(Photo 4)**. Just be sure to dry the slab along the location with a hair dryer so your adhesive will work properly.

MIX AND SPREAD THE RESURFACER

This is the time to recruit a helper. You'll need one person to mix and another to spread resurfacer. Take two minutes to read the directions before mixing. The key to a smooth, lump-free mix is to let the resurfacer "slake," that is, sit in the bucket for a few minutes after the initial mixing. Then mix a bit more **(Photo 5)**. It's also good to have a slat of wood on hand to scrape the sides of the bucket as you mix.

The concrete should be damp when you apply the resurfacer, but not wet to the touch. Pour the mix onto the slab and immediately spread it **(Photo 6)**. Work quickly and carefully, blending each stroke into the previous one until you get a nice, uniform look. Smooth the resurfacer along the side walls by pulling the squeegee toward you. As you reach the edge of the door weatherstrip, use your steel trowel to gently blend the resurfacer against the weatherstrip. You can remove the excess with the trowel and drop it into a bucket.

With the slab finished, let the mix set up. In hot, dry weather, it's a good idea to mist the hardened surface; keeping it damp longer will allow the resurfacer to fully harden. After several hours, the finish will support foot traffic. Depending on the weather, wait at least 24 hours before driving on your newly finished slab. After a few days of curing, you can apply a sealer if you'd like to protect the slab from oil and other stains.

Erase Your Mistakes

If you end up with ridges, shallow craters or squeegee marks, you don't have to live with them forever. Go to a rental store and rent a concrete grinder. It looks like a floor polisher, but it grinds down the surface, removing about 1/16 in. with each slow pass. It's a dusty job that might take all day, but you'll get a much smoother, flatter surface—perfect if you want to apply a finish such as epoxy paint.

5 MIX LIKE MAD. Recruit a helper to mix the resurfacer while you spread it. The material begins to stiffen quickly, so the faster you get it all mixed and applied, the better your results.

6 SPREAD IT SMOOTH, THEN LET IT SET. Push the squeegee forward to work the resurfacer into the concrete, then drag it back to smooth the coating. Aim for a thickness of 1/8 in. When you've covered the whole floor, let it cure for 24 hours before you drive on it.

Protect & Renew Stamped Concrete

Stamped concrete should be sealed every two to three years to protect it from the elements, make it last longer and keep it looking new. This stamped sidewalk was looking dull and faded with a whitish film on it, so it was time to reseal.

Sealers are either water- or solvent-based, and it's best to use what was previously used on your stamped concrete. If you apply solvent-based over water-based, you'll likely end up with an uneven, blotchy finish. That's because solvent-based sealer will darken areas where the old sealer has worn off but not areas where it's still visible. If you put water-based sealer over solvent-based, you're likely to get a poor bond.

If you don't know what the existing sealer is, do this quick test: Pour some xylene—a readily available solvent—on a small area that still has old sealer. After a minute or so, if it feels tacky, you know it's a solvent-based sealer. Water-based sealer gums up with this test. Ours was solvent-based. Switching to water-based would mean completely stripping the old sealer, which is a pain, so we used solvent-based.

1 WASH THE SURFACE. Pressure-wash using a surface cleaning attachment. The attachment has a spinning head, ensuring that you don't get lines in the concrete from a standard pressure tip. This step removes dirt, mold, mildew and old, flaking sealer. Some of the old sealer remained on ours, but that was fine. Think of it as scraping and repainting. You don't have to scrape off all the paint, just the loose stuff. After the surface cleaner, use a fan tip to rinse the dirt away. Let the patio dry thoroughly, no less than 24 hours. If there's moisture underneath the new sealer, it won't bond well.

2 BLOW OFF THE DIRT. After drying and before applying sealer, blow off any debris with a leaf blower. Sealing when the temperature is in the 60s or 70s is ideal. If the temperature is too high, the sealer might dry too quickly and blister.

3 BRUSH THE TIGHT SPOTS. To apply sealer, first brush areas that would be hard to reach with a roller, such as steps or where the concrete meets the house. Before applying the sealer, you can mix in an anti-slip agent, such as Sherwin-Williams' Sharkgrip.

4 ROLL ON THE REST. Finish with a 3/8-in. nap roller, applying two thin coats. A thin coat of solvent-based sealer is ready for recoating in 20 to 30 minutes. You could apply sealer with a pump sprayer and then back-roll it afterward, but you'd need a sprayer with hoses and seals that are made to stand up to solvent.

CHAPTER **THREE**

LANDSCAPE

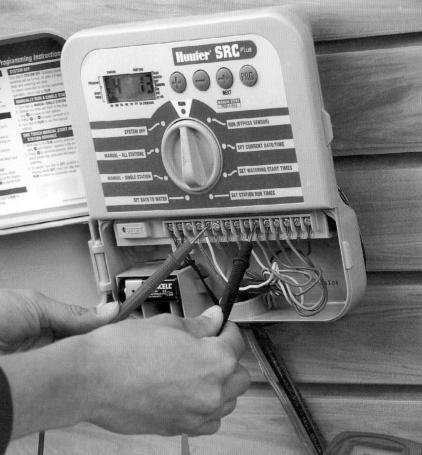

Touch Up a Vinyl-Clad Fence

Follow these steps for using the right paint and making quick work of the repair.

Vinyl-clad chain-link fence keeps its appearance for a long time. But the vinyl can get scuffed and worn where the gate latch locks onto the post. The repair is a little tricky because you're trying to paint over vinyl and metal. If you use a spray paint formulated for metal, it won't bond well to the vinyl. Instead, coat the damaged area with spray paint specifically designed for plastic (Krylon Fusion is one brand).

Start by cleaning the damaged area and beyond with a household spray cleaner. Then rough up the surface **(Photo 1)**. Finish the repair with special plastic paint **(Photo 2)**. Let the repair dry at least 24 hours before operating the gate latch mechanism.

1 SAND THE AREA. Lightly scuff the vinyl and metal with 120-grit sandpaper. Then wipe with a tack cloth.

2 COAT WITH PAINT. Apply a first coat of plastic paint and allow it to set up for the recommended time shown on the label. Then apply a finish coat.

Fix Dog Spots in Your Lawn

Take care of those burn spots caused by the family pet with a hose, some topsoil and grass seed.

Burn spots caused by dogs relieving themselves on the lawn are usually about 4 to 8 in. wide with dead grass in the middle and a ring of dark green grass around them. Dog urine contains high concentrations of acids, salts and nitrogen, which kill the grass. The only way to fix the burn spots is to plant new grass. Here are the steps.

1 Flood the dog spot with lots of water to dilute the urine. Let the hose run for a good three minutes.

2 Scrape up the dead grass with a hand rake and loosen the soil about 1/2 in. deep. Seeds germinate and take root better in loose soil.

3 Add a ½-in. layer of new topsoil over the spot and sprinkle on grass seed. Cover with a thin layer of soil and keep the area moist (don't overwater) until the grass grows about 3 in. tall.

Repair a Bent Fence Rail

With the right tools and supplies, it's an easy DIY fix that will save you the cost of hiring a pro.

When a tree limb falls on your property, you can bet it's going to damage something. And if that something happens to be a chain-link fence, consider yourself lucky because fixing a chain-link fence is an easy DIY repair. The pros would charge about twice what it would cost you to do the repair shown here. Take these steps.

Get a new section of top rail and some wire ties from a home center or fence supplier. The top rail should have one open end and one crimped end. Grab a hacksaw or a reciprocating saw with a metal-cutting blade, a file and pliers—and grab a helper too.

Start by removing the wire ties that hold the fence fabric to the top rail. Then rest the new rail on top of the damaged rail and have your helper hold it in place while you mark a cutting line on the old rail, as shown in the photo. Mark a cut on the opposite end of the new rail, where that end meets a rail joint.

Cut the damaged rail at the cutting line **(Figure A)**, slide it off the joint and toss it. Then cut the excess off the new top rail to mate with the existing joint.

Create some maneuvering room by unbolting the top rail from the corner post and sliding it away from the damaged area. Install the larger end of the new rail onto the crimped end of the old rail. Then make the final connection. Reconnect the rail end cap to the corner post.

MARK A CUTTING LINE. Slide the new rail down so the crimped end is located over a straight section of the damaged rail. Then mark the cutting line.

CRIMPED END

CUTTING LINE

FIGURE A
CUTTING GUIDE

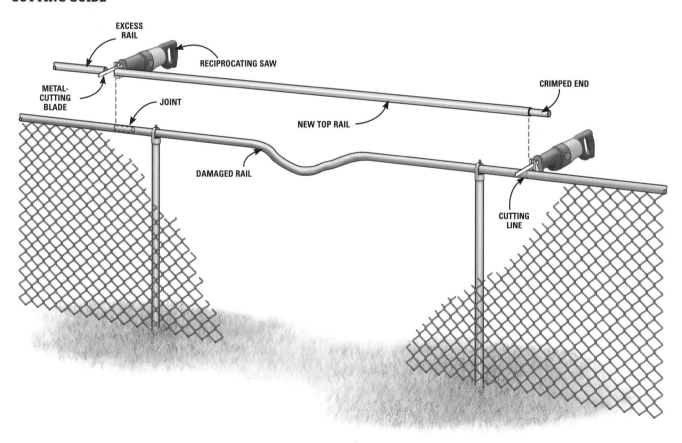

EXCESS RAIL

RECIPROCATING SAW

METAL-CUTTING BLADE

JOINT

CRIMPED END

NEW TOP RAIL

DAMAGED RAIL

CUTTING LINE

Restore a Weedy & Patchy Lawn

Work a little, water a lot—and then enjoy!

Reseeding is a job you can do in a weekend if you have an average-size lawn. You'll have to wrestle home a couple of engine-powered rental machines. Once your work is done, be prepared to keep the soil damp with daily watering for the first month or so. It's the key to a successful reseeding job.

Before you establish this beautiful new lawn, be sure to do any hardscaping or landscaping—such as retaining walls, patios or tree planting—that might tear up your new lawn with heavy equipment or excavating. If an in-ground irrigation system is in your future, install that beforehand as well. You'll avoid damaging your new lawn by trenching in

irrigation lines and sprinkler heads as well as have the benefit of using the system to water the new grass. Flag the sprinkler heads to avoid hitting them with the aerator or power rake.

GET BETTER GRASS

Grass has improved dramatically in recent years, with varieties now available that provide better color and thicker turf or are shade or drought tolerant. So reseeding doesn't just fill in the bare spots; it also improves the mix of grass varieties that you have in your lawn, which greatly improves your ability to grow a lush lawn.

1 KILL THE WEEDS. Use a hose-end sprayer to spray the lawn with a broadleaf weed killer at least three weeks before you plant the new grass seed. Wear eye protection, gloves, a long-sleeved shirt, pants and waterproof shoes.

SAVE THE EXISTING GRASS?

The steps we show here are for a lawn that's at least 50% grass. Take a close look at your lawn. If you see plenty of healthy grass among the weeds or large areas of good grass throughout the lawn, you can save the existing grass and fill in the rest of the lawn by planting new seed. That calls for applying a broadleaf herbicide, which kills the weeds but doesn't harm the grass. It should be applied three to four weeks before starting the project. A hose-end sprayer with concentrated weed killer is the fastest, easiest application method **(Photo 1)**. But if your lawn is hopelessly bare or completely covered with weeds, it's best to go "scorched earth" and kill all the vegetation with a nonselective herbicide such as Roundup to start over. If after two weeks some weeds reappear, apply another treatment to the survivors.

LATE SUMMER OR EARLY FALL IS BEST

Timing is important when it comes to lawn reseeding. When summer heat begins to wane, it's much easier to stay on track

POWER
AERATOR

2 AERATE THE SOIL. Make at least three passes from three different directions with an aerator to loosen the soil.

3 PREPARE THE SURFACE. Pulverize the aerating plugs and loosen dead foliage with a power rake. Rake up and remove any vegetation that completely covers the soil.

4 OUTLINE GARDEN BEDS. Sow seed with a drop spreader near or around gardens or other areas where you want to avoid sowing grass seed.

with watering newly sprouted grass shoots because they won't be stressed by high heat and humidity. Plus, there will be plenty of time for the grass to get established before winter.

You'll be far less successful planting and growing grass from seed during spring and summer. If you must seed in the spring, wait for soil temperatures to reach a consistent 55 degrees. Also watch for weeds! They can outcompete new grass seedlings as they both vie for space, sunlight and water. Using a seed-friendly herbicide is recommended in the spring or early summer if you have to treat emerging weeds after reseeding. And when choosing the starter fertilizer, look for one containing siduron or mesotrione pre-emergent herbicide, or be prepared for disappointing results.

Reseeding can be a crapshoot. A big thunderstorm could wash away your seed. So pay attention to long-range forecasts and plan accordingly. This is especially true if your yard is sloped enough that it doesn't take much water to wash away seed. Before you start the soil prep, set your mower to its lowest setting and give your yard a buzz cut.

RENT THE NECESSARY TOOLS

There's no reasonable way to prep the soil by hand, so you should plan to rent an aerator (**Photo 2**) and power rake (also called a dethatcher) (**Photo 3**). Hauling them home will require a helper, but operating them doesn't require an athlete's physique. The worst part is that you'll be marching around the yard following the self-propelled machines for many, many passes. Unless you have a small yard, plan to aerate it in one day, then return the aerator the following day and rent the power rake to finish the heavy work. Day two would also include planting, raking and fertilizing.

AERATE LIKE CRAZY

Aerators pull small plugs from the soil and deposit them on the surface (**Photo 2**). That loosens the soil, making it easier for roots to grow deep into the soil. The plugs will be pulverized with the power rake in the next step (**Photo 3**), forming loose soil in which the seeds can germinate. The holes you create will allow fertilizer and water to penetrate deep into the soil for better retention. When you're using a core aerator to prepare soil for reseeding, the key is to make at least three passes—more if you have the stamina—each from a different direction.

NEXT STEP: POWER RAKING

Power rakes spin metal tines at high speed to scarify and loosen the soil as well as break up the aerator plugs. These rakes also lift thatch from your lawn. Go over the whole lawn from two directions, then rake up and remove dead debris if it completely covers the ground and would prevent seed from contacting the soil.

CHOOSE THE RIGHT SPREADER

In most cases, a broadcast spreader **(Photo 5)** is the best choice because it evenly distributes seed or fertilizer for thorough coverage. If you have a large yard bordered by flower beds or vegetable gardens, use a drop spreader **(Photo 4)** to spread the seed near them before doing the majority of the yard with a broadcast spreader. Since the seed drops straight down, you won't be casting grass seed in your gardens by mistake.

Whichever spreader you use, set the feed rate at half (or less) the recommended rate. When using the drop spreader around border gardens, overlap subsequent passes slightly for more even seed distribution. But when using the broadcast or drop spreader for the open areas, make two or more passes from different directions for even distribution. This is especially true when you're using a drop spreader since you don't wind up with a striped lawn. If you don't own a broadcast spreader, buy one—don't rent it. You'll need it to keep your new lawn in tiptop shape after it's established.

SOW THE SEED

Applying too much or too little seed is a mistake. Here is a little hands-and-knees observation to let you know if you're applying the right amount. Picture a square inch of a freshly seeded area and count the seeds. Strive to get about 15 or so seeds per square inch. After spreading, lightly rake the seed

5 **SEED THE LARGE AREAS.** Spread seed with a broadcast spreader in large areas away from gardens. Use half the recommended drop rate to spread the seed in one direction. Spread the remaining seed in the opposite direction to ensure even distribution.

How to Buy Quality Seed

Quality seed mixtures contain different species and varieties of lawn grasses that will better adapt to your lawn's conditions. Don't try to save money when you shop for grass seed. Look for the highest-priced seed on the shelf and follow these tips:

- Pay attention to the label. The lower the amount of weed seed, crop seed and inert matter, the better.
- Consult your local county or university extension service for a list of recommended lawn seed varieties for your area. You can also check university websites for tips on how to purchase quality grass seed.
- For quality lawns in full sun, look for a high percentage of Kentucky bluegrass in the mix.
- Lawns in heavy shade should be seeded with a mix containing 70% or more fine fescue.
- Fine fescues (creeping red, sheep's, hard, chewings) use less water and need less fertilizer and fewer mowings.
- Avoid mixtures containing annual ryegrass because it lasts for only one year!
- Stay away from unnamed varieties or "Variety Not Stated" (VNS) ingredients.

6 **RAKE IN THE SEED.** Lightly rake in the seed to establish good seed-to-soil contact.

7 DISTRIBUTE THE FERTILIZER. Spread starter fertilizer over the yard. Follow the directions on the bag to determine how many pounds per 1,000 sq. ft.

8 WATER DAILY. Water lightly daily or twice daily in hot, dry or windy conditions to keep the soil damp, not wet.

into the soil for good contact **(Photo 6)**. It doesn't have to be completely buried. Some of the seed can still be showing.

FERTILIZE WITH A STARTER

Fertilizers used to contain nitrogen, phosphorus and potassium. But due to water pollution concerns, many states no longer allow phosphorus in ordinary lawn fertilizers. However, phosphorus is very helpful for root development, so it's important for starting new seed. At the garden center, look for fertilizer labeled "Starter" or "New Lawns." Your state may allow the sale of phosphorus for establishing new lawns or in gardens. Spread the starter fertilizer over the yard **(Photo 7)**.

WATER, WATER, WATER

An oscillating sprinkler works best. It covers a large area with even, light streams of water to prevent washing away seed **(Photo 8)**. You'll need to water only for about 20 minutes at a time depending on your soil type. Unless it rains, you'll likely need to water at least twice daily. On hot or windy days, you may need to water more frequently.

Closely monitor the soil to keep it damp, not saturated. Strive to maintain soil dampness to a depth of about 1/2 in. You'll need to do this for at least three weeks. If you are not diligent, you may throw away all your hard work and money. One dry, hot sunny day is all it takes to wipe out a new lawn. A timer for your hose, available at any garden or home center, might be helpful if you can't be home to water as needed. After the grass is 3 in. high, you can start mowing and begin a normal watering regimen.

Soil Watering Gauge

Your goal is to water to a depth of 1/2 in. As a test, water for about 20 minutes, then drive a spade into the ground and look for the dark line near the surface indicating water penetration. That'll tell you if you should water for longer or shorter periods.

Sprinkler System Fixes

Your irrigation system may seem complex, but it's made up of simple components you can repair or replace yourself in just an hour or two. Don't be intimidated: The pipes are plastic and much easier to repair than the plumbing in your house. The electrical lines are low voltage, so they're not hazardous. You may need a multimeter to diagnose electrical problems, but you can master that step in just a few minutes.

PROBLEM: SPRINKLER HEADS NOT WORKING

SOLUTION 1: REPLACE A BROKEN SPRINKLER HEAD

Broken sprinkler heads are easy to identify. Just look for cracked or broken plastic casings on the heads, heads that don't pop up, or heads that spray water wildly or not at all. It's common to find the top of a head completely broken off.

NEW SPRINKLER HEAD

COMBINATION ELBOW

RISER

BROKEN SPRINKLER HEAD

CAUTION
Before you dig, call 811 or go to call811.com to have your underground utility lines marked.

SCREW ON A NEW HEAD. Dig around the sprinkler head to expose the riser. Unscrew the broken sprinkler head from the riser and screw on the new one.

FIGURE A: HOW A SPRINKLER SYSTEM WORKS

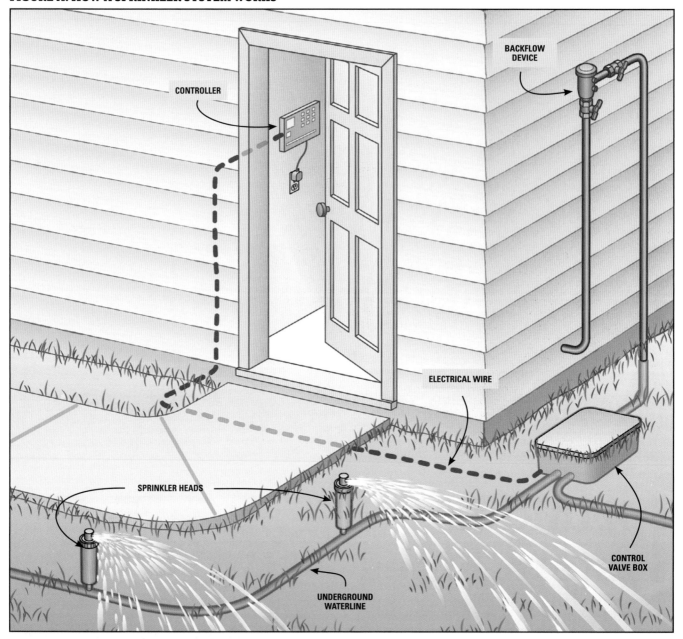

CONTROLLER

BACKFLOW DEVICE

ELECTRICAL WIRE

SPRINKLER HEADS

CONTROL VALVE BOX

UNDERGROUND WATERLINE

HOW A SPRINKLER SYSTEM WORKS. The controller sends a signal to the control valves in the control valve box. The valves open, sending water through the underground waterline, which causes the sprinkler heads to pop up and spray.

This typically happens to heads that are set too high and get run over by vehicles or hit by lawn mowers or other lawn care equipment.

Replacing a head is one of the simplest fixes. Replacement heads are available at home centers and online. Be sure to buy the same type that you're replacing so it fits properly.

To remove a broken sprinkler head, turn off the system and dig a 2-ft.-dia. hole around the head. Using a square shovel, slice the sod into easy-to-remove pieces. Set the sod on a tarp so you can put it back in place when you're finished.

Dig down to the "riser" (the vertical pipe that branches off the main line) that is connected to the sprinkler head. Dig gently to avoid damaging the plastic waterline, which is 8 to 12 in. underground.

Turn the head counterclockwise to remove it from the riser. While the head is off, take care not to spill dirt into the riser. Sprinkler heads are installed only hand-tight, but after they've been in the ground for several years, you may need a wrench to unscrew them. If the head doesn't turn easily, hold the riser with a slip joint pliers to keep it from twisting loose from the fittings below.

Attach the new sprinkler head by placing it on the riser and turning it hand-tight **(see bottom photo on p. 73)**. Don't use Teflon tape or joint compound on the riser threads.

Sprinkler heads are tested at the factory to make sure they work. As a result, they're often packaged still wet, so don't be surprised to see water in a new head that you purchase.

Before filling in the hole and replacing the sod, set the sprinkler pattern where you want it (see "Reset the Spray Pattern" below).

SOLUTION 2: CLEAN A CLOGGED HEAD

A head that's clogged with dirt may rise but not spray, stay up after watering or produce an erratic spray pattern.

To clean the head, dig it out and remove it from the riser **(see bottom photo on p. 73)**. Take the head apart by holding the bottom of the canister and turning the top of the head counterclockwise. Once it's unscrewed, lift it out of the canister **(Photo 1)**.

Remove the screen basket, which serves as a filter, at the base of the head. If you can't pop the screen out with your fingers, you can pry it out with a screwdriver or pull it free with a pliers.

Rinse the screen **(Photo 2)** and clean the rest of the sprinkler head. Reinstall the head. If it still doesn't work, replace it with a new head.

Reset the Spray Pattern: When you install a new sprinkler head or reinstall an old one, you may need to adjust it to water a specifically defined area. Adjustment methods vary. You can adjust some head types by turning a slot at the top with a screwdriver. Others require a special key that you insert into the head and turn **(Photo 3)**. Some heads also allow you to adjust the spray pattern by turning a tiny screw located next to the nozzle.

Adjust the heads before installing them, then fine-tune them once they're in place, with the sprinkler running.

First, turn the top clockwise until it stops. That nozzle location is the starting point (the head will turn counterclockwise from there). Adjust the head to set the watering rotation anywhere from 40 to 360 degrees counterclockwise from the starting point.

Set the head in the canister. Standing behind the head, align the nozzle with the right edge of the area you want to water, such as along a driveway. Then tighten the head in the canister. Next, carefully backfill the hole and put the sod back in place.

Turn on the sprinklers and allow the head to rotate a few times, and then make additional adjustments while the system is running.

Two Types of Pipe

Some sprinkler systems use black polyethylene pipe joined with barbed fittings and hose clamps. Other systems use PVC pipe, which is usually white and joined with PVC cement.

1 TAKE THE HEAD APART. Unscrew the top from the canister. Rinse away soil and debris in a bucket of water.

2 CLEAN THE SCREEN. Remove the screen basket from the bottom of the head, then rinse it clean.

3 ADJUST THE PATTERN. Set the watering range of the sprinkler head before installing it. Place the head in the canister so the nozzle is at the edge of the area to be watered. Make final adjustments with the water running.

MAKE SURE THE WATER IS ON. Check the valves on the backflow device to make sure they're open. Turn the valve on the horizontal pipe first, then the vertical pipe valve.

REPLACE DAMAGED PIPE. Cut out the damaged section of the line and replace it with a repair coupling. Repair couplings come in several styles. This one expands and contracts like a telescope.

PROBLEM: LOW WATER PRESSURE

SOLUTION 1: TURN ON VALVES AT BACKFLOW DEVICE

Low water pressure will result in the sprinkler heads barely shooting water. In extreme cases, many of the heads won't even pop up. Start with the easiest solution. Make sure the valves at the backflow device are fully open. The backflow device is located above ground, with the valves at least 12 in. above the highest sprinkler head in the yard. Most backflow devices have two valves, one on the horizontal pipe and one on the vertical. Turn the valves to their open positions. A valve is open when the handle is parallel with the pipe.

SOLUTION 2: FIND AND REPAIR LEAKS

Check for leaks in the waterline. Look for a series of sprinkler heads that aren't watering properly. A waterline problem is always located between the last working head and the first nonworking head.

Look for signs of leaking water, such as water bubbling up from the soil when the sprinklers are running, a depression in the ground or a very wet area. If you find running water, follow the water to the highest point to locate the source of the leak.

Once you locate the approximate leak site, dig straight down to the waterline. Then enlarge the hole along the line, following the flow of the leaking water until you find the break or crack. Before making the repair, be sure the system is turned off at the controller.

To fix the leak, cut out the damaged section of pipe. A hacksaw cuts plastic pipe easily. Replace the damaged section with a repair coupling (sold at irrigation supply stores). Turn on the system to check for leaks, then backfill the hole with dirt and replace the sod.

SOLUTION 3: CHECK FOR CRUSHED PIPES

If you can't locate a leak, the waterline may be crushed or obstructed. Sometimes roots wrap around the line and squeeze it closed over the course of several years **(photo above right)**. Or vehicles can compress the soil, causing the line to collapse.

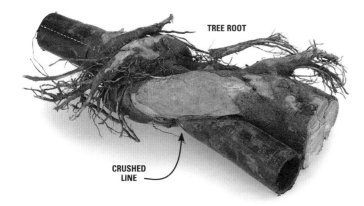

TREE ROOT

CRUSHED LINE

These problems are harder to find and often require a lot of digging. Again, look for the problem after the last working head. Dig along the waterline until you find the damaged section. If the line runs near a tree, start your digging there.

Once you locate the damaged section, cut it out with a hacksaw. If the line was damaged by tree roots, reroute the line by digging a new trench away from the tree.

Cut a new section of pipe to replace the damaged one. Then install the new section of pipe, connecting it at each end with regular couplings and hose clamps **(photo right)**.

PROBLEM: ONE OR MORE ZONES NOT WORKING

SOLUTION 1: CHECK FOR VOLTAGE TO THE BAD ZONES

Your watering system is divided into a series of zones. Each zone has an electrically activated valve that controls the heads for a designated area.

Generally, if you have a zone that's not turning on, you have an electrical problem. To solve the problem, make sure the zone wires are firmly attached to the terminals in the controller, the transformer is plugged in and the circuit breaker at the main panel is on.

Next, test for voltage to the nonworking zone using a multimeter (sold at home centers and hardware stores). Turn on the nonworking zone at the controller. Turn the multimeter dial to voltage and place one lead on the common terminal (marked "c" or "com"). Place the other lead on the terminal of the zone that's not working **(photo right)**. It doesn't matter which lead goes to which terminal.

Refer to your owner's manual to see whether the voltage reading falls within the required range (usually 24 to 28 volts). If it doesn't, the controller needs to be replaced. (If you don't get any voltage reading, see "Solution 2: Check Fuse and Transformer," p. 78.)

Fortunately, controllers rarely go bad unless they're struck by lightning. New ones can cost hundreds of dollars. Replace a damaged controller with the same brand and model as you currently have. To install the new one, label each wire that's connected to the existing controller with a piece of tape. Unhook the wires, and then attach them to the new controller in the same sequence.

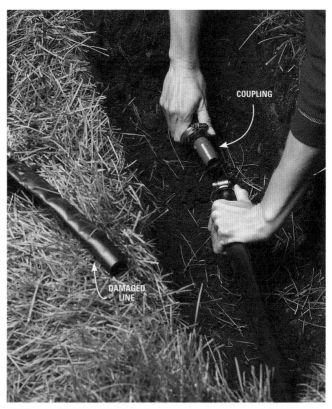

COUPLING

DAMAGED LINE

REPLACE CRUSHED PIPE. Cut out the damaged section. Replace it with a new pipe, making the connections with couplings and hose clamps.

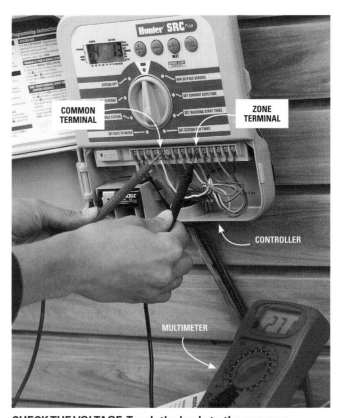

COMMON TERMINAL

ZONE TERMINAL

CONTROLLER

MULTIMETER

CHECK THE VOLTAGE. Touch the leads to the common terminal and zone terminal. If the voltage is too low, replace the controller.

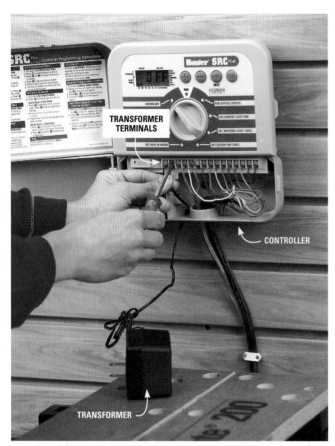

REPLACE THE TRANSFORMER. With the transformer plugged in, place the multimeter leads on the terminals marked "24 vac." If the reading is less than 22, replace the transformer.

SOLUTION 2: CHECK FUSE AND TRANSFORMER

If no zones will turn on, first turn the controller to the manual setting to see if the system will run. If it turns on manually, the controller is good but the rain sensor may be stopping the automatic programmed watering, which is what it's designed to do.

Rain sensors conserve water by preventing the system from running when the ground is already saturated. Some states require rain sensors on all new systems. (Your rain sensor is bad if the system runs when the ground is already wet.)

If the system doesn't run in the manual position, check the controller for power. If it has a fuse, make sure it's not blown. Or, if it has a circuit breaker reset button, press the button, then try the system again. If the system is plugged into a GFCI receptacle, press the GFCI reset button.

If it still doesn't turn on, make sure the outlet that the power transformer is plugged into is working by plugging in a power tool. If the outlet is working, plug the transformer back in, turn the system off and test the transformer for voltage. Using a multitester, place a lead on each of the two transformer terminals. It doesn't matter which lead goes to which terminal. The transformer terminals are marked "24 vac." A 24-voltage transformer should normally test between

24 and 28 volts. If the voltage falls below the manufacturer's range, replace the transformer. Simply unscrew the terminals that hold the two transformer wires in the controller and remove the transformer **(photo left)**. Insert the wires on the new transformer through the designated opening in the controller. Attach the wires to the controller terminals marked "24 vac" by placing the wire ends under the screws, then tightening them.

SOLUTION 3: REPAIR A BAD VALVE

If the controller, fuse and transformer check out OK, test the resistance "ohms" between the common terminal and the nonworking zone. Turn off the system, turn the multimeter to test for ohms (the omega symbol), and place the leads on the common terminal and zone terminal, just as you did to test for voltage.

Compare the ohms reading with the range listed in your owner's manual (usually 20 to 60 ohms). If the ohms fall below the required amount, the switch (solenoid) that operates the control valve for that zone is defective and needs to be replaced. The defective solenoid will be connected to the same color wire as the zone wire at the controller. (If the reading is too high, see "Repair Damaged Wires" below.)

Control valves are typically grouped with three to six valves in one box **(Photo 1)**. The boxes are located in the ground with a cover that simply lifts off. They can be located anywhere in the yard but are usually located close to the main water supply.

Although valves themselves rarely need to be replaced, solenoids do occasionally fail. Fortunately, replacing them is quick and easy.

Be sure the controller is in the off position (you don't need to shut off the power) and the water valves on the backflow device are turned off **(see top photo on p. 76)**. Inside the control valve box, remove the wire connectors and disconnect the two wires on the defective solenoid. Turn the solenoid counterclockwise to unscrew it from the valve **(Photo 1)**. Water will slowly seep out of the valve opening, even with the water turned off.

Place a new solenoid in the valve. Twist the ends of the new solenoid wires onto the same common wire and field wire that were attached to the old solenoid **(Photo 2)**. It doesn't matter which solenoid wire goes to the common and which one goes to the field wire. Twist a new waterproof wire connector over each connection **(Photo 2)**. To make waterproof connections, use a silicone-filled "direct bury" connector, sold at home centers.

Repair Damaged Wires: If the ohms reading between the common terminal and the nonworking zone terminal is too high (it's sometimes an infinity reading), the problem is a severed or bad wire to the control valve. If only one zone isn't working, the field wire is damaged. If none of the zones in a

1 REPLACE A SOLENOID. Disconnect the wires and unscrew the defective solenoid from the control valve. Insert a new solenoid and turn it until it's finger-tight.

WATERPROOF CONNECTOR

control valve box are working, the common wire is damaged, although the field wires could also be bad.

To find a bad wire, bypass each in turn by temporarily substituting a 14-gauge wire for the original that you run above ground. Make the wire connections with the controller turned off. Then turn the controller back on. Test the field wire first. If the zone turns on, the old field wire is bad. Replace it with an 18-gauge wire rated for underground burial. Bury the wire at least 8 in. underground. Follow the same procedure to test the common wire.

2 RECONNECT THE WIRES. Connect the two wires on the new solenoid to the common wire and field wire, using waterproof connectors.

Repair Wet Spots in Your Yard

Wet spots in your yard are a nuisance and an eyesore. Grass will die if it's underwater for too long. You can't mow over wet areas, and everyone tracks mud into the house. If the soggy area is close to your house, it can cause your basement to leak, or worse. So what's the answer? Listed here are your options. If you see a solution that looks right for you, go to familyhandyman.com and do a search on the topic for more details.

1. TRY SIMPLE FIXES FIRST

Before you start digging a trench or taking some other drastic action to get rid of a wet spot, step back and survey the situation to see where the water is coming from. The problem could be as simple as downspout or sump pump discharge that's draining into a low area of your yard. Or landscaping near the house may be creating a basin for water. Redirecting your downspout, extending it or running the discharge pipe from your sump pump to a different location might be all you need to do.

2. CONSTRUCT A CREEK BED

You can solve drainage problems and create an attractive landscape feature at the same time by building a dry creek bed. A creek bed such as the one shown can channel water away from a low spot or direct runoff into a rain garden or dry well. With the right landscaping, the creek bed will look good even when it's dry.

Start by making a swale—essentially a gentle, shallow drainage ditch. Then line it with gravel or stones and add interest with boulders, a bridge or plantings.

Of course, you don't have to turn your drainage project into a creek bed. A simple swale is an effective and subtle way to control surface water. Obviously it's easier to create a swale before you seed or sod your yard, but if necessary, you can cut out the grass with a sod cutter and replace it when you're done regrading.

Draw a Drainage Plan

If you can't find a simple fix for your soggy yard dilemma, you'll need another strategy. Start by making a sketch of your property, showing the house, driveway, patios, street and other features. Then use a line level, builder's level or some other leveling method to determine high and low spots. Draw arrows to show how water flows and make notes to indicate the relative height of high and low spots. Keep in mind that in most cases you shouldn't plan to direct water onto your neighbor's property. And if you're hoping to discharge water into the street or municipal storm sewer, contact the city first to see what regulations apply.

A sketch will help you decide which of the following strategies is best for your situation. For example, if you simply have no way to drain water from a low spot to another location, your best option may be to build a rain garden or dry well.

3. BUILD A RAIN GARDEN

If you have a low spot in your yard that tends to collect and retain water, consider building a rain garden. A rain garden is simply an area of your yard that is designed to catch water and is filled with water-loving plants. It doesn't really solve a soggy yard problem, but a rain garden looks a lot better than a muddy hole. Plus, rain gardens are good for the environment. They reduce runoff and the lawn chemicals, pet waste and sediment that go along with it.

A rain garden doesn't have to hold water like a pond. You can add drainage and use the rain garden to hold the excess water until it has a chance to drain away. A key part of a rain garden's design is choosing the right plants for the soil conditions. Typically, native plants with deep fibrous roots work well. Go to familyhandyman.com and search for "rain garden" to learn more about how to build one in your yard.

4. INSTALL A FRENCH DRAIN

A French drain is a versatile system for dealing with all kinds of drainage problems. It disperses water over a large area through a buried perforated pipe. The pipe must be surrounded by material that allows water to drain through. Conventionally this was gravel, but NDS sells a system called EZflow that includes the pipe and surrounding polystyrene aggregate in one convenient and lightweight package. A French drain system can be used alone or in combination with a dry well.

A properly designed French drain system does not require an outlet. The water will simply soak into the soil as it flows along the perforated pipe. In fact, a French drain doesn't require an inlet on just one end either. You can construct the drain to accept water along its length and then disperse the water underground.

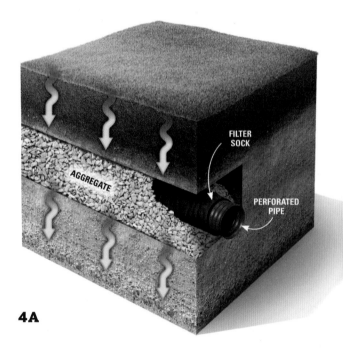

Anatomy of a French Drain (4A): A typical French drain consists of a perforated pipe—usually flexible lightweight plastic—sheathed by a fabric filter sock to keep dirt and sand from clogging the pipe. The pipe is buried in a trench and surrounded by aggregate. Water enters the pipe from an inlet at one end, through the earth or through long narrow grates spaced along its length and then is dispersed through the aggregate and into the ground.

Install the Pipe in a Trench (4B): Connect the lengths of tubing and place them over a bed of gravel. Then add gravel on the sides and over the top before covering the pipe. Perforated drainage pipe is also available with the sock already in place.

5A

5. CREATE A DRY WELL

A dry well is simply a large hole filled with gravel or some other aggregate that catches excess water and holds it while it soaks into the ground. You can increase the capacity of a dry well by burying special dry well barrels **(5A)**. These plastic containers collect water and hold it while it drains out through holes in the sides and bottom. Commercially available dry wells such as the one shown are easy to assemble. The containers must be surrounded by gravel or another porous material to allow drainage. You can stack these plastic dry wells or place them side by side. In general, a dry well should be large enough to collect the first 10 or 15 minutes of a large rainstorm. Websites like ndspro.com provide guidance and calculators to help you determine the size of your dry well. You can also consult with a landscape contractor or soil engineer. You can increase the capacity of a dry well by connecting it to a French drain system **(5B)**. Search for "French drain" at familyhandyman.com.

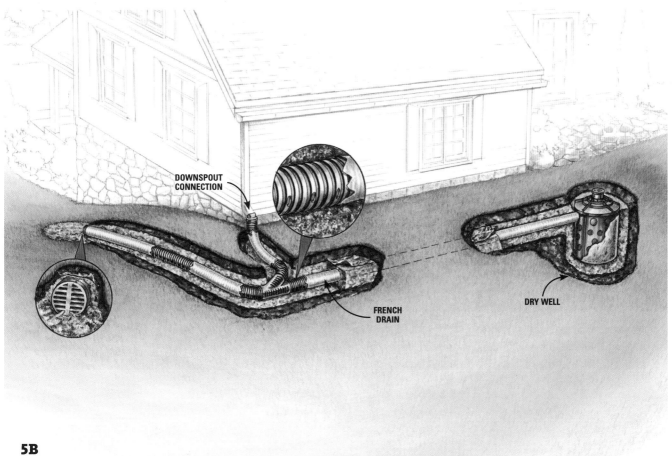

DOWNSPOUT CONNECTION

FRENCH DRAIN

DRY WELL

5B

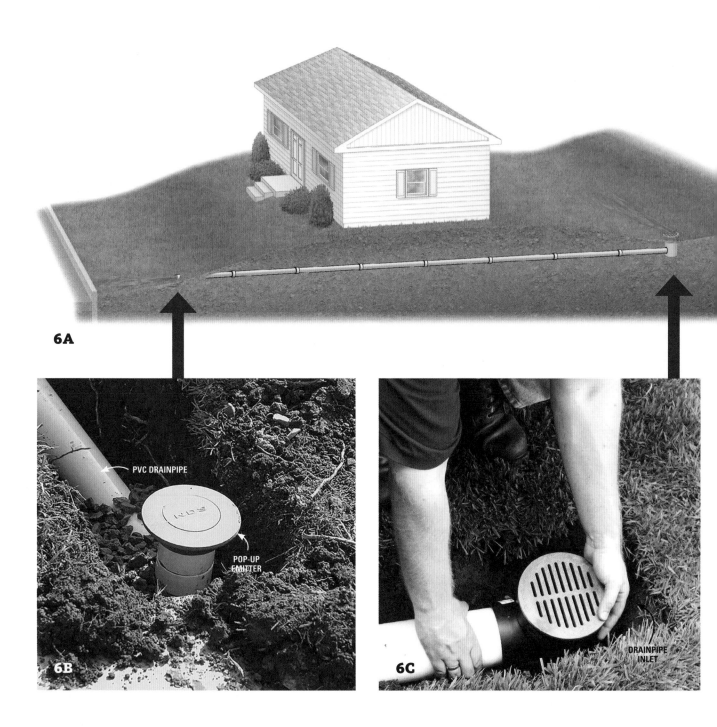

6A

PVC DRAINPIPE

POP-UP EMITTER

6B

DRAINPIPE INLET

6C

6. ADD A DRAINPIPE

One of the best ways to get rid of water from a low spot is to simply drain it away through an underground pipe **(6A)**. For this to work, you need an area to discharge the water that's lower than the inlet area. The drainpipe should slope downhill at least 1/8 in. per foot. If you had a discharge outlet 100 ft. from the inlet, it would have to be about 1 ft. lower than the inlet area.

To create the drain, you'll have to dig a gradually sloping trench from the source to the outlet. Then bury a plastic catch basin at the source and connect it to the discharge with PVC drainpipe. This system has a few advantages over

a French drain **(see p. 82)**. Since the pipe is solid and not perforated, there's no need to provide gravel for drainage along the length of the drainpipe. Also, smooth-wall pipe drains water quickly, and if it gets clogged, you can use a drain snake to clean it out.

Drainpipe discharge (6B): The discharge end of your drainpipe can be connected to a pop-up emitter that sits flush to the lawn when no water is flowing.

Drainpipe inlet (6C): Position the inlet catch basin at the low spot of your soggy area. The grate will sit flush to the lawn for easy mowing.

An Outside Cure for Wet Basements

The basic solution is often the best solution.

Water in your basement? Don't call the basement waterproofing company yet. Many basement leaks can be cured with a weekend's work and several hundred dollars' worth of dirt and plastic (still less expensive than the pro!).

A huge percentage of wet basements can be remedied by simply regrading the landscape, and adding or upgrading gutters and downspouts. The **graphic on pages 86 and 87** shows the key elements for an effective solution.

Of course, this fix will work only if the water entering your basement is coming from rain or melting snow. But it's pretty easy to tell. If you get water in your basement shortly after a storm or when the snow is melting, or if a wet inverted-V pattern appears on the wall, the cause is most likely improper grading or a downspout that's emptying water near your foundation. And even if there are other factors contributing to your wet basement, the solutions we show here will help keep your basement dry and should be done before you take more extreme measures.

4 STEPS TO FIXING A LEAKY BASEMENT

1. CHECK THE LANDSCAPE AROUND YOUR HOUSE

You'll need to do a thorough check of the ground around your foundation. For this you'll need a 4-ft. level, a tape measure and a notepad. First draw a simple sketch of your house and yard on your notepad. Then use the level to check the slope of the ground around your foundation. Look for areas of sunken soil, garden beds with edging that protrudes to form a dam, and ground that slopes toward the house. Make notes on your sketch with arrows to show which way the ground slopes. This step will help you develop a plan for redirecting the water away from the foundation.

2. MAKE A PLAN AND ORDER MATERIAL

With the sketch in hand, you can figure out where the problem areas are and what you need to do to fix them. The goal is to create a 6-ft.-wide perimeter that slopes away from the house. Aim for a slope of about 1 in. per foot, but if this isn't practical, get as close to it as you can. There are two ways to change the slope of the ground near your foundation. You can add soil or some other compactable fill near the house, or you can move soil from the high area to

USE A TAMPING TOOL OR POWER TAMPER TO COMPACT THE FILL AND CREATE A SMOOTH, HARD SURFACE.

YOU'LL NEED:
COMPACTABLE FILL
6-MIL POLY
EDGING
MULCH OR GRAVEL

the foundation. In either case, keep in mind that you should maintain 6 in. between the soil surface and the siding to prevent rot and discourage insects.

If you need a lot of fill, it may be cheaper to have a dump truck deliver a load. Otherwise you can buy bags of soil at most landscape supply stores or home centers. You'll also need enough 6-mil black poly sheeting to cover the area between the foundation and 6 ft. out. And if you like our idea of using bricks for the edging **(see illustration on pp. 86-87)**, you'll need to order these too. Finally, you'll need some mulch or other decorative material to cover the poly.

3. CREATE THE SLOPE

If you have shrubs or trees near the foundation, they may be part of the problem. In some cases, their roots form a channel for water to reach the foundation, or they penetrate cracks in the foundation and create new paths for water to enter. Remove shrubs and trees that you don't need. You'll have to work around any that are a valued part of your landscape.

Next, spread the new fill, using a level to check the slope. Or simply regrade the soil near your foundation to create the slope. Use a garden rake to smooth and level the ground. When you're happy with the slope, tamp the soil to compact it. If you're doing the entire perimeter, it may be worth renting a gas-powered tamper for this. Otherwise a hand tamper will work.

If your plan includes adding bricks along the edge, dig a trench deep enough so that the top edge of the brick is level with the ground. Then lay 6-mil poly over the ground and into the trench. Finish up by placing the bricks and covering the poly with mulch, wood chips, or some type of decorative stone or gravel.

4. CHECK YOUR GUTTERS AND DOWNSPOUTS

If you don't have gutters and downspouts, consider adding them. Otherwise, most of the water from the roof ends up right near the foundation where you don't want it. If you do have gutters, or if you're adding them, make sure to attach extensions to the downspouts so that the water discharges at least 6 ft. away from the house.

If at First You Don't Succeed ...

These four simple steps will solve most basement leaks caused by surface water such as rain and snow melt. But if your basement still leaks after you've made these corrections, consider hiring an engineering firm experienced in solving water leakage problems to propose other remedies. Be cautious about hiring companies that offer only their own solution because it may not be the best one for your situation. And if you're looking for more information on solutions to wet basements, how to deal with wet carpet, how to fix plumbing leaks, or how to add an interior drain and sump pump, search for the key words at familyhandyman.com.

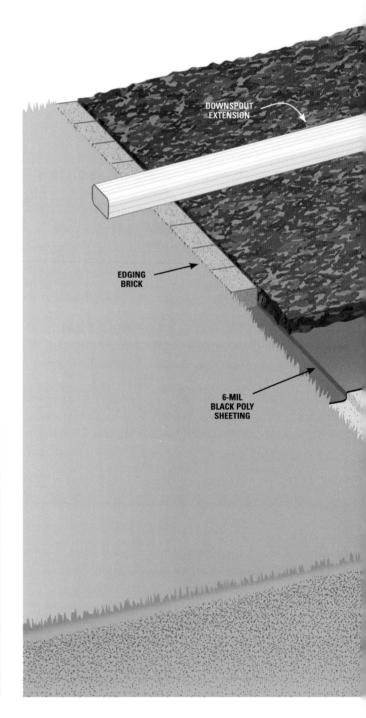

DOWNSPOUT EXTENSION

EDGING BRICK

6-MIL BLACK POLY SHEETING

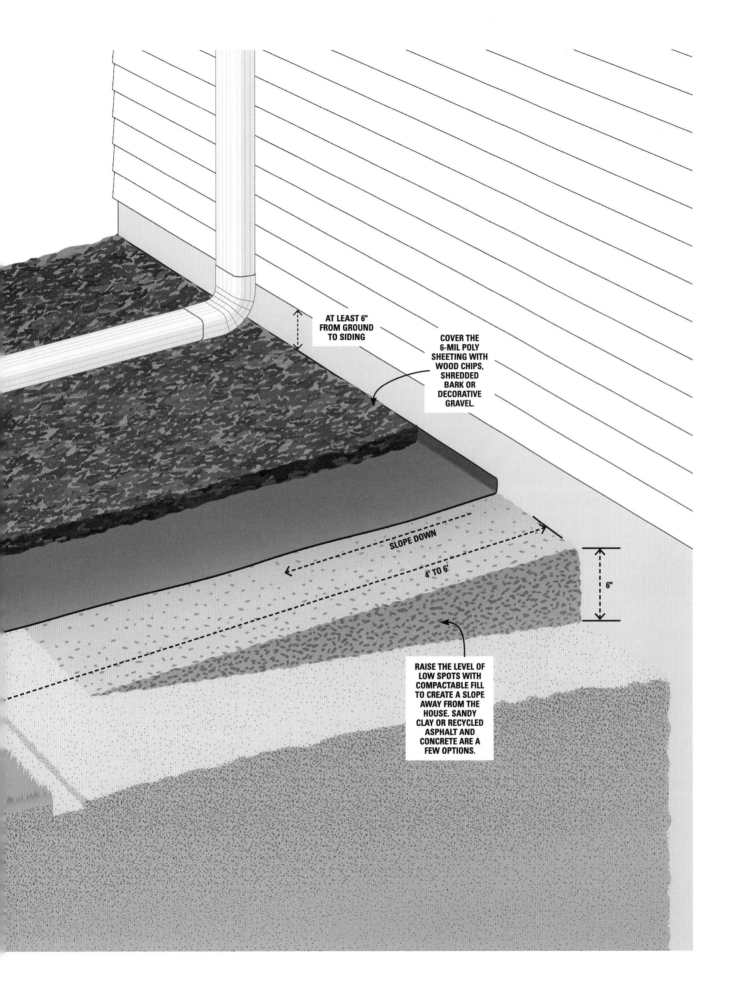

AT LEAST 6"
FROM GROUND
TO SIDING

COVER THE
6-MIL POLY
SHEETING WITH
WOOD CHIPS,
SHREDDED
BARK OR
DECORATIVE
GRAVEL.

SLOPE DOWN

4' TO 6'

6"

RAISE THE LEVEL OF
LOW SPOTS WITH
COMPACTABLE FILL
TO CREATE A SLOPE
AWAY FROM THE
HOUSE. SANDY
CLAY OR RECYCLED
ASPHALT AND
CONCRETE ARE A
FEW OPTIONS.

CHAPTER **FOUR**

ELECTRICAL & PLUMBING

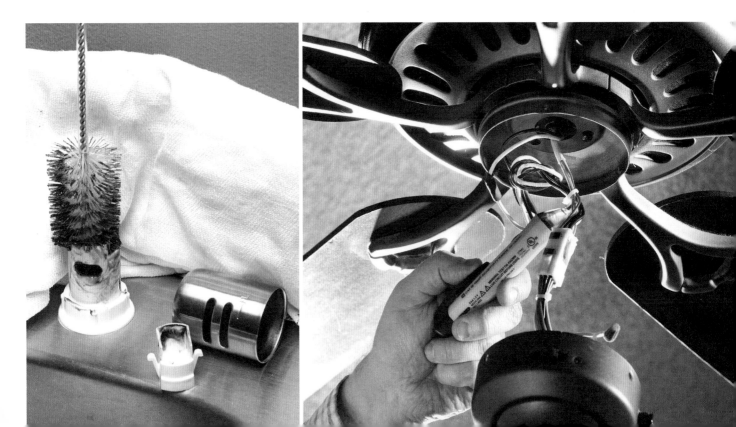

LIQUID TAPE

Fix a Broken Phone Charger

Charger cables for cell phones usually last only a few years before the insulation starts fraying on the ends. Replacement cables can be purchased, but there's a cheaper solution. If the insulation is cracked but the copper wire inside is still intact, try covering the crack with a couple of layers of liquid electrical tape. Performix and Gardner Bender are two brands that get lots of positive reviews online. Just be sure not to let the cable touch anything until the liquid tape dries completely.

Knob-and-Tube Insulation Repair

The insulation on knob-and-tube wiring gets brittle with age. When you're working with it, the insulation may just crumble in your hands. You can easily reinsulate a section using a length of the plastic jacket from a piece of nonmetallic sheathed cable (often referred to as Romex).

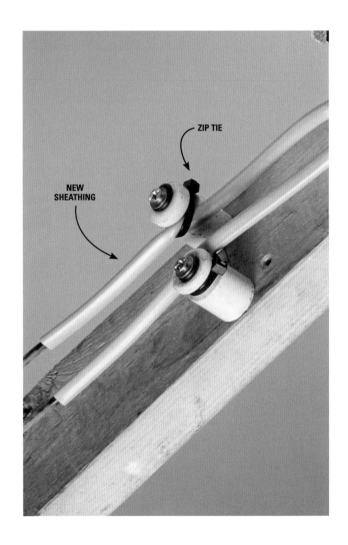

ZIP TIE

NEW SHEATHING

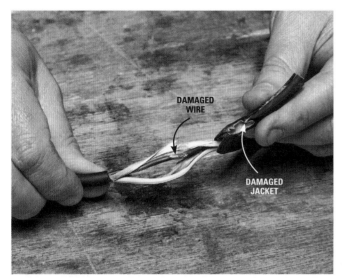

1 **SLIT AND PEEL THE JACKET.** Slice around the outer jacket about 3 in. on both sides of the damage. Then slit the jacket down the center and peel it off.

DAMAGED WIRE

DAMAGED JACKET

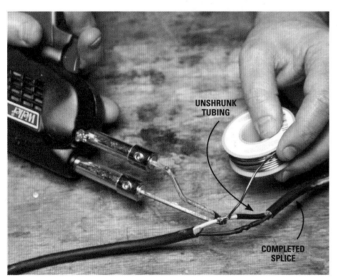

2 **STRIP, TWIST AND SOLDER.** Strip insulation off each wire. Then twist the strands together and solder. Solder each splice.

UNSHRUNK TUBING

COMPLETED SPLICE

3 **COVER AND SHRINK.** Slide the shrinkable tubing over the splices and the outer jacket. Shrink the tubing using a heat gun.

SHRINKABLE TUBING

Patch a Power Tool Cord

Got a nicked or cut power tool cord? Here's how to restore it to "almost new" condition.

You'll need some basic supplies to make the repair, including heat-shrinkable tubing in both small and large diameters, a soldering gun and rosin-core solder, a utility knife, a heat gun and wire strippers.

Start by removing a 6-in. section of the outer jacket **(Photo 1)**. Save it for later use. Then cut the wire insulation and the reinforcement cord. Slide a piece of large-diameter heat-shrinkable tubing onto the cord and push it out of the way for the moment.

Slide a small piece of heat-shrinkable tubing onto each wire. Stagger the splices and solder **(Photo 2)**. Let the solder cool, then slide the tubing over each splice and shrink it.

Reinstall the outer jacket. Cover the entire patched area with the large heat-shrinkable tubing and shrink it **(Photo 3)**.

Fix a Ceiling Fan

**When a ceiling fan stops working or starts making noises, don't panic.
It's likely an easy and inexpensive DIY fix.**

A ceiling fan can run nonstop for years without a hint of a problem. Then, out of the blue, it can quit completely, stop working on some speeds or start making a loud humming sound. You may think the motor is shot, but it's probably not. Those are all symptoms of a burned-out capacitor. The capacitor and the pull-chain switch are the only two components that control the fan speeds. Switches rarely wear out. But they can break if you pull the chain too hard or it gets caught in the blades. You can hedge your bets and replace both the capacitor and the switch in less than an hour. Here's what you need to do.

Start by shutting off the power to the fan and the lights (if equipped). You'll have to gain access to the housing where the speed and direction switches are located. In fans without lights, just remove the bottom cover. Double-check the power with a voltage sniffer before you stick your fingers in the housing. If your fan has lights, remove the globes and

bulbs. Then remove the light kit. That will expose the wiring in the housing.

Next, remove the capacitor **(Photo 1)**. A burned-out capacitor might have a burnt smell, swollen sides or scorch marks. Those are sure signs it's bad. But even if yours appears to be in good shape, replace it anyway because it's still the most likely cause of your speed/humming problem **(Photo 2)**. If you have any doubts about the fan switch, replace it too.

Remove the pull-chain switch by unscrewing the knurled outer knob. Pull the switch into the housing and disconnect the wires. Take both pieces to a ceiling fan or appliance parts store to get replacements.

If you don't have a local source for parts, go to eceilingfans .com. Click on the "Capacitors" or "Wall Switches" tab to find replacements.

Finish the job by connecting the new parts and tucking everything back into the housing **(Photo 3)**.

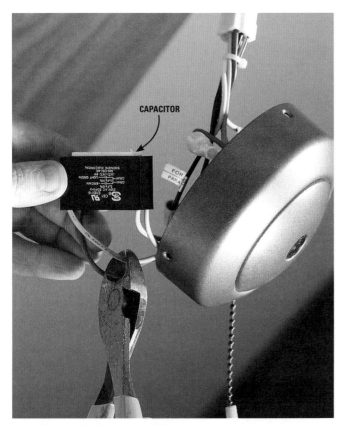

CAPACITOR

1 **REMOVE THE CAPACITOR. Reach into the housing and gently pull out the capacitor. Untangle it from the other wires. Then cut the capacitor lead wires one at a time, or remove the wire nuts and cut off the wire strands.**

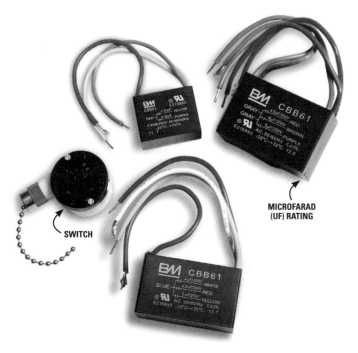

SWITCH

MICROFARAD (UF) RATING

2 **SHOP FOR A NEW CAPACITOR AND SWITCH. Note the number of wires and the microfarad (UF) rating on the old capacitor. Buy a new one with the same number of wires and UF rating.**

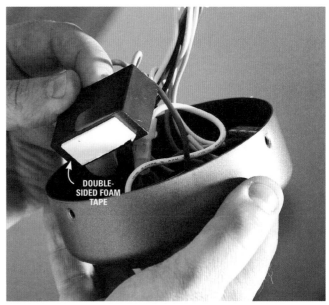

DOUBLE-SIDED FOAM TAPE

3 **INSERT THE CAPACITOR, THEN THE WIRES. Apply double-sided foam tape to the capacitor and stick it to the housing cap. Then pack the wires into the center, making sure the wire nuts stay connected.**

Fixing a Remote Control Fan

Ceiling fans with factory remote controls don't use traditional capacitors to control fan speed. The remote receiver varies the voltage and current to change the fan motor's speed. But remote control units can go bad too. Before you even think about tearing the fan apart to diagnose a problem, replace the batteries in the transmitter first. Then press the transmitter buttons to see if the LEDs light up. If you're not sure whether the problem is in the transmitter or receiver, you can send both units to eceilingfans.com for testing (testing and repair is inexpensive). The receiver is usually tucked into the fan's mounting bracket, which is connected to the electrical box.

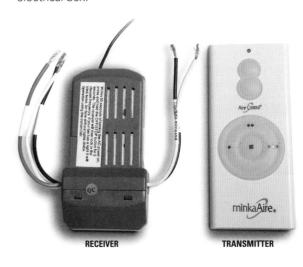

RECEIVER   TRANSMITTER

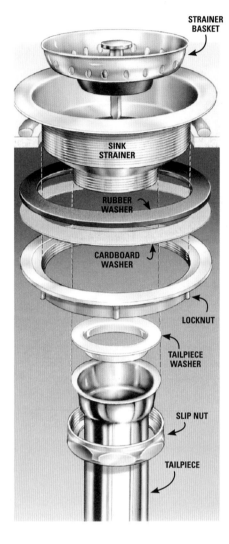

STRAINER BASKET

SINK STRAINER

RUBBER WASHER

CARDBOARD WASHER

LOCKNUT

TAILPIECE WASHER

SLIP NUT

TAILPIECE

LEAKY STRAINER

SLIP NUT

1 Take apart the drain assembly so you can remove the leaky strainer. Turn slip nuts counterclockwise, using a second set of pliers if necessary to keep the pipes from turning.

LOCKNUT

STRAINER

LOCKNUT WRENCH

2 Turn the locknut counterclockwise to remove the strainer. Have a helper stick the handles of a pair of pliers into the strainer holes and keep the strainer from turning using a screwdriver.

STUBBORN LOCKNUT

3 Cut the locknut with a hacksaw if you can't unscrew it. Make sure to cut at a sharp diagonal angle and be careful that you don't cut into the sink as you work.

PLUMBER'S PUTTY

4 Put plumber's putty or waterproof caulk around the drain opening. Install the rubber and cardboard washers. Tighten the locknut with the same method you used to take off the old one.

Reseal a Leaky Strainer

The primary seal around a basket strainer is plumber's putty, which doesn't last forever. Over the years it can harden, shrink or crack. Sometimes you can stop a leak by tightening the locknut. But in many cases the only cure is a new dose of putty. **Photos 1-4** above show how to reseal a strainer. You can reuse the old strainer if all the parts are in good shape, but it usually makes sense to replace it. Expect to spend money to get a quality strainer—cheaper ones are less reliable. Since you have to take apart most of the drain assembly to get at a leaking strainer **(Photo 1)**, consider replacing drain lines if they're old.

The hardest part of this job is unscrewing the old locknut, which is often welded in place by mineral deposits or corrosion. A special wrench designed just for locknuts,

called a spud wrench or locknut wrench **(Photo 2)**, can help. Big slip-joint pliers with a 3-1/2-in. jaw opening will work too, plus you can use them for other jobs.

Whatever tool you use, you might find that the locknut won't budge. In that case, a single cut with a hacksaw blade is the only solution **(Photo 3)**. It's almost impossible to do this without cutting into the strainer threads, so plan on buying a new strainer.

With the locknut removed, pull out the strainer and scrape the old putty off the sink with a plastic putty knife. Installing a new strainer is simple **(Photo 4)**. Just remember that the rubber washer goes on before the cardboard washer. Tighten the strainer using the same method you used to remove it.

Quiet a Noisy Toilet

Whenever you flush a toilet, the fill valve inside the tank opens, letting fresh water back into the tank. The sound of the water rushing into the tank can be quite noisy, which is really a problem only if it's the middle of the night and people are trying to sleep.

Try this trick to quiet things down: Find the water shutoff for the toilet underneath the tank and close it a little bit. That will reduce the amount of water flowing into the tank and take the noise level down a bit. Of course, the toilet will take longer to fill.

WATER
SHUTOFF
VALVE

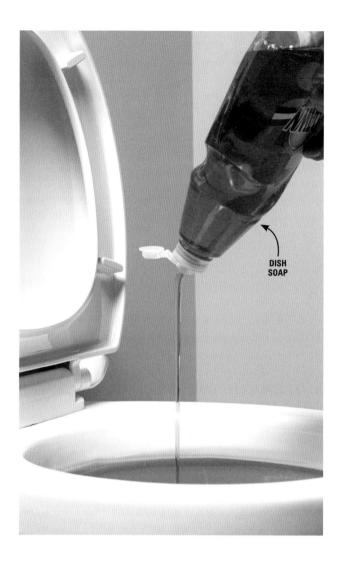

DISH
SOAP

Unclog a Toilet with Dish Soap

When your attempts to unclog a bathroom toilet are futile, try this trick with a little help from a staple cleaner from the kitchen.

Pour in about 1/2 cup of liquid dish soap and don't flush. Instead, let it sit for a while. It works like magic! As it sits, liquid soap coats the toilet and reduces friction, which allows the contents of the bowl to slide on through.

Toilet Tune-Ups

The toilet is arguably the most important seat in the house. If your toilet isn't flushing well, don't just live with it! You can probably fix the problem in less than 30 minutes. We've put together nine simple tips to help you get the best possible flush every time.

1. SWITCH TO SINGLE-PLY

Sometimes a poor flush is caused by partial drain clogs. The majority of these clogs are caused by toilet paper, particularly the luxuriously soft two- and three-ply varieties. Switching to single-ply toilet paper can help because it breaks down faster, even if you use the same amount of toilet paper.

2. OPEN THE WATER SUPPLY ALL THE WAY

When you flush, it's not just the water from the tank that's making the flush. The fill valve also opens, allowing more water to immediately enter the tank. The more water flowing in, the better your flush will be.

3. GET A FLAPPER WITH A CHAIN FLOAT

A chain float helps the flapper stay open a bit longer, allowing more water to enter the bowl for a better flush. You can adjust the float up or down on the chain to fine-tune how long the flapper remains open.

4. TRY A DIFFERENT FLAPPER

The flapper is the part inside the tank that goes up when you press the flush handle. Hundreds of flapper styles are available, including some that allow you to adjust the amount of water per flush—but not all flappers are compatible with every toilet. Plumbers often carry a variety in their truck and, through trial and error, choose the one that works best. If you've tried everything else, buy a few different flappers and see which one works the best on your toilet. Check map-testing.com to find flappers compatible with your specific toilet.

5. CLEAN THE RIM JETS

Over time, particularly if you have hard water, mineral deposits can plug the rim jets. If you notice the sides of the bowl aren't clean after flushing, the rim jets likely need cleaning. You'll need a mirror to see them. Depending on the size of the jets, use a coat hanger or small screwdriver to clean them out.

SINGLE-PLY

TWO-PLY

1

2

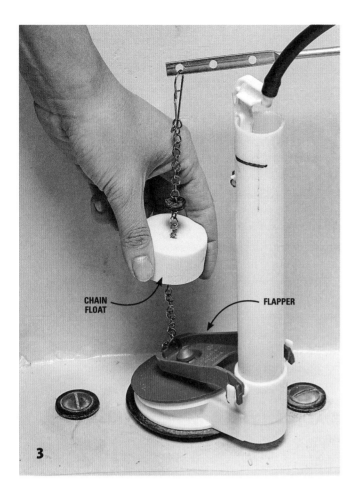

CHAIN
FLOAT

FLAPPER

3

4

5

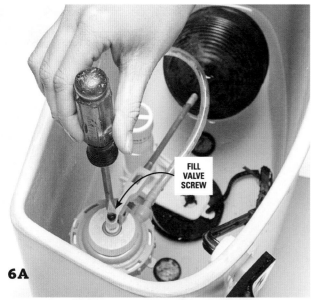

6A

FILL VALVE SCREW

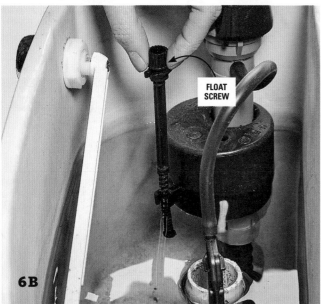

FLOAT SCREW

6B

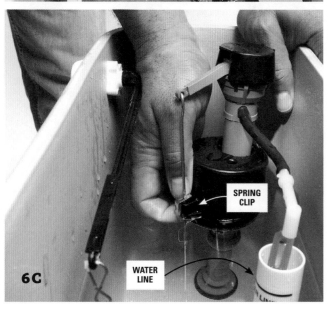

SPRING CLIP

WATER LINE

6C

6. ADJUST THE WATER LEVEL

Most toilets have an indicator line showing the proper water level. If yours doesn't, set the fill level 1 in. below the top of the overflow pipe. Closer than that might be asking for trouble. In the evening, the demand on your municipal water supply drops, which can increase water pressure. This can cause the water level in your tank to rise a bit.

If water is continuously flowing into the overflow pipe, you're flushing money as well as water down the toilet. Many different mechanisms can help you adjust your tank's water level. The most common ones are an adjustment screw on the fill valve **(photo 6A)**, an adjustment screw connected to the float **(photo 6B)** and a spring clip connected to the float **(photo 6C)**.

7. ADJUST THE FLAPPER CHAIN

Adjust the chain so that it just allows the flapper to seat. If the chain is too long, the flapper will close too soon for a good flush. If the chain is too short, the flapper won't seal. To adjust the length, move the clip to a different chain link. Be sure there are no kinks in the chain, then squeeze the clip closed and cut off the excess chain.

8. AIM THE REFILL TUBE

Make sure the refill tube is aimed directly into the overflow pipe; you don't want any water spraying outside it. That little tube refills the bowl with water from the tank after flushing. A low water level in the bowl contributes to a weak flush and fails to clean the sides of the bowl.

9. TIGHTEN THE FLUSH HANDLE

A nut inside the tank holds the flush handle in place. If it's loose, it can throw off the chain adjustment. Tighten the nut, being careful not to overtighten; it just needs to be snug.

Basement Toilet Trouble?

Basement toilets are notoriously bad flushers. There often isn't enough of a drop from the toilet to the horizontal drain that leads to the main sewer line, which limits the assist of gravity. This can also be a problem if you have a toilet in a building with no basement. A pressure-assist toilet might be your only option in this case.

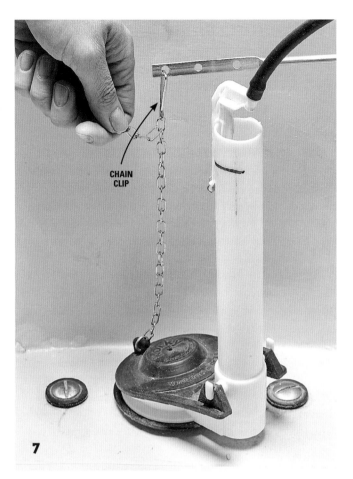

CHAIN CLIP

7

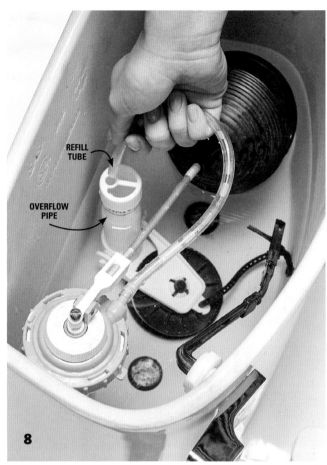

REFILL TUBE

OVERFLOW PIPE

8

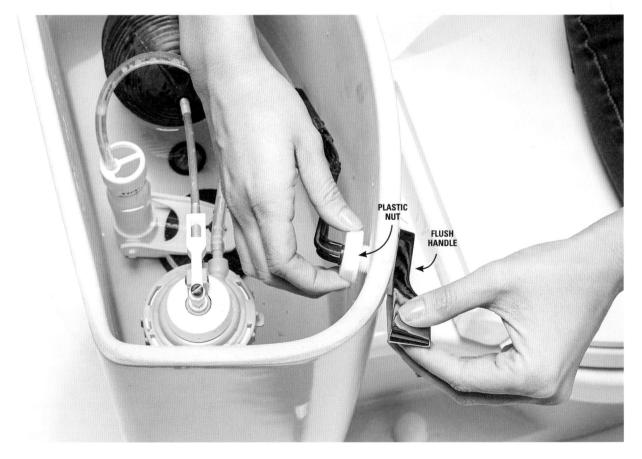

PLASTIC NUT

FLUSH HANDLE

9

Improve Low Water Pressure

When a showerhead or faucet isn't delivering enough water, everyone complains about low "pressure," but pressure is the force. "Flow" is more likely the culprit in most homes.

1

1. CHECK THE WATER PRESSURE

"Pressure," measured in pounds per square inch (psi), is the physical force exerted on water by a municipal pumping station or private well pump. Go to your local home center to get yourself a water pressure test gauge. Then just screw it onto an outdoor hose bib and turn on the water **(photo 1A)**. If the gauge reads 40 to 60 psi, you've got good pressure.

INSPECT YOUR PRESSURE-REDUCING VALVE (PHOTO 1B) If your pressure test reads lower than 40 psi, see if you have a pressure-reducing valve (PRV) mounted on your water main. It'll look similar to the one pictured here, and it needs to be adjusted correctly. Most come set from the factory for 50 psi, but you can adjust them up or down by turning a screw on top. PRVs can also go bad after 10 to 20 years and cause too little (or too much) pressure. So if yours is old, it might be time to replace it. Just about any DIYer with a little plumbing experience can handle the job. A new PRV may have to be special-ordered.

CALL CITY HALL If after all that you've still got low water pressure, call your local water department to see if there's a problem with the pressure coming from the street to your house. If you get your water from a private well and suspect that your well pump might be the cause of your pressure woes, visit familyhandyman.com and search for "well pump" for some solutions.

INSTALL A WATER PRESSURE BOOSTER (PHOTO 1C) If your water department can't deliver more pressure and you have a 3/4-in. or bigger copper or plastic water main coming into your house, consider installing a water pressure booster. It takes the water coming in from the street and increases its pressure by means of an electric pump and a pressure tank. The tank holds a reserve of pressurized water so that the pump doesn't have to run every time somebody opens a faucet. It also helps boost flow when the demand for water is high (like when your teenagers are all showering at the same time). Water pressure boosters such as the one shown here are available at home centers and online.

TOO MUCH WATER PRESSURE? When it comes to water pressure, it's actually possible to have too much of a good thing. Pressure that's over 80 psi can cause you to waste water and the energy required to heat it. It can also damage water softeners, water heaters, faucets, appliances and seals. If your pressure test shows more than 80 psi, make sure you have a working pressure-reducing valve that you've set between 50 and 60 psi.

1A

BOOSTER
PUMP

PRESSURE
TANK

WATER
WORKER

1C

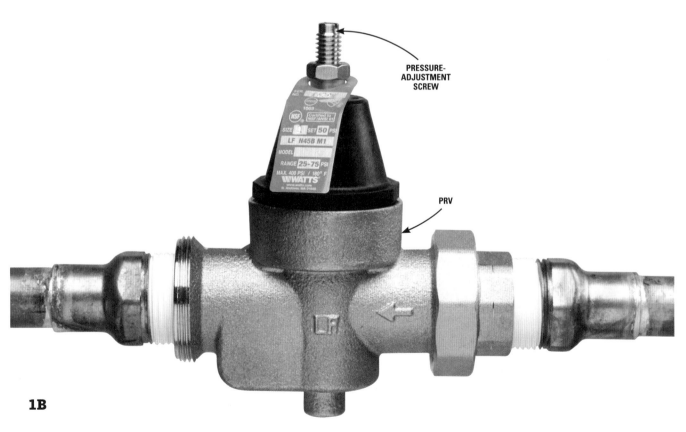

PRESSURE-
ADJUSTMENT
SCREW

PRV

1B

2A

2B

2. IMPROVE WATER FLOW

START WITH THE SMALL STUFF If you have poor water flow at most or all of your faucets, think about things such as old galvanized steel pipes or a busted water softener. But if just one faucet is weak, look for isolated causes such as clogged aerators and shutoff valves. Start with the small stuff, not the big stuff.

CLEAN AERATORS Remove the aerator with a pair of groove-joint pliers **(photo 2A)**. Cover the jaws with electrical tape so you don't scratch the finish.

Next, scrub all the parts clean with an old toothbrush **(photo 2B)**. Be sure to close the drain or cover the hole with a rag so your parts don't fall down it, and set all the parts on the side of the sink in the order you removed them to make reassembly easier. Soak the parts in vinegar overnight if you have a lot of mineral buildup. If they just won't come clean, buy a replacement aerator. Exact replacements can be hard to find locally, so you might have to special-order one. To find online retailers, search for "faucet aerator."

UNCLOG SHOWERHEADS If your showerhead used to work fine but now just spits at you, it's probably clogged with mineral buildup (you'll usually see a ring of deposits surrounding each hole). Remove the showerhead and soak it in vinegar overnight. (Test the vinegar on an inconspicuous spot first to make sure it doesn't harm the finish.) Use a toothpick to poke the holes clean, then rinse it with water **(photo 2C)**. Some newer showerheads have rubber-lined holes that you can just pick with a fingernail to unclog—you don't even have to remove the showerhead.

OPEN PLUMBING VALVES Make sure all the fixture shutoffs in your kitchen and bathrooms, as well as the plumbing valves in your basement or crawl space, are fully open. Stop valves and gate valves have round handles that you turn counterclockwise to open. Ball valves have straight handles and are open all the way when the handle is in line with the piping to which it's connected.

You might find a smaller version of a ball valve, called a quarter-turn valve **(photo 2D)**, under your sinks and toilets. If the handle is even slightly askew, it could be impeding water flow.

REPLACE WATER FILTERS Water filters do a great job of keeping crud out of your plumbing system and make water smell and taste better, but they can also slow down the flow of water if you don't replace them regularly. If you have a whole-house sediment filter and you're always forgetting to check it, replace it with one that has a clear housing so you can easily see when it needs changing. And don't forget to change the filters under your sink and the water and ice filter inside your fridge too **(photo 2E)**.

CLOGGED PIPES AND ELBOWS If you have old galvanized steel pipes and elbows in your plumbing system, they're probably reducing your water flow. Any type of pipe or

2C

VALVE NOT FULLY OPEN

2D

UNDER-MOUNT SINK FILTERS

2E

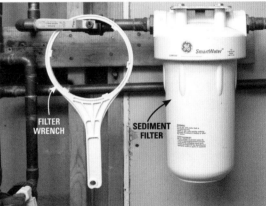

FILTER WRENCH

SEDIMENT FILTER

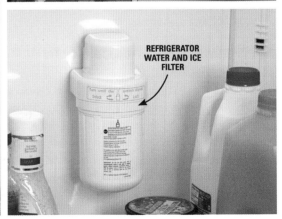

REFRIGERATOR WATER AND ICE FILTER

tubing can clog, but these ancient relics are especially notorious for corroding internally to the point that water can barely pass through **(photo 2F)**.

Consider replacing galvanized steel piping with copper, CPVC or PEX tubing. Complete replacement is a huge job that usually requires tearing into walls and ceilings. But in many cases, just replacing the exposed horizontal pipes in your basement or crawl space is enough to dramatically increase water flow.

GALVANIC CORROSION This type of corrosion occurs when you join pipes made of dissimilar metals, such as galvanized steel with copper. You'll often see it happening on the tops of water heaters, where galvanized steel nipples are connected to copper pipes. The corrosion can get so bad that it clogs the inside of the pipes. The photo **(2G)** shows a dielectric union that was supposed to prevent corrosion by separating the two metals, but they were still close enough for serious corrosion to occur.

For maximum protection against galvanic corrosion on water heaters, use both dielectric unions AND dielectric nipples. Both have nonmetallic liners that keep the two different metals from touching or being close enough to cause corrosion.

3. WATER SOFTENERS

Water softeners do a great job of keeping mineral deposits (hardness) from forming and clogging faucets, fixtures and pipes—but they can do that only if you keep them in good working order. For tips on maintaining and repairing water softeners, visit familyhandyman.com and search for "water softeners."

FLUSH PIPES AFTER WORKING ON THEM

Whenever you do plumbing work, there's a chance that bits of solder, Teflon tape and crud that break loose can clog a faucet or fixture if you don't flush the pipe or hose supplying it. Disconnect hoses downstream from the part of the plumbing system you were working on, then open the shutoffs (one at a time) and let some water flow into a bucket before reconnecting them.

IS IT TIME TO REPLACE YOUR WATER MAIN?

If you've tried everything and you're still not getting enough flow, you might need a new water main—the underground pipe that carries water from the street to your house. Remember that pressure and flow are different. You might have good pressure at the main, but the main's flow might be restricted. This is especially common with older galvanized steel mains, which often clog over time from corrosion buildup.

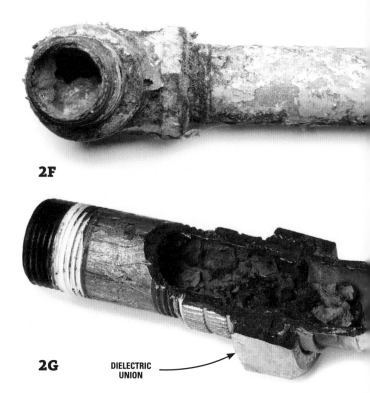

2F

2G   DIELECTRIC UNION

3

Old mains are also often just too small. A modern water main—usually 3/4-in. or bigger copper or plastic—could make a huge difference. You might also be able to avoid tearing up your yard to install one if your contractor uses an underground boring machine. Also see if your municipal water department will give you a water meter with larger-diameter fittings.

WELLS AND WELL PUMPS

Whether you get your water from a private well or your local water department, everything discussed here about troubleshooting and fixing flow problems still applies. For pressure problems related to well pumps, visit familyhandyman.com and search for "well pump."

Clear a Clogged Air Gap

An air gap prevents dirty dishwater from backflowing into fresh water lines. But over time, ground-up food and grease can build up inside the air gap and form a clog. If water squirts out the air gap's vent holes or you notice a foul smell coming from it, it's time to clean it. All you need is a bottle brush and some household disinfecting cleaner.

Yank the cover off the air gap and remove the snap-in or screw-on diverter. Remove any loose food particles, then clean it with the bottle brush as shown. If you still have a water leak after cleaning the air gap, clean the drain line where it meets the garbage disposer or drain wye (aka Y).

CLEAN THE AIR GAP WITH A BRUSH.
Soak the bottle brush in household cleaner
and plunge it up and down into the air gap.

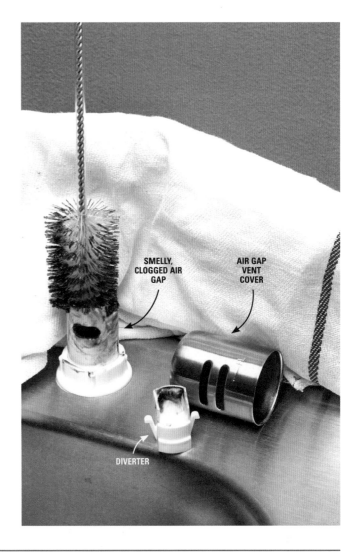

SMELLY, CLOGGED AIR GAP

AIR GAP VENT COVER

DIVERTER

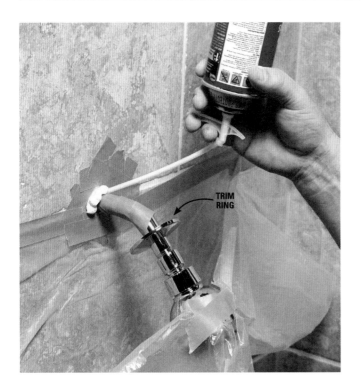

TRIM RING

Foam a Loose Showerhead

To fix a wobbly shower arm, there's no need to tear into the wall and refasten the plumbing. Instead, use expanding foam. Shield the wall with plastic and inject a few shots of the foam. The foam encases the pipes in the wall and should eliminate the wobble.

Fix Roots in a Sewer Line

Hire a pro to determine how much damage you have and then decide which of four options is the best fix.

Your sewer line is a particularly attractive water source for tree roots, especially if you live in an arid climate. Roots can bore right through the tiniest cracks and holes in any pipe. Once inside the pipe, roots will eventually fill or even break a pipe. If you suspect you have roots in your drain, the best starting point is to hire a professional to run a camera down the drain to see the extent of the problem. Depending on the situation, you have four options.

DRAIN CAMERA

SEARCH AND REMOVAL. A pro can use a cable with a camera attached to determine the exact location and extent of a root problem. The cable can also be used to cut out roots.

1. LINE REPLACEMENT

This can cost several thousand dollars, depending on the length of the line. If you're on a city sewer system, it could be particularly expensive because hand-digging may be required if there are other utility lines nearby.

2. SPOT REPAIR

With the use of a camera, an isolated damaged area can be located, cut out and replaced for under $1,000.

3. LINING OR PIPE-BURSTING

These options can cost $10,000 or more. A pipe, either MDPE (medium-density polyethylene) or HDPE (high-density polyethylene), is forced through the old pipe, breaking the old pipe as it progresses. The upside of this method is that you need a hole only at each end of the pipe instead of having to dig a trench to replace the old pipe with a new one.

4. CABLING

A spinning steel cable with cutters on the end snakes through the line, cutting out the roots. It's a temporary, inexpensive solution that's done regularly. You can rent or buy a machine, but it can be dangerous to do cabling yourself. The cable can whip and backlash, causing cuts or even lost fingers. Cuts from dirty cable can cause serious infections.

MONSTER ROOT REMOVED FROM SEWER LINE

CLAY PIPE

1A

Repair a Well Yourself

When trouble strikes, you might be able to make the repairs yourself, saving time and money.

If you own a home with a well, you know that trouble can hit at the worst possible times, such as at the start of a long holiday weekend when off-hour repairs done by a pro can cost a small fortune.

If you're comfortable replacing electrical and plumbing components, you can save money by not having to make a service call as well as save money on the cost of any replacement parts. Conveniently, all the parts that can be replaced by a DIYer are located inside the house. But you'll need to call a professional for outside electrical, piping, pump and check-valve failures.

Most of the time you'll find the parts you need at home centers. But those stores may not carry the highest-quality parts. If you want to get long-lasting components, shop at a plumbing supplier.

THREE COMMON PROBLEMS

The most common symptoms of well trouble are having no water at all, pulsing water pressure and a pump that runs constantly. If you experience any of these, there's a good chance you can solve the problem yourself. We show you how on the following pages.

PROBLEM 1: NO WATER AT ALL

FIRST, BE SURE THE POWER IS ON
Start by checking that the well switch located near your pressure tank hasn't been switched off. Then check the well's double-pole circuit breaker to make sure that it hasn't tripped. If it has, reset it. A breaker that keeps tripping likely means a problem with the well pump, and you'll need to call a pro for that.

THEN CHECK THE PRESSURE SWITCH You'll find the pressure switch mounted on a 1/4-in. tube near the pressure tank. The switch senses when water pressure has dropped to the point where the pressure tank requires more water. The switch then powers up the well pump.

If the switch is bad, it won't start the pump and you won't have water, so testing the switch is your first step. Remove the cover and tap a screwdriver handle sharply against the tube below the switch to jar the electrical contacts **(photo 1B)**. If you see a spark and the pump starts, the pressure switch is the problem. Replace it. If there's still no spark, you'll have to replace the controller.

IF THE SWITCH IS BAD, REPLACE IT
If you find the pressure switch is bad, test the pressure tank to make sure it isn't waterlogged (see "Problem 2: Pulsing Water"). To replace the switch, remove the wires to the old switch (be sure to label them as you remove them) and unscrew the switch **(photo 1D)**. Coat the tubing threads with pipe dope or Teflon tape and screw on the new switch so it sits in the same orientation. Then reconnect all of the wires.

> **WARNING: CONFIRM THE POWER IS OFF!**
> Before you replace the pressure switch or file the contacts, turn off the power at the main panel and then check the wires with a noncontact voltage tester (photo 1C).

1B TAP HERE

1C NON-CONTACT VOLTAGE TESTER

1D PRESSURE SWITCH — DRAIN OPEN — VALVE OFF

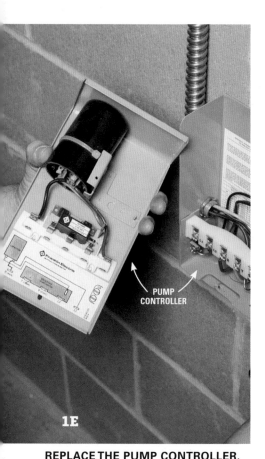

1E

REPLACE THE PUMP CONTROLLER.
Remove the screw at the bottom of the
pump control cover; lift it off the box
to disconnect it. Take the cover to the
store and buy an exact replacement.
Snap the new cover onto the old box
(no need to rewire if you buy the same
brand). Then start the pump.

IF ALL ELSE FAILS, REPLACE THE
CONTROLLER The pump controller
houses a capacitor to help start the
pump. Most pump controls are
mounted in the house near the pressure
tank, but others are mounted inside the
well pump itself and the fix requires a
pro. If you don't have the box shown
above, this fix isn't for you.

There's no way to test the controller,
so you either have to risk buying a
replacement when it might not be
needed or call a pro. Replacing the
pump controller as shown above is easy,
and it's your last, best shot at avoiding
a service call. If you've replaced the
pressure switch and the pump still
won't start, we think it's worth the
risk to replace the pump controller.

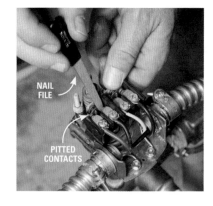
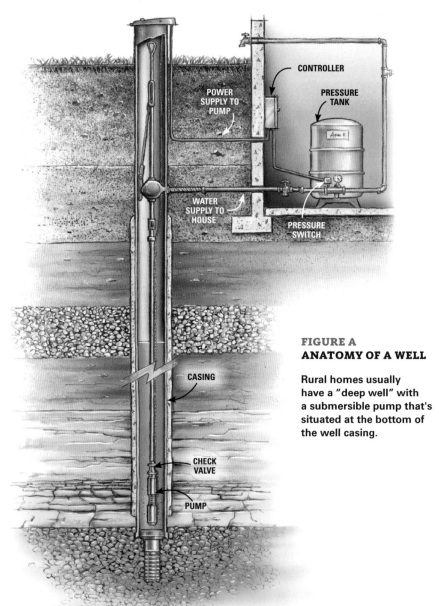

**FIGURE A
ANATOMY OF A WELL**

Rural homes usually
have a "deep well" with
a submersible pump that's
situated at the bottom of
the well casing.

PROBLEM 2: PULSING WATER

CHECK PRESSURE TANK When water "pulses" at the spigot, it usually means you have a waterlogged tank. In that case, replacement is your only option. There are two methods for diagnosing a bad tank: checking for water at the air valve and shaking the tank **(photos 2A and 2B).**

A typical pressure tank stores about 6 to 10 gallons of water inside a balloonlike bladder on the bottom half of the tank. The top portion is filled with air. As the pump fills the tank, the water compresses the air above the bladder. The compressed air is what powers water through your house when you open a faucet. When the bladder fails, water seeps into the top half, reducing the tank's ability to force out more than 2 or 3 gallons of water. The water also rusts the tank from the inside.

These are the symptoms of a bad pressure tank:

- Water pressure in one faucet drops dramatically when someone opens another faucet or flushes a toilet—because the tank has lost its capacity to store and pressurize water.
- Water pressure fluctuates while taking a shower or filling a tub—the tank can pressurize only a few gallons of water, forcing the pump to cycle on and off.
- Water leaks onto the floor around the tank, or water starts to look rusty.
- Your electrical bill jumps for no apparent reason—because the pump has to start so many times, and frequent starting takes more power than longer run-times.

PROBLEM 3: PUMP RUNS NONSTOP

When a pump turns on, you'll hear the clicking of the pressure switch opening and closing. If you hear frequent clicking when no water is flowing, you have problems outside the house and you'll need to hire a pro. It could be a broken water line from the well to the house (usually you'll have a wet area between the well head and the house), a bad check valve just above the submersible pump at the bottom of the well, a bad connector leaving the well casing or even a broken water line inside the well casing. Each of those problems requires a professional to repair.

TEST FOR WATER AT THE AIR VALVE. Unscrew the plastic cover from the air valve on the top of the tank. Use a small screwdriver to depress the air valve to see if any water comes out.

VALVE CORE

2A

2B

ROCK THE TANK. Push against the top of the tank to rock it slightly. If you can't rock it or it feels top heavy, it's bad. Drain it and replace it.

Tank Replacement Tips

- Buy a larger pressure tank. Frequent starts wear out well pumps, controllers and pressure switches much faster than longer run-times. The larger the pressure tank, the fewer times your well pump must start. Since well pumps are much more expensive, the longer pump life more than offsets the higher tank cost. This is particularly good advice if your home uses more water than an average home (for example, if you run a business with high water needs, irrigate a large area or raise animals that require large amounts of water).
- Don't buy a tank based on price alone. Cheap tanks will cost you far more in the long run because of shorter bladder life and accelerated tank rust-out.

Quiet Noisy Pipes

Noisy pipes are a common problem with a variety of causes. Here are four ways to silence pipes.

FIX A: CUSHION THE PIPE HANGERS

Pipes expand and contract when they heat up and cool down. This can cause them to tick, creak and groan as they slide by the hangers or straps holding them in place.

Minimize the sounds by pulling off the straps and inserting strips of felt or heavy fabric under the straps before reinstalling them. You may have to fix only the hot water supply line because that's the one that changes temperature the most.

FIX B: SPRAY FOAM ON VIBRATING PIPES

Supply lines can vibrate when water is running through them. Those vibrations can be amplified through the framing.

To fix the problem, isolate the pipes from wall and floor framing with expanding foam. If you can reach the offending area, spray foam between the wood and the pipes. If the area is sealed, drill a small hole and squirt in some expanding spray foam. Don't overdo it though; too much foam could literally bow out your drywall. Patch up the hole when you're done and touch it up with a little paint.

FIX C: REPLACE A WORN WASHER

An outdoor faucet with a worn-out washer can make a loud vibrating noise when it's turned on or off. You can easily replace the washer without removing the entire faucet. First, turn off the water to the faucet. Then use a wrench to remove the retaining nut.

Slide the handle and stem assembly out of the sill cock. Remove the screw at the end of the stem and remove the washer. Buy a new washer that matches the old one. Then reassemble. Occasionally the washer is fine but the screw holding it is loose. If so, put a drop of thread-locking sealant (sold at hardware stores) on the threads and tighten screw.

FIX D: INSTALL A WATER HAMMER ARRESTER

Solenoid valves, like the ones in washing machines and water softeners, shut off almost instantly, causing a ferocious clunk in your plumbing. This also strains hoses and fittings.

A water hammer arrester isolates the air pocket from the water in the pipes with a rubber-gasketed piston. The closer the arrester is to solenoid valves, the better. The model shown is designed to mount between the spigot and the washing machine feed lines with simple hose bib connections.

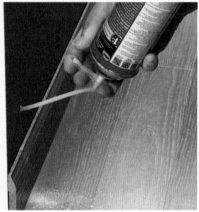

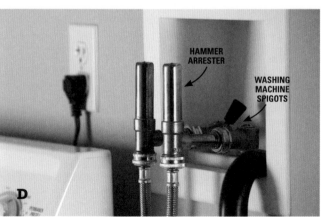

Fix a Shutoff Valve

Nothing is worse than starting a sink or toilet repair only to find that the shutoff valve won't shut off. Some shutoff valves are easy to replace. For those that aren't, turn off the main water valve, remove the packing nut, then unscrew the stem and take it to the hardware store to find a replacement washer. Clean any grit out of the valve body and pop on the new washer. The valve should work like new.

PACKING NUT

STEM

WASHER

NEW WASHER

SHUTOFF VALVE

Cut Rusted Faucet Nuts with an Oscillating Tool

Sometimes you just can't muscle off rusted-in-place faucet nuts with even the best basin wrench. And you can forget about using a reciprocating saw under the sink deck—there simply isn't enough room.

But you may be able to pull off the impossible by using an oscillating tool that's equipped with a high-quality bimetal cutting blade.

Angle the tool against the nut and start it off at slow speed until it cuts a groove. Increase the speed and keep sawing until you're about three-quarters of the way through. Then break off the remaining portion with pliers.

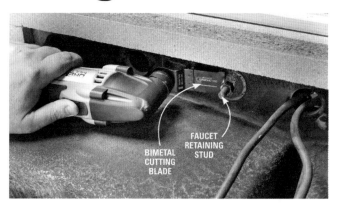

BIMETAL CUTTING BLADE

FAUCET RETAINING STUD

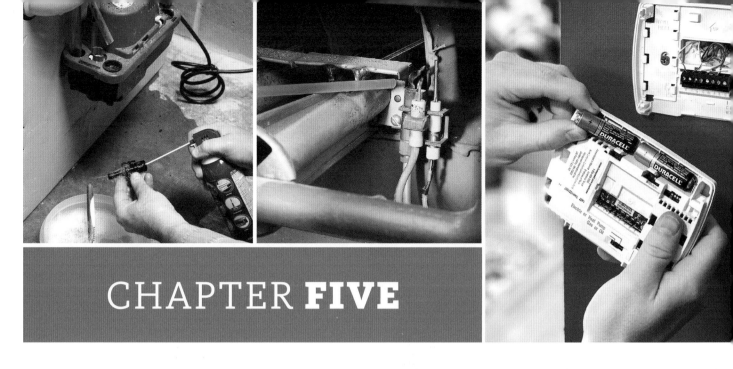

CHAPTER **FIVE**

HVAC

PRO TIP

Buy the Right Parts

Buy replacement parts from your local appliance parts store or A/C dealer. You will need the make, model and serial numbers from the nameplate on your outdoor condensing unit—not from the furnace nameplate. Or, if you're willing to pay for overnight delivery, you can buy discount parts online (source1parts.com is one site).

Fix Your Central A/C

You can repair several problems yourself with minimum tools, saving the wait and the cost of a service call.

You can't cool off in front of the open fridge forever. It's time to decide: You can either wait four days for the service person to show up or try fixing your central air conditioner yourself. We'll show you which A/C failures can be handled by a DIYer and how to safely replace the three parts that cause the majority of all outdoor condenser unit failures. You'll need a standard multimeter, an insulated needle-nose pliers and ordinary hand tools. (We'll assume you've checked the A/C and furnace circuit breakers in the main electrical panel, as well as any cartridge fuses in the outside disconnect.)

You can replace all three parts at once (see "Buy the Right Parts"). Of course, that might mean you'll replace some good parts. But if the fixes work, your A/C will be up and running much sooner and you'll save the cost of a service call. Or

you can replace the parts one at a time and test the unit after each one.

If these fixes don't work, at least you've covered the most common failures and your service person can concentrate on finding the more elusive problem. Plus, with the new parts, you'll likely add years of breakdown-free air conditioning.

MAKE SURE THE PROBLEM ISN'T WITH THE FURNACE

Set your thermostat to A/C mode and lower the temperature setting. If the furnace fan kicks in, the problem isn't in the furnace. If the fan doesn't run, try resetting the furnace circuit breaker. If the fan still won't start, call a pro—the fixes shown here won't work.

Next, check the outside condensing unit. The compressor (sounds like a refrigerator) and fan should be running. If not, follow the troubleshooting and repair procedures here.

CLEAN OR REPLACE THE CONTACTOR RELAY IN THE CONDENSER UNIT

The contactor relay switches power to the condenser fan and the compressor. It rarely fails. But it often gets jammed with beetles, bugs and spiders that perished checking things out. Remove the condenser unit's access cover and locate the contactor relay—it'll have at least six wires attached to it. Try cleaning out the critters with compressed air **(Photo 1)**. If that works, fine. But if you can't remove all the fried bug parts, replace the contactor with a new unit. Don't think you can file the contacts to clean them. That fix won't last and you'll end up still having to replace the contactor.

REPLACE THE CAPACITOR(S)

The "start" and "run" capacitors store electrical energy to jump-start the compressor and fan motor. You may have

CAUTION

Turn off the A/C and furnace breakers in the main electrical panel before pulling the outdoor disconnect or removing the condensing unit's access panel. Then use a voltage sniffer on the wires coming into the contactor to make sure the power is really off.

1 BLOW OUT THE CONTACTOR. Blow compressed air into all sides of the contactor relay to clean out dead insects. If you're not able to remove all the debris, you'll have to replace the contactor. Then try starting the unit.

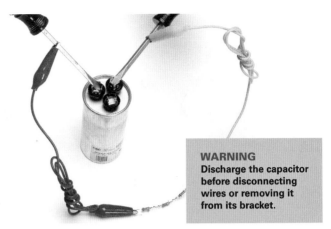

WARNING
Discharge the capacitor before disconnecting wires or removing it from its bracket.

2 DISCHARGE THE OLD CAPACITOR. Attach a jumper lead to each end of the resistor pack. Clip the other ends to insulated screwdrivers. Then touch the screwdrivers to the capacitor terminals.

3 SWAP CAPACITOR WIRES TO THE NEW UNIT. Wiggle each wire off the old capacitor, noting the terminal markings. Place the wire on the matching terminal on the new capacitor. Then secure the new capacitor in the mounting bracket.

4 INSTALL THE NEW FAN MOTOR. Align the fan motor studs with the holes in the fan guard or condenser cover. Then spin on the acorn nuts and tighten. Install the fan blade and the electrical connector. Tuck the new fan wires into the old conduit.

a combination start/run capacitor or two individual ones. Both styles have a very high failure rate. When they go, the compressor or fan won't start, so replace them.

First, discharge any remaining electrical charge from the capacitors before you work on them. Fabricate a shorting resistor pack by twisting four 5.6k-ohm, 1/2-watt resistors in series (part No. 030113 sold at kelvin.com). Then discharge the capacitor **(Photo 2)**. Use a multimeter to double-check its voltage output; it should read zero.

Next, move each wire lead from the old capacitor to the new capacitor **(Photo 3)**.

REPLACE THE FAN MOTOR

Remove the fasteners that hold the fan guard in place or remove the entire cover assembly from the condenser unit. Lift out the fan assembly and mark the bottom of the blade so you replace it in the right direction. Then loosen

the blade-retaining nut and pull it off the motor shaft. Disconnect the fan motor electrical connector. Then swap in the new fan motor **(Photo 4)**. Reconnect the fan guard or condenser cover.

CHECK OUT THE OPERATION

Reinstall the access cover and the outside disconnect block. Raise the temperature on the thermostat. Then flip the A/C and furnace breakers to "on." Wait 15 minutes for the thermostat and furnace electronics to reset. Then lower the temperature setting. The condensing unit should start up.

If it doesn't, your system may need more time to reset. Wait one hour and then try it again. If it still doesn't work, you'll need to schedule a service call. Be sure to explain exactly what you did. That will keep the repair person from replacing brand new parts, and you'll be able to have your work checked by an A/C expert.

1 TEST THE PUMP. Hold a bowl over the pump outlet to direct water into a bucket. Then slowly pour water into the pump reservoir until the pump kicks in. If water shoots from the outlet, the pump is good.

Repair or Replace a Condensate Pump

In the summer, central air conditioning units remove moisture from the air. And in the winter, condensing gas furnaces generate an enormous amount of wastewater. Plus, if your furnace has a humidifier, it also drains off extra water. All that water has to go somewhere. In newer homes, it goes right into a nearby floor drain.

But many older homes don't have a floor drain next to the furnace. So furnace installers mount a condensate pump right on the furnace and route the drain line to a far-off sink or floor drain. If that pump fails, the water overflows the pump and spills onto the floor. That doesn't necessarily mean the

pump is bad; the problem could be just algae buildup in the pump's check valve.

Start your diagnosis by unplugging the pump. Disconnect the drain line and empty the water into a bucket. Then remove the check valve and plug in the pump **(Photo 1)**. If the pump doesn't work, buy a new one (sold at home centers or online HVAC stores) and swap it for the old one. However, if the pump works, you've got a stuck check valve.

Try cleaning the valve by soaking it in warm, soapy water. Then flush it. Clean out any remaining crud with compressed air and test it **(Photo 2)**.

2 **CLEAN THE CHECK VALVE.** Soak the check valve in warm, soapy water. Scrub it with an old toothbrush. Then rinse it. Next, blow it out with compressed air before testing.

CHECK VALVE OUTLET

CHECK VALVE

3 **CATCH THE WATER WHILE YOU WAIT FOR PARTS.** Remove the pump and aim the drain tubes into a bucket. Empty often to prevent overflowing. Then reinstall the pump with the new check valve when it arrives.

A/C CONDENSATION LINE

If you can't remove all the crud or the valve is still stuck, replace it with a new valve (purchase from the pump manufacturer's parts department). The furnace or A/C will continue to drain while you're waiting for the new part to arrive, so jury-rig a bucket system **(Photo 3)**.

Clean out any algae buildup from inside the pump using soapy water and a brush before you install the new valve. Then install the new valve and test it.

To prevent future algae clogs, place algae reduction tablets (such as Pan Tablets, No. AC-912, sold at homedepot.com) in the pump reservoir.

Diagnosing Noise in Ductwork

If you hear a banging noise from a large rectangular return air duct when the furnace shuts off, you can try to silence it by reinforcing the troublesome duct with strips of sheet metal S-cleat that you screw on. This may very well stop the banging, but the fix might also mask an underlying problem that needs investigating.

HVAC contractors intentionally score creases into the air ducts to prevent flexing and to stiffen the metal. So if the duct is scored but flexing, it's an indication of either a restriction in the return air line or an improper fan speed. Either way, it should be checked by a pro.

However, if the noise is coming from uncreased flat sheet metal installed between two floor joists, you can crease it yourself **(photo below)**.

CREASE A RETURN AIR DUCT. Hold a straightedge diagonally across a section of the sheet metal. Then drag an awl or screwdriver along the straightedge to crease the metal. Score a second line in the sheet metal to form an "X."

22 Instant Heating & A/C Fixes

Even a beginner can solve common problems—and save money!

When your heating and cooling system isn't working properly, you might throw up your hands and call for help, thinking that whatever the problem is, solving it must be outside your skill set. Well, you might be surprised: The most common problems have simple solutions. Here are 22 extremely easy fixes that take minutes or less and can save you a wad of cash.

1. HOW'S YOUR FILTER?

A dirty filter causes your system to work harder, resulting in premature failure of parts. A dirty filter can also cause a shutdown. How often your filters need changing depends on many factors. Do you live in a high-traffic zone? Do you have pets? Do you leave the windows open? Write the date on your filter to help keep track of when it needs to be changed.

2. CHECK THE THERMOSTAT

Most thermostats have a switch so you can set the system to "heat" or "cool." Make sure yours is set to the proper function.

3. RUN A QUICK POWER TEST

To see if the furnace is getting power, set your thermostat to the "fan" position. If you don't hear the fan turn on, there's a good chance no power is going to the furnace. If there is power to the furnace, it's time to check the furnace itself.

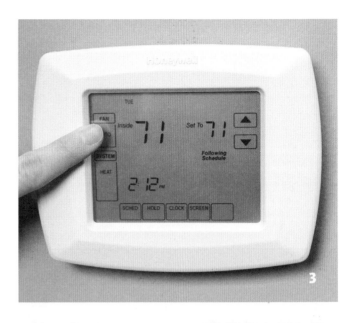

4. CHECK INSIDE THE FURNACE

New furnaces, like cars, have fault codes. Check for codes or flashing lights, then look in your owner's manual or online to diagnose the problem. If you can't decipher the code or don't want to bother with it, send a video to the repair technician. It's helpful for the tech to know what the problem might be before coming out.

5. CHECK THE CIRCUIT BREAKER

A breaker can trip without fully moving to the "off" position, so flip it to the "off" position and then back to "on" to be sure that's not the issue.

6. REPLACE THERMOSTAT BATTERIES

If your thermostat doesn't seem to be working, try changing the batteries. They typically need to be replaced annually. After you've replaced the batteries, your thermostat might revert to its default settings and need to be reprogrammed.

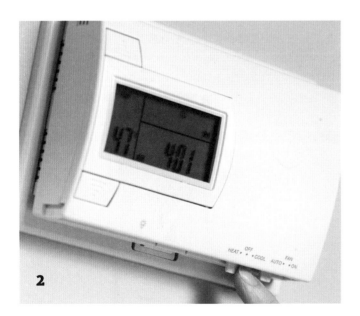

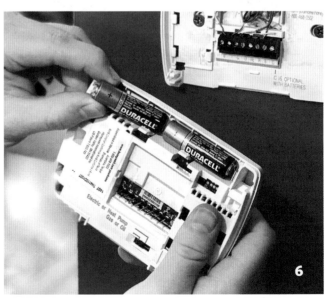

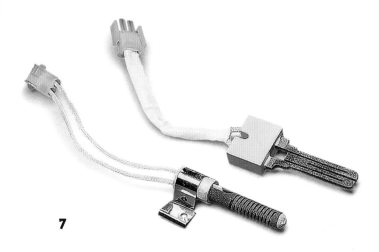

7

7. CLEAN THE HOT SURFACE IGNITER

This most common ignition system on modern furnaces takes the place of standing pilot lights and electronic igniters. Clean dust off the igniter by leaving it in place and blowing air on it through a straw. The part breaks very easily; don't even touch it. In fact, when you replace the furnace cover panels, do so gently to avoid breaking the igniter.

8. CLEAN THE PILOT

A dirty pilot light can cause the flame sensor (or thermocouple) to get a false reading indicating the pilot isn't lit. Clean the pilot with a blast of air. Direct air to the exact spot with a drinking straw.

9. CHECK THE CONDENSATE PUMP

If you have a condensate pump, listen closely to make sure it is running. If not, try resetting the GFCI outlet that powers it. If that doesn't work, you may need a new pump.

10. CHECK FOR POWER

A furnace has a power switch nearby, often right on its housing. It looks just like a light switch. Check to make sure the power hasn't inadvertently been switched to "off."

11. CHECK THE SAFETY SWITCH

Furnace cover panels often activate a safety switch when the panel is removed or left even slightly ajar. Check to see that the panel is fully closed.

12. MAKE SURE WATER CAN DRAIN

High-efficiency furnaces collect water as a byproduct of combustion. In cooling mode, your A/C collects water from the air. In either case, that water needs to drain away. If not, your furnace will leak water or just shut down. First, make sure water is dripping from the end of the tubing when the system is running. If you don't see drips, clear the line by blowing through it with your mouth. Don't use a compressor; too much pressure can blow connections apart.

PILOT LIGHT

8

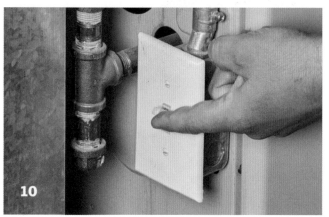

9

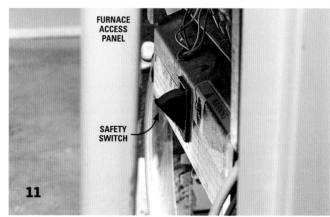

FURNACE ACCESS PANEL

SAFETY SWITCH

10

11

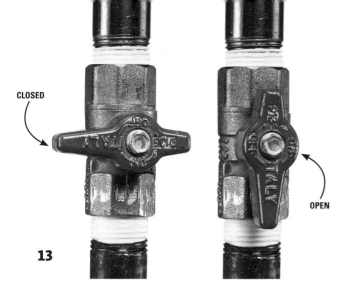

CLOSED

OPEN

13

FURNACE EXHAUST

FURNACE INTAKE

14

MAKEUP AIR DUCT

15

16

17

13. IS THE GAS VALVE ON?

Find the gas line for your furnace, then find the valve. The valve's handle should be parallel to the gas line. If it's perpendicular, there's no gas going to the furnace.

14. CHECK AIRFLOW

Outside of your house, you may have a couple of PVC pipes sticking out of the wall. One points downward (furnace air intake); one points horizontally or upward (furnace exhaust). Drifting snow, ice buildup or nesting animals can block one or both, causing a high-efficiency furnace to shut down.

15. CAN YOUR FURNACE BREATHE?

Your furnace room is likely supplied with a "makeup air duct." It's a large, flexible, insulated duct that probably drops into a bucket. It supplies your house with fresh air to replace oxygen lost in combustion. Because furnace rooms often double as storage areas, it's easy to inadvertently block that duct. If it's blocked, kinked or squashed, it can cause your furnace to shut down, as there's no oxygen for combustion and it won't ignite. Typically, this isn't a problem in old, drafty homes, but in super insulated ones it can be an issue.

16. A HUMIDIFIER CAN CAUSE YOUR FURNACE FILTER TO CLOG

If you use a portable humidifier, always use distilled water to fill it. Non-distilled water can cause a calcium buildup on your furnace filter and completely clog it in a matter of days. The buildup is white, so a white filter will still look clean when it's actually clogged.

17. CHECK FOR BLOCKED REGISTERS

Have you noticed large temperature swings in certain rooms or an unusually short furnace cycle time? Make sure there's nothing blocking the air returns. Returns pull air out of the room and back to the furnace, while supply registers blow air into the room. You can check the return airflow by holding a piece of paper against the return register. The paper should stick to the register. If it doesn't, there's an airflow problem.

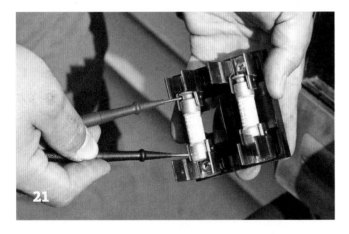

18. ADJUST THE DAMPERS

If your heating ducts also serve as air conditioning ducts, they likely have dampers that require adjusting for seasonal changes. The seasonal settings should be marked on the duct. Two-story homes often have separate supply trunks to serve the upstairs and downstairs. To send more warm air downstairs (winter setting) or more cold air upstairs (summer setting), adjust the damper handle on each supply trunk.

19. CHECK FOR MICE AND OTHER PESTS

Your condenser has an access panel behind which you'll find the wiring and connections. Because this is an outdoor unit, it's often an appealing residence for critters. After shutting off power at the breaker, remove the access panel and check for broken or chewed wires. Replace them as needed.

20. INVESTIGATE YOUR A/C'S CONDENSER UNIT

Is your A/C blowing air but not cold air? Does the condenser seem louder than usual? If it's having to work too hard, it may just shut off. The condenser coil, located inside the outdoor unit, is probably dirty. To clean it, spray off the condenser coil. Don't use high pressure. Put your thumb over the end of the garden hose or use a sprayer nozzle. More pressure than that can bend the fins. The cleaning schedule for condenser coils—like the timing of filter changes—depends on environmental conditions. Cottonwood seeds can blanket a condenser coil in a day. Plan to clean the coil regularly.

21. CHECK FUSES IN THE DISCONNECT BLOCK

These fuses are typically located in a box mounted to the house near the condenser. Set your multimeter to the lowest ohms value and touch the red and black leads to opposite ends of each fuse. If you get a numerical reading, the fuse is good. But a zero, a minus symbol or an infinity symbol (∞) indicates a blown fuse.

Take your old fuses along to the home center to verify that the new ones match. Replacing a fuse can get you up and running again quickly, but if your unit regularly blows fuses, there's something else wrong with your system.

22. DOES IT SEEM LIKE THE A/C ISN'T WORKING?

Condensation in your A/C attracts dust. When the condensation flows out the drain line, that dust can plug the line. Check the end of the drain line to see if water is coming out. If not, blow the line clear. Usually lung power is sufficient. Compressed air may cause something unseen to come apart. Also, remove the cap from the evaporator coil and clean out the tube with your finger.

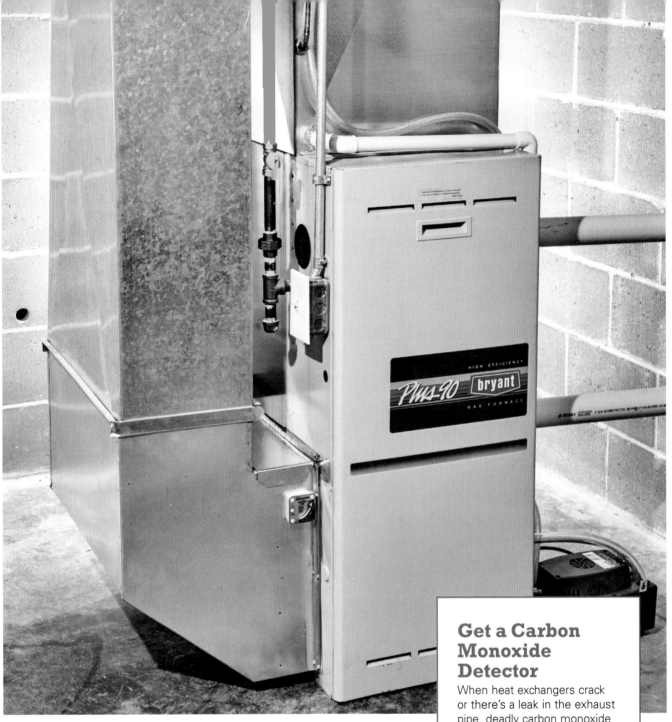

Know Your Furnace

A little knowledge can save you big bucks!

Furnaces might seem complicated, but the basics are surprisingly easy to understand. Once you know them, you'll be able to avoid breakdowns and solve simple problems yourself. Plus, you'll be able to understand what a repair technician is saying, make smarter decisions and avoid rip-offs. This knowledge can add up to huge savings over the life of your furnace.

Get a Carbon Monoxide Detector

When heat exchangers crack or there's a leak in the exhaust pipe, deadly carbon monoxide can seep into your home's living space. That's why it is critical you have a working carbon monoxide detector. At home centers you can buy two-in-one carbon monoxide and smoke detectors or stand-alone  units that you just plug into a wall (with backup batteries).

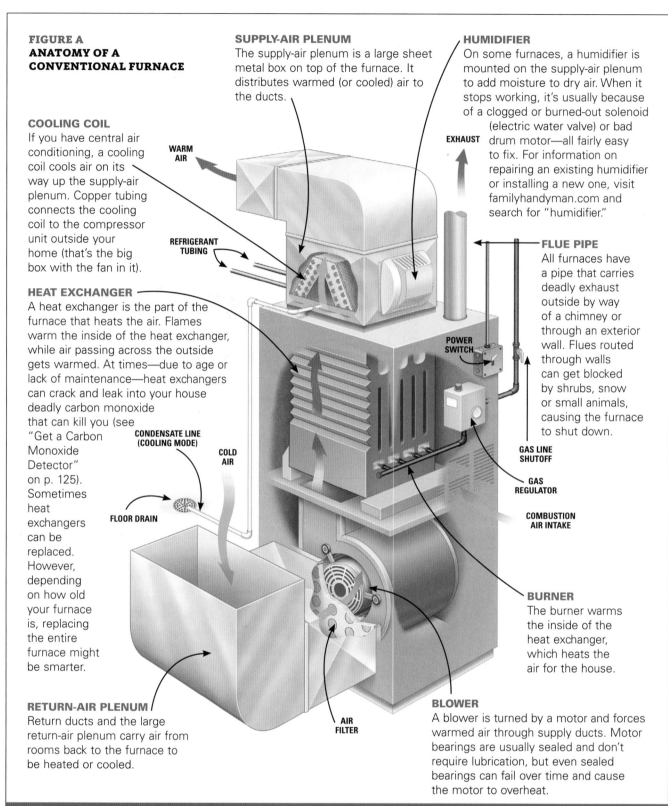

FIGURE A
ANATOMY OF A CONVENTIONAL FURNACE

SUPPLY-AIR PLENUM
The supply-air plenum is a large sheet metal box on top of the furnace. It distributes warmed (or cooled) air to the ducts.

HUMIDIFIER
On some furnaces, a humidifier is mounted on the supply-air plenum to add moisture to dry air. When it stops working, it's usually because of a clogged or burned-out solenoid (electric water valve) or bad drum motor—all fairly easy to fix. For information on repairing an existing humidifier or installing a new one, visit familyhandyman.com and search for "humidifier."

COOLING COIL
If you have central air conditioning, a cooling coil cools air on its way up the supply-air plenum. Copper tubing connects the cooling coil to the compressor unit outside your home (that's the big box with the fan in it).

FLUE PIPE
All furnaces have a pipe that carries deadly exhaust outside by way of a chimney or through an exterior wall. Flues routed through walls can get blocked by shrubs, snow or small animals, causing the furnace to shut down.

HEAT EXCHANGER
A heat exchanger is the part of the furnace that heats the air. Flames warm the inside of the heat exchanger, while air passing across the outside gets warmed. At times—due to age or lack of maintenance—heat exchangers can crack and leak into your house deadly carbon monoxide that can kill you (see "Get a Carbon Monoxide Detector" on p. 125). Sometimes heat exchangers can be replaced. However, depending on how old your furnace is, replacing the entire furnace might be smarter.

BURNER
The burner warms the inside of the heat exchanger, which heats the air for the house.

RETURN-AIR PLENUM
Return ducts and the large return-air plenum carry air from rooms back to the furnace to be heated or cooled.

BLOWER
A blower is turned by a motor and forces warmed air through supply ducts. Motor bearings are usually sealed and don't require lubrication, but even sealed bearings can fail over time and cause the motor to overheat.

WARM AIR

REFRIGERANT TUBING

EXHAUST

POWER SWITCH

CONDENSATE LINE (COOLING MODE)

COLD AIR

FLOOR DRAIN

GAS LINE SHUTOFF

GAS REGULATOR

COMBUSTION AIR INTAKE

AIR FILTER

How It Heats

A conventional "forced-air" furnace is a pretty simple system. A thermostat calls for heat, which triggers the furnace to burn fuel, which warms a heat exchanger. A motor spins a blower wheel, which moves cool air past the heat exchanger and pushes the newly warmed air through supply ducts and into the rooms of your house. Meanwhile, cooler air in each of the rooms gets pulled back toward the furnace through cold-air return ducts. You'll usually see return grilles mounted in the floor or low on a wall.

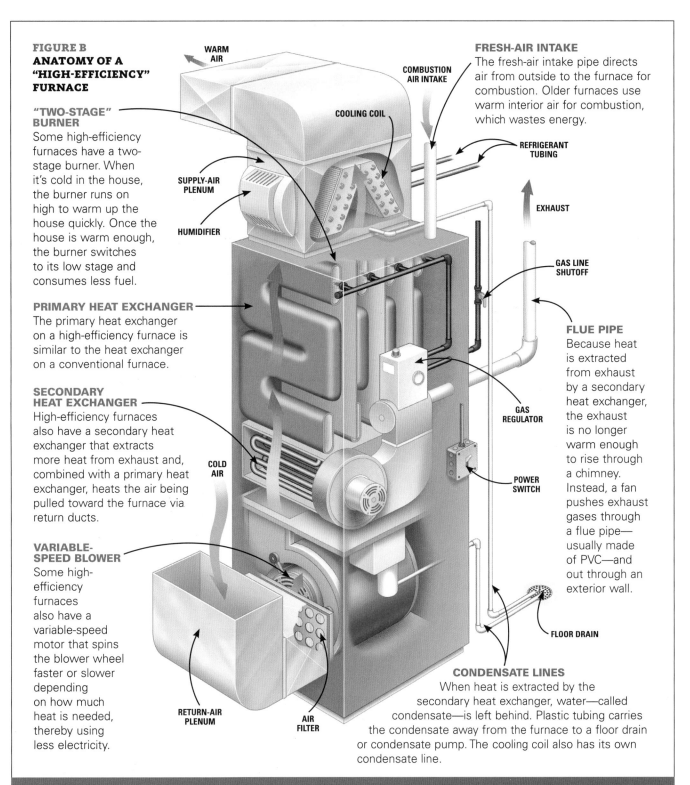

FIGURE B
ANATOMY OF A "HIGH-EFFICIENCY" FURNACE

"TWO-STAGE" BURNER
Some high-efficiency furnaces have a two-stage burner. When it's cold in the house, the burner runs on high to warm up the house quickly. Once the house is warm enough, the burner switches to its low stage and consumes less fuel.

PRIMARY HEAT EXCHANGER
The primary heat exchanger on a high-efficiency furnace is similar to the heat exchanger on a conventional furnace.

SECONDARY HEAT EXCHANGER
High-efficiency furnaces also have a secondary heat exchanger that extracts more heat from exhaust and, combined with a primary heat exchanger, heats the air being pulled toward the furnace via return ducts.

VARIABLE-SPEED BLOWER
Some high-efficiency furnaces also have a variable-speed motor that spins the blower wheel faster or slower depending on how much heat is needed, thereby using less electricity.

WARM AIR

COMBUSTION AIR INTAKE

COOLING COIL

SUPPLY-AIR PLENUM

HUMIDIFIER

COLD AIR

RETURN-AIR PLENUM

AIR FILTER

FRESH-AIR INTAKE
The fresh-air intake pipe directs air from outside to the furnace for combustion. Older furnaces use warm interior air for combustion, which wastes energy.

REFRIGERANT TUBING

EXHAUST

GAS LINE SHUTOFF

FLUE PIPE
Because heat is extracted from exhaust by a secondary heat exchanger, the exhaust is no longer warm enough to rise through a chimney. Instead, a fan pushes exhaust gases through a flue pipe—usually made of PVC—and out through an exterior wall.

GAS REGULATOR

POWER SWITCH

FLOOR DRAIN

CONDENSATE LINES
When heat is extracted by the secondary heat exchanger, water—called condensate—is left behind. Plastic tubing carries the condensate away from the furnace to a floor drain or condensate pump. The cooling coil also has its own condensate line.

How It Heats

Like conventional furnaces, high-efficiency models use a heat exchanger to warm the air. In fact, they actually have two heat exchangers—a primary one and a secondary one.

The secondary heat exchanger extracts heat from exhaust—heat that would otherwise go out the flue— and uses it, combined with heat from the primary heat exchanger, to warm the air in your home. Because heat is removed from the exhaust, it's not warm enough to rise, so it can't be vented up through a chimney. A small PVC exhaust pipe running through an exterior wall is all that's needed. These units also require a second PVC pipe—usually located close to the exhaust pipe—to deliver fresh outside air to the furnace for combustion.

Cleaning Air Ducts

Many benefits come from cleaning the ducts in your home. But it's a job best done by a pro. Here's what to expect.

Man wrestles octopus, trains it to clean houses. OK, that's not really true. Actually, a professional duct cleaner used that black and yellow tube you see here—an extra-large vacuum hose—to suck all the dust and dirt from a home's ductwork. It was a 15-year-old house and the ducts had never been cleaned. Here's how the pro tackled the job.

First, access holes were cut (they were patched later) in the main supply and return ducts near the furnace. The vacuum hose was then connected to pull out dust and dirt before it could get into the furnace and blower fan.

With rubber cords at the end of a compressed air hose (top photo), the whip system goes into ductwork and agitates the dirt and dust to be vacuumed out. With a smaller shop vacuum (second photo), wall spaces behind return-air grilles are cleaned by hand.

SHOULD YOU HAVE YOUR HOME'S AIR DUCTS CLEANED?

Yes. Think of it this way: Just as your house gets dirty, so do your ducts.

HOW OFTEN SHOULD YOU HAVE YOUR AIR DUCTS CLEANED?

It's really personal preference. Different people have different sensitivities. According to the National Air Duct Cleaning Association, duct cleaning should be done every two to four years. We think this might be overkill and instead suggest that your ducts be cleaned by a professional every three to five years. If you have pets or a smaller home with a large family, consider having the ducts cleaned more frequently.

WHAT ARE INDICATORS OF DIRTY DUCTS?

If you find that you need to replace your furnace filter more frequently than usual, your ducts are most likely dirty. You can also take off return vent covers and look inside the ducts using a flashlight. Check for dirt. It's a common place for dirt to collect.

WHAT TOOLS ARE USED?

Primarily, a giant vacuum is used. One pro we spoke to uses a vacuum with a 31-hp engine attached to a fan, which then pulls dirt and dust into a bag outside of the house. The vacuum moves 7,000 cfm (cubic feet per minute) of air and creates negative air pressure in the home while the home is cleaned. Meanwhile, he and his team agitate and disrupt the ducts with snake tools equipped with compressed air "whips" on the end. The vacuum continues to pull out dirt as they agitate inside the ducts. They also use a HEPA-filtered backpack vacuum for precleaning.

WHAT SHOULD HOMEOWNERS EXPECT FROM CLEAN DUCTS?

The house should look and feel cleaner, and you should notice a reduction in dust.

PLUS:

- Duct cleaning can help your furnace work more efficiently.
- Cleaning only some ductwork does no good.
- Be wary of services marketing chemical biocide treatments.
- Hire a pro who will explain the process and tools.
- Change that furnace filter often!

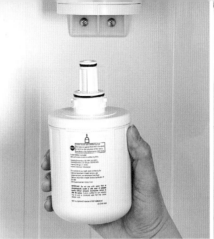
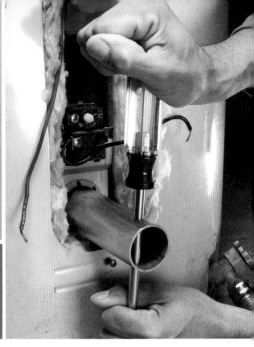

CHAPTER **SIX**

TOOLS, APPLIANCES & EQUIPMENT

Is Your Square Square?

Framing squares—even brand-new ones—aren't reliably square. Here's how to check them.

1 To test your square, place the tongue (the short part) against the factory edge of a sheet of plywood and make a line along the body (the long part) using a sharp pencil.

2 Flip the square and line up the body with the line you just made. If it lines up perfectly, you have a square that is truly square.

3 If it doesn't line up perfectly, you can try to fix it (next step). You'll need a center punch, a hammer and something to use as an anvil, such as your vise (a wood surface doesn't work).

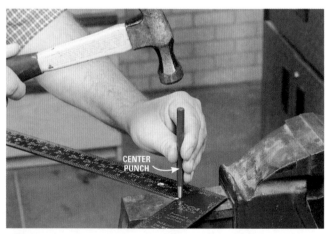

CENTER PUNCH

4 If your square is less than 90 degrees, set it on your "anvil" and punch the inside corner hard enough to make a dimple. Squeezed between the punch and the anvil, the metal moves outward. Recheck the square, starting with a new line. Increase the dimple as needed, rechecking each time you strike the square.

5 If your square is more than 90 degrees, dimple the outside corner. If you're shopping for a new square, grab a handful of them, take them to the plywood aisle of the store, sharp pencil in hand, and test them before you purchase one. Any that are square are the winners!

Sharpen Drill Bits in 30 Seconds

You can tell a drill bit has become dull when it squeals, smokes or takes five minutes to bore a hole. A close look usually reveals a cutting edge that reflects light, meaning it's no longer an edge but a surface, which won't cut anything.

When running out for a new bit isn't an option, use this technique to make a bit "sharp enough" in a hurry. You can use a bench grinder, a belt sander, an angle grinder or the narrow benchtop belt sander shown here.

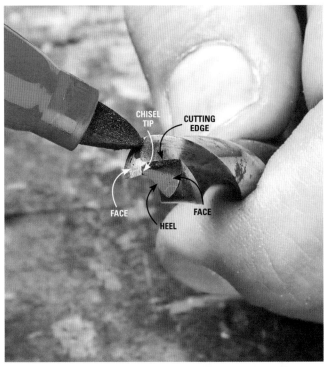

BEFORE

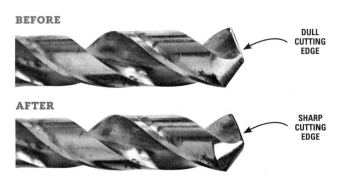

DULL CUTTING EDGE

AFTER

SHARP CUTTING EDGE

1 **MARK THE FACES.** Color each face behind the cutting edge using a permanent marker. You'll have a reference to track your progress and make sure your angle is correct when you start grinding. (Wear eye protection!) The goal is to lightly grind each face evenly, from the heel to the cutting edge, without changing the angle or the size of the chisel tip. It sounds complicated, but if you're careful, you'll have a sharp bit in about 30 seconds on your first try.

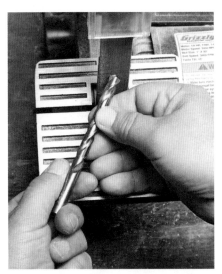

2 **FIND THE ANGLE.** Before turning on the sander, looking from the top, eyeball the angle of the cutting edge. On larger bits, you can even press the bit's face against the belt and feel the angle.

3 **FIND THE HEEL.** Keeping the first angle, drop the end of the bit until the heel is touching the belt. Feel that position in your muscle memory.

4 **GRIND AWAY!** Turn on the machine and touch the bit to the belt. Using very light pressure, rotate the bit, starting from the heel, until you've reached the cutting edge. Check your progress by looking at the colored face. When the marker ink is gone and the cutting edge no longer catches light, you're done!

Busted Dryer?
Replace the Motor

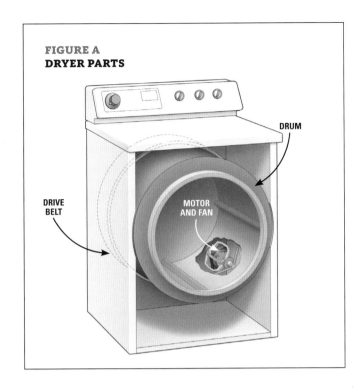

FIGURE A
DRYER PARTS

DRUM

DRIVE BELT

MOTOR AND FAN

1 REMOVE THE DRUM. Pop the lid and remove the front panel. Then disconnect the drive belt from the motor and lift the drum out of the front of the machine.

When a dryer motor goes bad, the loud grinding and rumbling from the worn-out bearings make it seem as if the dryer's going to blow up at any second. It won't, but fairly soon after the noise starts it will stop dead in its tracks when the bearings seize. If you think the repair cost compares favorably with the cost of a new dryer, you might be right to hire a pro. But if you have basic mechanical skills and aren't afraid to dig in, buck up and deal with it yourself. You can replace a dryer motor in a morning and be back in business cheap. Buy a genuine factory motor or an aftermarket motor for about half the cost (depending on the make and model).

Since you have to remove the drum to get to the motor, you may as well replace the belt, idler and drum rollers at the same time. That'll add to the cost. But in the end, your dryer could last more years than you spend raising your kids.

The motor and blower wheel on our dryer were located at the back of the machine, but they may be near the front on other models. However, the motor replacement procedure is similar for both. You'll need nut drivers or sockets, screwdrivers, a shop vacuum, slip-joint pliers and two large adjustable wrenches.

We'll show you how to replace a motor on a typical Whirlpool electric dryer and how to remove the motor without having to use special tools. And we'll show you how to avoid damaging the blower wheel.

POP THE TOP AND REMOVE THE FRONT PANEL AND DRUM

Unplug the dryer (and shut off the gas valve if you have a gas model). Then slide a putty knife between the front and the top panels to depress the latches located near the corners.

Lift the top panel up and support it in the open position. Then disconnect the electrical connector to the door switch. Next, remove the screws that hold the front panel in place and pop it off. Then disconnect the drive belt from the motor and lift out the drum **(Photo 1)**.

For more information on removing the dryer's top and front panels and the drum, search for "clothes dryer repair" at familyhandyman.com.

REMOVE THE BLOWER WHEEL AND SWAP IN THE NEW MOTOR

Pay attention here: The blower wheel is screwed to the motor shaft with *left-hand* threads. To remove it, hold the wheel while you turn the motor clockwise—the opposite of what you'd normally do.

Hold the blower wheel by sliding an adjustable wrench over the flats on the neck where it meets the motor shaft. Tighten the wrench jaws so they fit snugly. Then grab the other end of the shaft with a pump pliers and turn it to break it loose **(Photo 2)**. Once you break it loose, spin the motor shaft clockwise with your hand until the blower wheel is loose. Then remove the motor clamps using the technique shown in **Photo 3**. Disconnect the electrical connector and then lift out the old motor.

Slide the new motor into place and screw on the blower wheel **(Photo 4)**. Then set the motor into the motor mount and install the clamps. Hook one end of the clamp to the base and force the other end over the catch using a flat-blade screwdriver.

ADJUSTABLE WRENCH ON BLOWER WHEEL FLATS

2 CLAMP THE BLOWER WHEEL. Rotate the adjustable wrench clockwise until it wedges against a drum roller or the side of the cabinet. Grab the flats on the other end of the motor shaft and turn it clockwise too. Don't grab the belt pulley—it will break.

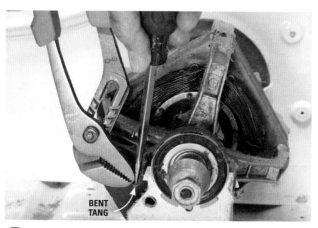

BENT TANG

3 RELEASE THE MOTOR CLAMPS. Grab the bent tang on the motor clamp with slip-joint pliers. Then jam a flat-blade screwdriver between the clamp and the pliers jaws, and pry the clamp outward until it pops off. Repeat on the opposite end.

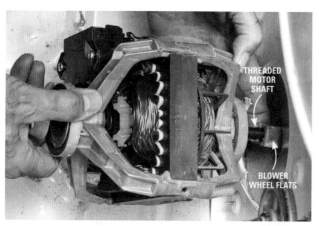

THREADED MOTOR SHAFT

BLOWER WHEEL FLATS

4 CONNECT THE BLOWER WHEEL. Tilt the threaded portion of the motor shaft down to mate it to the blower wheel. Spin the shaft counterclockwise until it's snug. Hold the blower wheel with the adjustable wrench and tighten by turning the opposite end with pump pliers.

Quick Fix for a Dryer Door

If your dryer door won't stay closed, chances are the latch is either bent or missing, or the strike is worn. The fix is cheap and easy. Buy the parts from any appliance parts store. Then grab pliers, a couple of small straight-slot screwdrivers and a roll of masking tape.

Grab the bent or broken latch and yank it out. Then install the new one **(Photo 1)**. Next, protect the door's finish with tape and remove the old strike **(Photo 2)**. Snap in the new strike and you're back in the laundry business.

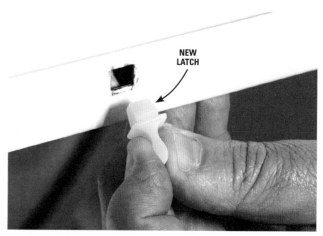

NEW LATCH

1 POP IN THE NEW LATCH. Line up the replacement latch with the hole and push it in firmly until the locking tabs seat themselves.

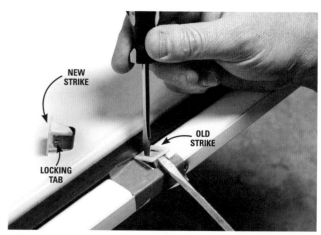

NEW STRIKE

OLD STRIKE

LOCKING TAB

2 PRY OUT THE OLD STRIKE. Jam a small screwdriver into the strike and bend the metal locking tab inward. Pry upward with a second screwdriver to pop it out.

How to Clean a Refrigerator

Food is only as clean as the refrigerator you store it in. Here's how to deep clean (and then keep clean) your fridge.

Your refrigerator may be the most important appliance in the kitchen. It certainly has a critical job, keeping the food you eat fresh and bacteria-free. Regular cleanings help on both counts. Find out how to do the job right so you can go longer between deep cleans.

HOW TO CLEAN YOUR FRIDGE

Step One: Empty the refrigerator. Toss spoiled, smelly or expired items as you go. Have a cooler ready to hold highly perishable foods (e.g., milk or raw fish), and set the rest in an out-of-the-way spot.

Step Two: Detach all removable refrigerator drawers and shelves. Carefully set them aside while you ready a sink full of soapy water. Wait to soak the shelves and drawers until they've come to room temperature, so the warm water doesn't cause them to crack.

Step Three: Wipe the fridge interior with a non-toxic, food-safe solution of mild dish soap and water, using a soft cloth, sponge or scrubby pad. To remove tough stains or serious smells, scrub with a paste made of baking soda and water. Clean crumbs and debris from the rubber door seal with an old toothbrush or a butter knife wrapped in a rag.

Step Four: Once the interior is sparkling, shut the door to give the interior a chance to re-cool and wash the removable components in the sink. While they're drying, do a quick-clean of the freezer by tossing any old or unwanted items and wiping up crumbs or spills. Then wipe down the refrigerator's exterior with a sponge or microfiber cloth, using a solution of mild dish soap and water. If you have a stainless steel fridge, use a cleaning product made for stainless steel. Wipe from the top down and in the direction of the grain.

Step Five: Reinstall the removable components and restock your fridge. While restocking, wipe off any crumbs, drips or sticky residue on the items before returning them to their proper spots.

HOW TO CLEAN A REFRIGERATOR WITH VINEGAR

A 50-50 solution of plain white vinegar and water makes a great, food-friendly fridge cleaner. Consider keeping a small labeled spray bottle of it in your fridge for quick and easy daily spot-cleaning.

HOW TO KEEP YOUR FRIDGE CLEAN

Have better things to do than deep clean your fridge? Try these fridge-cleaning hacks to keep it cleaner longer:

- Get in the habit of quick-cleaning the fridge before loading it with new groceries. Toss old food and wipe up crumbs or spills so the fridge is clean for the fresh stuff.
- Line shelves with one-side-sticky plastic wrap. Instead of scraping up stuck-on spills, just peel off and replace.
- Use a Lazy Susan for condiments and small jarred items, such as olives or sauces, to keep them from inadvertently getting shoved into the back and forgotten.
- Make sure you slide the fridge out and clean underneath and behind it every couple of months.
- To keep everything running in optimal condition (and to save operating costs), clean the refrigerator coils, which are exposed on the back side or hidden behind a panel on the front or back.

17 Quick Appliance Tips

Little fixes can save big bucks.

When an appliance stops working, you might feel the itch to call a repair service right away. Don't. Take a breath and think it through. Sometimes the solution to a broken appliance is so easy you'll regret calling for service. Plus, you'll feel the glow of satisfaction that comes from making your own repairs. Here are 17 appliance fixes you can tackle yourself and save some money.

1. THE OVEN TEMPERATURE IS INACCURATE

If your food is taking longer to cook in the oven, recalibrate your oven's temperature setting. First, check the instruction manual for how to adjust this. You can find the manual online by searching for your oven's model number and "instruction manual." Then, place an oven thermometer in the oven for an accurate heat reading. Compare the thermometer reading with your oven's digital display when recalibrating the temperature setting.

INSERT NEEDLE TO CLEAN BURNER HOLES

2

GFCI OUTLET

3

2. GAS BURNER WON'T LIGHT

A quick cleaning will usually remedy this. First, scrub the stove igniter with a toothbrush, making sure to remove all the gunk. Then, clean out the burner holes with a needle.

3. CHECK THE POWER

Often, a repair person shows up at a home and finds that the appliance isn't broken at all: It's either switched off or unplugged, or else a breaker is tripped. A less obvious cause is a tripped GFCI outlet. To check a GFCI, first press the "test" button, then "reset." GFCI outlets can protect other outlets downstream. If your fridge isn't working, a GFCI above your countertop may be the culprit.

4. INDUCTION COOKTOP WON'T HEAT

Induction cooktops can be used only with ferromagnetic pots and pans, such as enameled steel, cast iron and stainless steel. So it might sound silly, but the first thing to check would be the pots and pans you're using; they might not be compatible with your cooktop.

5. OVEN WON'T HEAT EVENLY

This problem can often be solved in seconds if your racks are wrapped in foil. People will often do this to keep the racks clean, but that prevents heat from transferring evenly. To fix the problem, just remove the foil.

6. WASHING MACHINE WON'T DRAIN

If your washer won't drain after a completed cycle, you might need to clean the washer filter.

A front-loading washer filter is located behind the bottom panel. Tilt the washer back, slide blocks under the front legs and unscrew the panel. Locate the filter and unscrew it by turning counterclockwise. Clean it and reinstall.

For most top-loading washers, you need to remove the agitator to reach the filter. Remove the fabric softener cap on the agitator. Shine a flashlight down in the middle of the agitator and you'll find a bolt fastener. Use a socket wrench with an extension bar to reach inside and unfasten the bolt. Remove the agitator. At the bottom of the drum, you'll find one large filter or several small filters that need to be cleaned.

Bad Habits Lead to Breakdowns

Many appliance problems are caused by misuse and abuse. Breaking a few bad habits now will save you some expense and frustration later.

- Don't push the keypad buttons too hard. If you do, the plastic liner can crack, allowing moisture to seep in and damage the circuit board.
- Never put coffee grounds, celery, green beans or anything stringy in the disposal.
- Don't use too much laundry detergent in your washer—use about a tablespoon per load. At the bottom of the tub is a hose attached to a water level switch, and sometimes foam travels up the hose and destroys the switch.
- Don't slam appliance doors. This will break switches, which are expensive to replace.
- Set a date on your calendar to clean the front-loading washer filter every six months or so. Pop out the filter and rinse it clean.
- Don't overload your washer or dryer. This can fry drive belts, break couplers and wear out motors—all very expensive repairs.
- Clean the dryer lint filter after each load and wash it with detergent every six months.
- Clean fridge gaskets with warm water and a sponge. Sticky gaskets reduce the seal on the fridge, making it work harder and increasing your electricity bill; plus, you might pull so hard on the door that you tear the gasket.
- Don't drag clothes out of the washer unless you want to pay a lot of money to replace the door gasket. Buttons and zippers can get caught on the gasket and tear it.
- Don't spray appliance switches and buttons with a cleaner. The moisture can work its way behind them and short out sensitive electronics. A shorted control panel will cost hundreds of dollars. Instead, spray cleaner on a rag and then wipe down these areas.

7. WASHING MACHINE IS LEAKING

A washer can leak from lots of places, but the most obvious is where the hoses connect. Corroded hoses should be replaced with no-burst hoses. If they look OK though, first try to tighten them with pliers. If that doesn't stop the leak, turn off the water valves and unscrew the hoses. Remove the old gaskets and install new ones in both hoses.

8. LAUNDRY DRIES SLOWLY

If your dryer doesn't dry clothes as fast as it used to, the vent pipe might be clogged with lint. To see how to unclog it, go to familyhandyman.com and search for "dryer vent."

9. LOOK FOR ERROR CODES

Many new appliances display an error code on their LCD screen to indicate what's wrong. Often the problem is then easy to fix. Look for a guide to the codes on the appliance—for example, on the door or behind the kick plate. If you can't find the guide, search online using the appliance brand and your model's number.

6

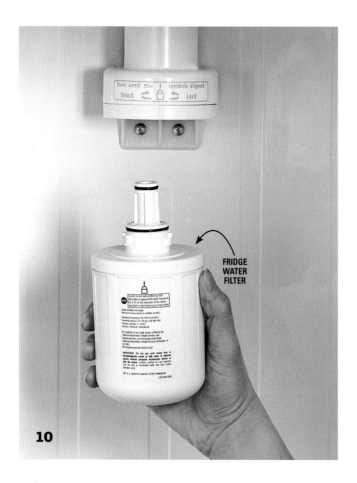

10

FRIDGE WATER FILTER

10. NO WATER FROM THE FRIDGE DISPENSER

There are a few reasons this might happen, but the least obvious and easiest to fix is the fridge water filter. If you recently replaced the fridge water filter, double-check that it's twisted all the way. Homeowners often don't turn it completely; all you have to do is give it a firm twist and the dispenser works again.

11. DISHWASHER WON'T RUN

In very cold climates, dishwashers placed near an exterior wall might stop working because the waterline is frozen. You can place a space heater next to the dishwasher to thaw a frozen pipe.

12. DISHWASHER WON'T DRAIN

If your dishwasher is flooded with dirty water, you should check the drain hose. Often the connection under the sink gets plugged with food. Turn off the power to the dishwasher, take off the hose (it's usually the one with ridges) and clean the end of the hose. You can also blow into the hose if there's junk clogging the other end. If this doesn't produce results, the next fix might be the solution.

13. SMELLY DISHWASHER

Dishwashers have a filter at the bottom that many ignore or aren't aware of. When you don't clean out the filter regularly, it will clog and make the dishwasher stop draining properly, but mostly it just makes the interior smell bad. It's an easy fix. Take off the bottom rack and remove the spray arm. Some filters can be removed by hand, but others may need a screwdriver. Empty out the filter with a vacuum and clean it.

11

COVER PANEL REMOVED

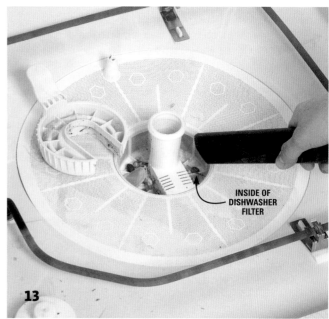

13

INSIDE OF DISHWASHER FILTER

TOO MUCH
FOOD BLOCKING
AIR VENTS

14. DISPOSAL DOESN'T START

If the disposal doesn't start, don't fret; it's a common problem that's easy to fix. Look under the disposal for a red reset button (you might need a flashlight). With the switch on the wall turned off, push the reset button. Then try the switch again and see if the disposer runs now.

15. FRIDGE ISN'T COLD ENOUGH

There are three instant fixes for this: First, make sure the temperature isn't set too warm (little kids like to adjust the temperature dial). Second, make sure food containers aren't blocking the air vents at the back of the fridge. Finally, make sure your fridge isn't overstuffed. Airflow is needed to keep food cold. If you overstuff your fridge, it can prevent airflow, overwork the system and damage expensive components.

16. GARBAGE DISPOSAL SHOOTS OUT GARBAGE

When a disposal splash guard wears down, it allows junk to fly back into the sink. To replace the guard, disconnect the disposal, place books underneath it and insert a screwdriver into the quick-connect fitting, pushing it away from you. Peel the old guard off and slip the new one on, pushing it down so it seals. When you reattach the disposal, insert shims under the books until the locking ring touches the sink flange. Rotate the lock back into place.

SPLASH
GUARD

17. DISPOSAL MAKES A GRINDING NOISE

Turn off the power to the disposal. Shine a flashlight into the drain to see if there's a hard object jamming the blades. Use a long screwdriver to dislodge the object.

Stinky Washing Machine?

There's a pill for that.

If your front-loading washer has developed a moldy odor, here's the problem: Unlike top loaders, front loaders seal up airtight. The drum doesn't dry out between uses, and that dark, damp space is perfect for mold.

There are several home remedies for this—usually using bleach or vinegar—but our appliance pros recommend washing machine cleaners, which are available as tablets, liquids or powders. Just put the product in the machine and run through a wash cycle. You'll find washing machine cleaners at discount stores or online.

ANTI-VIBRATION
PADS

Stop Washer and Dryer Vibration

Locating a laundry room near living areas rather than in the basement is much more convenient. But vibrations caused by washers and dryers can reverberate through floors and cause quite a racket. The noise can be eliminated or greatly diminished by the installation of anti-vibration pads under the legs of both the washer and the dryer. These pads, sold at home centers, are not a fix for appliances that are out of level; that's a different issue altogether.

Loosen a Stuck Throttle Cable

If your lawn mower's throttle cable is hard to move or stuck, here's a fix. Disconnect both ends of the cable from the mower. You'll probably have to remove a bolt and disassemble the lever assembly near the handle to get the cable out. Take a photo to help you remember how to put it back together when you're done.

At the engine end, loosen the clamp that holds the cable to the engine and unhook the cable from the carburetor. Pour penetrating oil into the cable **(Photo 1)**. Grab the inner cable with pliers, and work it up and down to loosen it. When the cable moves freely and all the penetrating oil has drained out, squirt silicone lubricant into the funnel to keep the cable sliding freely. Reinstall the cable **(Photo 2)**.

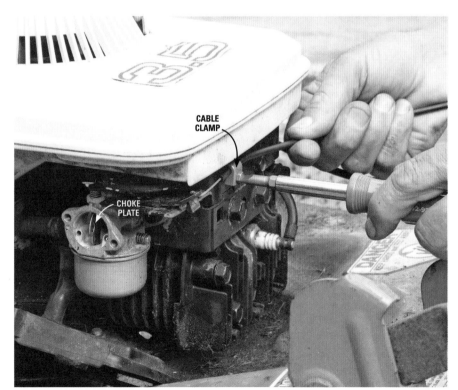

1 **SOAK WITH PENETRATING OIL.** Stick the end of the cable into a funnel and wrap electrical tape around it to create a seal. Spray or pour penetrating oil into the funnel. Position the opposite end of the cable over a small container to catch the penetrating oil as it drips out. Then lubricate the cable.

2 **REINSTALL THE CABLE AND ADJUST THE CHOKE.** Remove the air cleaner assembly so you can see the choke plate. With the throttle control lever in the "choke" position, pull on the outer jacket of the cable near the clamp until the choke plate opens. Tighten the clamp with the cable in this position. Reassemble the air cleaner.

DRAIN VALVE

Quiet Water Heater Gurgle

Popping or gurgling coming from your water heater is a sign of excessive sediment buildup in the tank. The sound is caused by steam bubbles percolating up through the muck. On a gas water heater, the sediment creates hot spots that can damage the tank and cause premature failure. On an electric water heater, sediment buildup can cause the lower heating element to fail. Flushing offers a payback in lower energy bills and extended heater life.

Start by shutting down the water heater. Turn the breaker off, and turn the thermostat to "Pilot" if you have a gas model. Shut off the water supply to the appliance and let the water cool. Then hook a hose to the drain valve at the bottom of the tank. Put the other end of the hose into a bucket and open the drain valve. Dump the bucket outside so the sediment doesn't clog your pipes. Keep draining until only clear water discharges. If the tank empties before the water turns clear, open the water valve and allow more water into the tank to further rinse it. Once you're done rinsing, close the drain valve, let the tank refill and turn the water heater back on.

Simple Dishwasher Rack Fix

As dishwashers age, the plastic coating on the rack posts wears off and the exposed metal begins to rust and stain dishes. Here's a simple fix: Get some of the plastic end cap covers that are used for wire shelving and glue them over the posts (we used polyurethane glue). No specialty kits or expensive dish rack replacement necessary. The fix is inexpensive and takes just a few minutes.

Fix an Electric Water Heater

A one-hour DIY fix saves the cost of a service call.

If your electric hot water heater is slow to heat, runs out of hot water faster than it used to or doesn't deliver any hot water at all, there's a 90% chance that simply replacing one or both of the heating elements will solve the problem. The fix is straightforward, and replacement elements are inexpensive and readily available at home centers, hardware stores and appliance parts dealers.

We'll show you how to test the heating elements, remove one if it's bad and install a new one. Just keep in mind that water heaters have a typical life span of 10 to 15 years. If your heater is approaching old age, replacement may be smarter than repair.

Of course, there are other potential causes of a lack of hot water. Before you test the elements, check to make sure the circuit breaker is on and not tripped. Also press the reset button on the high-temperature cutoff located just above the upper thermostat. Resetting either the circuit breaker or the high-temperature cutoff may resolve the problem, but the fact that they were tripped in the first place may indicate an electrical problem. If they trip again, test the heating elements.

If the heating elements are good, the problem could be the thermostats or cutoff switch. Testing these is complicated, but since they're inexpensive, you could simply try replacing them.

What's Inside and How It Works

Most residential electric water heaters have two heating elements: one near the top of the tank and one near the bottom. Power enters the top and runs to the high-temperature cutoff switch, and then to the thermostats and elements. The top and bottom elements are controlled by separate thermostats. When the water near the top of the tank is hot, the top element turns off and the lower one heats. The upper and lower heating elements never come on at the same time.

FIGURE A
ELECTRIC WATER HEATER

- HOT WATER
- COLD WATER SUPPLY
- GROUND WIRE
- HOT WIRES
- PRESSURE RELIEF VALVE
- ANODE ROD
- HIGH-TEMPERATURE CUTOFF
- UPPER THERMOSTAT
- UPPER HEATING ELEMENT
- LOWER THERMOSTAT
- LOWER HEATING ELEMENT
- DRAIN VALVE

TURN OFF POWER TO TEST ELEMENTS

You don't need electrical experience to check and replace the heating elements. But you do need to make very sure the power is off before you perform any tests or repairs.

First, find the circuit breaker in the main electrical panel that's labeled for the water heater and switch it off. Then go back to the water heater and test for power with a noncontact voltage detector. Make sure the tester is working by putting the tip into an outlet you know has power. The tester should indicate power by lighting up or beeping.

Now test the wires leading into the water heater. If they're covered by metal conduit, the tester won't read voltage. Instead you'll have to remove the metal thermostat cover on the side of the water heater, pull out the insulation and hold the tester near the wires leading into the top of the high-temperature cutoff switch **(see Figure A)**.

Test both hot wires. Then hold the tester against the metal water heater shell. If the tester doesn't light up, it's safe to test the elements.

COVER PLATE

1 REMOVE THE COVER PLATES. Turn off the power at the circuit breaker and remove the metal covers and insulation to expose the thermostats and elements. Make sure the power is off by touching the electrical connections with a noncontact voltage detector.

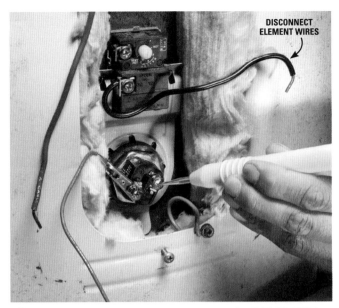

2 **TEST CONTINUITY FOR A BURNED-OUT ELEMENT.** Clip the alligator clamp onto one of the element screws and touch the other screw with the tester probe. If the tester doesn't light, replace the element.

3 **TEST FOR A SHORT CIRCUIT.** Clip the alligator clip to one of the element screws and touch the tester probe to the element mounting bracket. Repeat on the other screw. If the tester light comes on either time, there's a short. Replace the element.

TEST FOR A BURNED-OUT ELEMENT

For this you'll need a continuity tester. It's basically a lightbulb and battery with two wires attached. Touching the end of each wire to a continuous circuit will cause the bulb to light. You'll find these tools near the electrical testers in any hardware store or home center. You may also find a continuity tester called a water heater tester near the replacement elements.

If you own and understand a volt-ohm meter, you can test with it instead. To expose the elements for testing, remove the two metal covers, the insulation and the plastic covers on the side of the water heater **(Photo 1)**.

First perform a continuity test to see if an element is burned out. Electricity won't flow through a burned-out element. Disconnect the wires from the terminal screws. Then connect the alligator clip to one terminal and touch the probe to the other one **(Photo 2)**. The tester should light up, indicating there's a complete circuit. If there is no light, the element is bad.

TEST FOR A SHORTED ELEMENT

Next, test to see if the element is shorted out. If the element has a short, power will flow through the metal tank of the water heater. With the wires still disconnected, touch one probe (or connect the alligator clip) to one screw terminal and touch the other tester probe to the element mounting bracket **(Photo 3)**. Repeat the test on the second terminal. If the tester lights on either test, the element has a short; replace it. Test both terminals on both elements.

The Secret of the Red Button

Rarely, both elements will test OK but you're still not getting hot water. Try pushing the button on the high-temperature cutoff, located just above the upper thermostat. It may solve the problem, but if the problem recurs, check your heating elements.

HIGH-TEMPERATURE CUTOFF RESET BUTTON

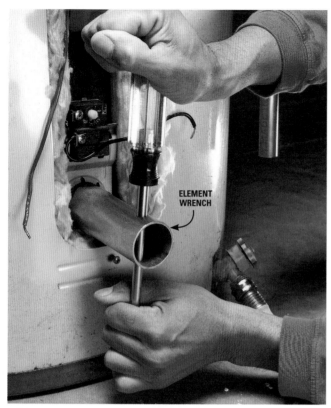

ELEMENT WRENCH

4 REMOVE THE BAD ELEMENT. Drain the water from the tank and unscrew the old element using a heating element wrench. You'll need a long, sturdy Phillips screwdriver to turn the socket. If it won't unscrew, use a cold chisel and hammer to loosen the threads.

5 INSTALL THE NEW ELEMENT. Thread the new element into the water heater and tighten it with the heating element wrench. Then reconnect the wires, making sure the connections are tight. Replace the insulation and reattach the metal covers.

REPLACE AN ELEMENT

To replace an element, start by draining the tank. With the power still turned off, close the cold water supply valve **(Figure A)**. Open the hot water faucet in the kitchen. Then connect a garden hose to the drain valve and open it to drain the tank. For thread-in–type elements as we show here, you'll need a water heater element wrench (sold at home centers and hardware stores).

Try unscrewing the bad element by turning it counterclockwise **(Photo 4)**. If it's stuck, you can try breaking it free with a cold chisel and ball peen hammer or a small maul. Set the chisel at an angle against the nut so that pounding on it will turn the nut in a counterclockwise direction. Then install the new element, using the wrench to tighten it, and reconnect the wires **(Photo 5)**. Close the drain valve and fill the tank before switching on the circuit breaker.

If testing reveals the elements are good, the thermostat may be faulty. The thermostat testing procedure is complex, so we recommend simply replacing the thermostat(s). You don't have to drain the tank to replace a thermostat. Simply remove the old thermostat—they're usually held by a metal clip—transfer the wires to the corresponding terminals of the new thermostat and attach the new thermostat.

Buying Heating Elements

Replace your heating element with one of the same wattage. If your old element isn't labeled with the wattage, refer to the nameplate on the water heater or your instruction manual, or search online using the model number from the nameplate.

Heating elements are held to the water heater either with a large thread and nut as shown here or by four bolts and nuts. Most home centers stock the version we show, but you can buy an adapter kit if you're replacing the four-bolt version.

Simple U-shape elements are the cheapest. More expensive low-density elements are usually folded back like the one shown **(Photo 5)**. These provide the same amount of heat but spread out over a larger surface area, which lowers the surface temperature, making them less prone to mineral buildup.

If your old element was caked with minerals, replace it with a low-density element for more efficient operation and longer life.

Free Up a Stuck Trailer Hitch

When the ball mount on your trailer hitch is rusted in place, don't whack at it with a sledgehammer. Here's what to do instead: Buy a can of penetrating oil and an air chisel fitted with a "hammer" bit. Both are inexpensive.

Spray the opening to the hitch receiver. This style of penetrating fluid chills the metal, causing it to contract to help break the rust seal. Then use an air chisel fitted with a hammer bit to knock everything loose. The air hammer will break up the rust, spread the penetrant and free up the ball mount. Once it's free, just tap out the rusted ball mount with a regular hammer. If you plan to reuse the rusty mount, coat it with a rust converter or waterproof marine grease.

Rap the sides, top and bottom of the hitch receiver with blows from the air hammer for 15 seconds. Spray again. Repeat the rapping until the ball mount loosens.

AIR HAMMER

HAMMER BIT

Misfiring Gas Nailer

If you own a cordless gas nailer, you know how convenient it is. But that convenience quickly gives way to aggravation when it starts acting up. If you can hear the fan running on your nailer but it fires only intermittently when you pull the trigger, don't take it to the repair shop—new gas may be all you need! Fuel cells have a "best used before" date printed right on the can. Old fuel cells lose internal pressure over time, so manufacturers recommend buying only as much fuel as you need to finish the job. You can buy new fuel cells at home centers.

FUEL CELL

CHAPTER **SEVEN**

WALLS, CEILINGS & FLOORS

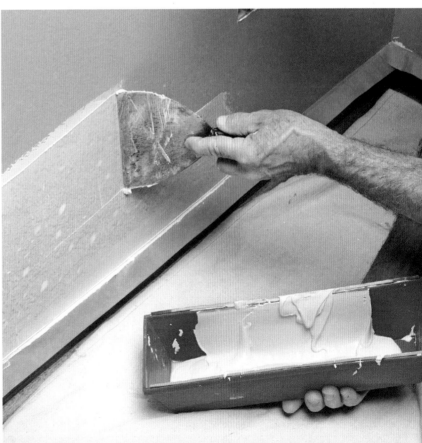

Patch a Wall

Preparing walls for paint inevitably involves patching—it's one of the most important steps. But sometimes it takes more than just a can of spackling and a small putty knife to get good results. We'll show you some wall patching tips and products that will help you speed up the job and avoid problems.

1. USE SELF-PRIMING FILLER

Patches made with traditional patching materials need to be primed with a sealing-type primer before painting. Otherwise the patched areas could show through the finished paint job as foggy spots. But if you patch with a self-priming patching material, you can avoid this extra step. Several brands exist; just look for "self-priming" or "with primer" on the container.

2. USE SETTING COMPOUND FOR BIG HOLES

It's fine to fill screw holes and other small wall dings with patching compound, but for dime-size and larger repairs, and for holes that are deep, it's best to use a joint compound that sets up by a chemical reaction. These are available in powder form with setting times ranging from five to 90 minutes.

The reaction starts when you mix in the water, and the compound hardens in the specified time. The five-minute version is nice because you can buy the powder in a convenient 5-lb. box, and the compound hardens quickly, so you can apply another coat right away. Remember, setting-type compounds are harder to sand than regular patching materials, so make sure to strike them off flush to the surface when you fill the hole. You'll find setting-type compounds wherever drywall taping supplies are sold.

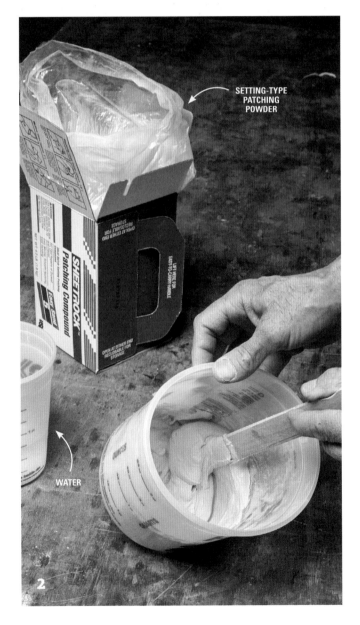

SETTING-TYPE PATCHING POWDER

WATER

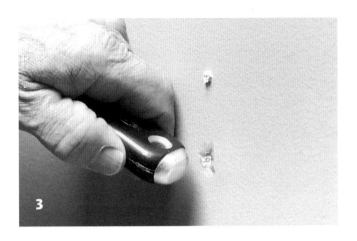

3. MAKE A DENT FOR THE PATCHING COMPOUND

When you remove a nail, drywall anchor or picture hanger, there is usually a little ridge of old paint or drywall sticking out that's hard to cover with patching material. The solution is to make a dent over the hole and then fill the dent. Most good-quality putty knives have a rounded hard plastic or brass end on the handle that works perfectly for making the dent. The rounded end of a screwdriver handle or the handle of a utility knife will also work. Press the handle against the hole and twist it slightly while applying pressure to dent the surface or, if you have good aim, use a hammer.

4. COVER CRACKS WITH REPAIR SPRAY

Stress cracks usually show up around window and door openings. The cracks are the result of framing movement and are hard to fix permanently. But using spray-on crack repair is a good way to at least extend the life of your repair. The spray forms a flexible membrane over the crack that can stretch and relax as the building moves.

If the crack is open, fill it first with patching compound. Then follow the instructions on the can to cover the crack with the crack-repair spray. Let it dry and cover it with paint to finish the repair. You'll find crack-repair spray at hardware stores, paint stores or online.

5. FILL A ROW OF HOLES WITH ONE SWIPE

Professional drywall tapers always fill a row of screw holes with one long stripe of joint compound, rather than filling every screw hole separately. In addition to being faster, this method disguises the screw holes better and makes it easier to sand the patch. Instead of sanding around each hole, you can just sand the whole stripe.

You can take advantage of this tip whenever you're filling a series of holes that are lined up and close together, like the holes left from a shelf standard or a row of pictures. Use a 6-in.-wide putty knife and apply the compound as shown in the two photos.

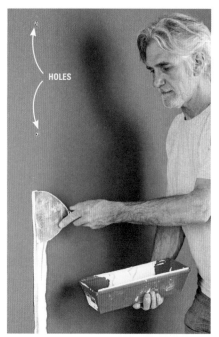

1 FILL THE HOLES. Use a 5- or 6-in.-wide putty knife and apply the compound with the knife held parallel to the line of holes.

2 REMOVE THE EXCESS. Turn your knife so the blade is perpendicular to the stripe of joint compound and remove the excess. To completely fill the holes, you'll probably need to apply another coat after this one dries.

6

6. SKIM-COAT AREAS WITH LOTS OF DINGS OR HOLES

In areas with a lot of dents and holes, like in mudrooms where boots, hockey sticks and golf club bags leave their marks, don't try to fill every dent individually. Instead, get a wider taping knife—a 6-in.-wide putty knife will do—and simply skim the entire area with joint compound. For the best results, use "topping" or "all-purpose" joint compound.

Mix 1 or 2 tablespoons of water into 3 or 4 cups of the joint compound to make it easier to spread. Then put a few cups into a drywall pan and use your 6-in. knife to spread it. Spread a thin coat of joint compound over the area. Then scrape it off, leaving just enough to fill the recesses and holes. You may have to apply two or three coats to completely fill the holes, but the thin layers dry quickly and are easy to apply. Sand the wall after the final coat dries.

7. SEAL EXPOSED DRYWALL PAPER BEFORE PATCHING

When you peel off old adhesive or self-sticking picture hangers, you often tear off the top layer of drywall paper, leaving fuzzy brown paper exposed. If you try to patch over this without sealing it first, the water in the patching material will cause the paper to bubble and create an even bigger problem. The key to patching torn drywall paper is to seal it first with an oil- or shellac-based sealer (KILZ Original and BIN are two brands). These are available in spray cans or a liquid that you can brush on. Don't use a water-based product or you'll likely have the same bubbling problem. After the sealer dries, sand the area lightly to remove the hardened paper fuzz. Then cover it with patching compound as you would for any other wall repair.

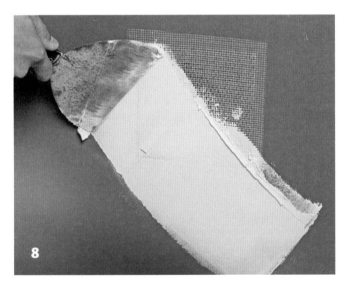

8. USE STICK-ON PATCHES FOR MIDSIZE HOLES

You can patch doorknob-sized holes in all kinds of ways. But the quickest and easiest way is to use one of these stick-on mesh patches. They're available in a few different sizes at paint stores, hardware stores and home centers. To use the patch, just clean the wall surface and sand it to give the surface a little "tooth." Then stick the patch over the hole and cover it with two or three thin layers of joint compound. You can speed up the patching process by using setting-type compound for the first coat.

9. SPRAY-ON WALL TEXTURE

Orange peel texture on walls or ceilings is nice for hiding defects and adding interest, but it can be a real pain if you have to make a big patch. Luckily you can buy spray-on orange peel patch that will allow you to match the texture of the patch without hiring a pro. You can purchase the patching material in a few different versions: regular, quick-drying and pro. The pro version gives you the most control over the spray pattern.

Make sure to practice spraying the texture onto a scrap of drywall or cardboard to fine-tune your technique before you spray it on the wall patch. Let the test piece dry before you decide whether you need to adjust the nozzle for a coarser or finer texture. Remember, you can always add another coat if there's not enough texture after the first coat dries.

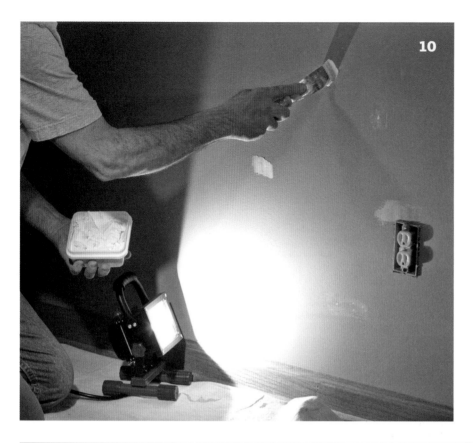

10. USE A RAKING LIGHT WHEN PATCHING WALLS

When you're preparing your walls for paint, position a bright light so the beam rakes across the wall as shown here. This will accentuate any defects, making them easier to see and fix, and will alert you to patches that need more fill or additional sanding. If your walls look smooth in raking light, you can be sure they'll look awesome when you're done painting.

Bleach Away a Water Stain

A second-floor pipe that leaks or an upstairs toilet that overflows can cause nasty-looking stains on the ceiling below. If the drywall wasn't damaged by the water, try this tip before you head to the store for paint to recoat the ceiling.

Fill a spray bottle with a bleach-and-water solution (10% bleach) and spray the stain. Then wait a day or two. If it's an old stain, try spraying with Tilex Mold & Mildew Remover. It works on both flat and textured ceilings.

Be sure to wear safety goggles, and protect nearby walls and floors with plastic.

STAIN

PLASTIC

BLEACH AND WATER MIXTURE

Ceiling Cover-Up

The ultimate solution for an ugly ceiling.

Covering an old ceiling with new drywall is a big job with heavy lifting, a serious time commitment and a major mess. But in some cases, it's the smartest way to go. We talked to a dozen remodelers, and every one of them made the same point: Sometimes covering up an old ceiling saves time, money and headaches in the long run. In the following pages, we'll focus on the details that make this job different from other drywall projects. For everything else you need to know about hanging and finishing drywall, go to familyhandyman. com and search for "drywall."

1 SHIM OUT EXPOSED JOISTS. If you have a hole in the ceiling, hold a straightedge across it, measure to the framing and cut spacers to that thickness. Screw a spacer to the joist or truss to create a flush surface for the new drywall.

2 MARK THE JOISTS. Locate joists with an electronic stud finder, or just probe for joists by driving a nail through the drywall. All the joists should be centered either 16 or 24 in. apart, but double-check with a nail. Mark each joist location with a chalk line on the ceiling and with tape placed on the wall.

TIME AND MATERIALS

For a 12 x 12-ft. room, with a helper or two, you can cover an average-size ceiling in one day. Finishing, or "taping," all the joints is much more time-consuming and requires drying time between coats. Then comes sanding and painting. Even if you can devote a few hours every evening to this work, you should expect it to span at least a week.

We recommend 1/2-in.-thick "lightweight" drywall for this project. It's not only lighter than standard drywall but also stronger so you can hang it from joists centered 24 in. apart. UltraLight, High Strength Lite and ToughRock are some brand names you'll find at home centers. If possible, get sheets that are long enough to span the room. Shorter sheets are easier to handle, of course, but you'll pay dearly for that convenience when it's time to finish the "butt joints" where the ends of sheets meet. Unlike the tapered joints along the long edges of drywall, butt joints are tough to finish. It's best to avoid them if you can.

Most home centers carry 8- and 12-ft. sheets. Specialty drywall suppliers usually carry those lengths, plus 10-, 14- or even 16-ft. sheets. Just be sure you can get long sheets into the room before you buy them; sometimes 8-ft. sheets are the only option. Everything else you'll need is available at home centers: 2-in. screws, 10-ft. lengths of 1/2-in. tear-away bead, mud rings for junction boxes, joint tape and compound, primer and paint.

HANGING THE ROCK

This project is a lot like any other drywall job, but there are a few differences. For starters, you'll have to "fur down" joists at holes in the drywall **(Photo 1)**. Don't try to simply span holes larger than 6 in. with drywall; your screws will pop right through the hollow space above the drywall. Also, shut off the power and remove any light fixtures in the ceiling.

Next, take your time to carefully locate and mark the centers of joists **(Photo 2)**. The rest of the project will go a lot more smoothly if your marks are accurate.

The final prep step is to extend junction boxes with "mud rings" **(Photo 3)**. If you have recessed lighting in the ceiling, you'll have to lower the "cans" by loosening screws inside the housings, but it's best to do that after the new drywall is up.

Now you're ready to head for the rental center to pick up a drywall lift and hang the drywall. You can hang drywall without a lift, of course, but a lift makes the job faster, easier and better. When you cut the rock to length **(Photo 4)**, remember to subtract 1/4 in. for the gap along walls. But you don't have to be exact about this: As long as the gap is between 1/8 in. and 1/4 in., you'll have no trouble installing the tear-away bead.

3 **EXTEND ELECTRICAL BOXES.** Screw a 1/2-in. mud ring to any junction box in the ceiling. This extends the box so that it will be flush with the new drywall.

4 **MEASURE TO JOISTS AND CUT THE ROCK.** Cut sheets so that the ends fall on the centers of joists. Measure from the wall to the chalk line and subtract 1/4 in. to allow for a gap along the wall. Also cut off the tapered edge that will run along the wall.

Joist Direction Matters

Drywall is normally hung perpendicular to the joists. But sometimes it's smart to break that rule. Let's say that you have an 11 x 14-ft. room with joists spanning the 11-ft. length (as shown here) and that you can't get sheets longer than 12 ft. into the room. You could run sheets across the joists as usual, creating three hard-to-finish butt joints **(Figure A)**. Or you could run the sheets parallel to the joists **(Figure B)** and eliminate butt joints completely.

FIGURE A
DRYWALL PERPENDICULAR TO JOISTS

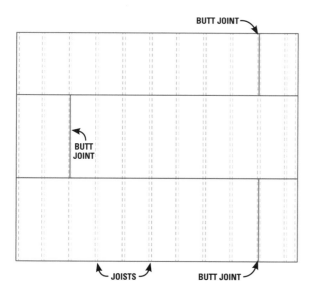

FIGURE B
DRYWALL PARALLEL TO JOISTS

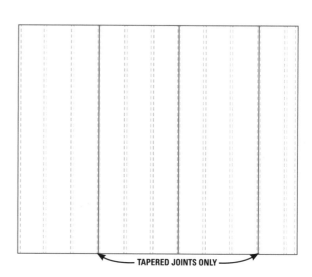

5 RAISE ROCK THE EASY WAY. Hoist each sheet with a rented drywall lift. Be sure to leave gaps between the sheet and the wall. Those gaps will allow you to slip tear-away bead behind the edges of the drywall bead later.

6 SCREW TO THE JOISTS. Screw each sheet along the tapered edges, then add a couple of screws near the center. That will be enough to hold it in place. Later, when all the sheets are up, snap chalk lines and drive the remaining screws.

The Ultimate Screw Gun

I love self-feed screw guns because they're fast: You just pull the trigger and push to automatically load and drive screws. Plus, the gun itself is long, so you can reach an 8-ft. ceiling without a ladder. Aside from drywall, I've used my gun for screwing down subfloors and decking too. The only thing I don't like about it is that it's usually missing from my toolbox, on loan to friends. You can get a corded version at any home center for about $100. A cordless one costs about $150.

Here's another critical thing to remember: Along walls, cut the tapered edges of the sheets. Because tapered edges are thinner than the rest of the sheet, they'll cause trouble when you mud the tear-away bead later.

Raise and position each sheet **(Photo 5)**. Take your time on this step. Make sure each sheet is aligned with a chalk line that marks the center of a joist. There's no need to completely fasten the sheets before removing the lift. Just drive enough screws to safely hold the sheet **(Photo 6)**.

When all the sheets are up, snap a fresh set of chalk lines and add the remaining screws.

TERRIFIC TEAR-AWAY BEAD

The usual way to finish the joints where walls meet the ceiling is to apply coats of joint compound. Making it all smooth, straight and square takes patience and practice. Plastic tear-away bead lets you skip all that. The bead is typically used where drywall meets a different material, such as brick, a shower surround or paneling. But for this job it's an even bigger timesaver because it makes taping much easier—and you may not even have to paint the walls when you're done.

The bead is easy to cut using metal shears. Make miter cuts at corners. Some installers simply overlap the beads, but that leaves an uneven guide for your knife. The same goes for splices along a wall: Butt the two sections together neatly; don't overlap them. Staple the bead to the drywall every 8 in. **(Photo 7)**. Take your time and make sure the bead is tight against the wall. Gaps will look bad and possibly cause you more work later. When the tear-away bead is up, you're ready to skim on the joint compound **(Photo 8)**.

Paint the ceiling before you pull off the tear-away bead's flange. The flange will keep ceiling paint off the wall. For extra protection, run a strip of painter's tape below the bead (we skipped this step—and regretted it).

When the paint is dry, run your utility knife along the bead at the point where the flange will tear off. Press lightly; the purpose is to slice through the paint so the paint film doesn't tear when you pull off the flange. A needle-nose pliers helps you get a grip on the flange as you begin to tear it off. Then simply pull down to remove the bead **(Photo 9)** and check out the result.

It won't look exactly like a standard wall-to-ceiling joint. Instead, you'll see a tiny crack between the wall and the ceiling. If your walls are a deep color, that crack will be almost invisible. With white walls, the crack is visible, but only if you're looking for it. If you're especially fussy—or if you didn't fasten the bead tightly along the wall—you can caulk the crack. Even with caulking and paint touch-up, tear-away bead saves hours of time and effort.

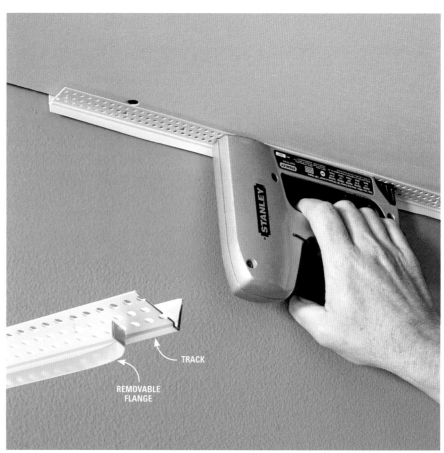

TRACK

REMOVABLE
FLANGE

7 INSTALL TEAR-AWAY BEAD. Staple the bead to the drywall every 8 in. Be sure to hold the bead tight against the wall before you fasten it.

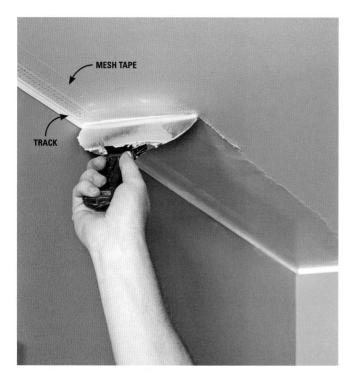

MESH TAPE

TRACK

8 MUD THE BEAD. Skim joint compound over the bead, using the track to guide your knife. Mesh tape isn't essential, but it's cheap insurance against cracks.

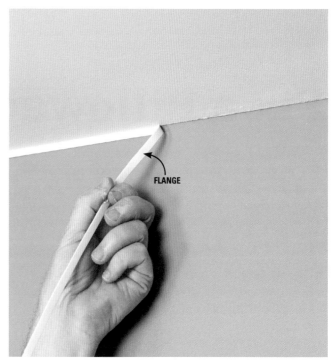

FLANGE

9 TEAR OFF THE FLANGE. After sanding and painting, rip the protective flange off the bead. To avoid scraping off the fresh paint, pull the flange downward along the wall, not outward along the ceiling.

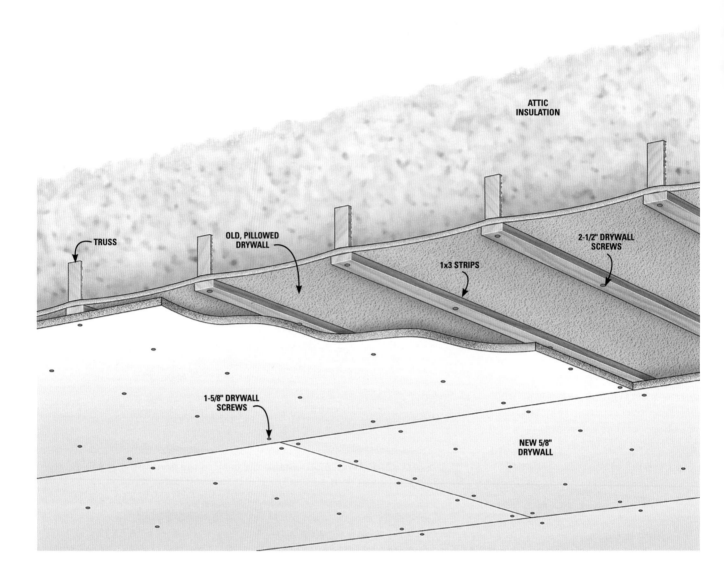

ATTIC
INSULATION

TRUSS

OLD, PILLOWED
DRYWALL

1x3 STRIPS

2-1/2" DRYWALL
SCREWS

1-5/8" DRYWALL
SCREWS

NEW 5/8"
DRYWALL

Fix a Pillowed Ceiling

If your ceiling drywall is sagging between joists, sometimes called pillowing, it's probably on the top floor and probably 1/2-in. drywall instead of 5/8-in. Half-inch drywall can sag if it's hung on framing spaced every 24 in. It isn't strong enough to handle the span, and the weight of the attic insulation just makes the sagging worse.

You have two choices: Rip out and replace the sagging ceiling, or add spacers and new drywall below it. In either case, you can use 5/8-in. drywall or lightweight, sag-resistant 1/2-in. drywall. Ripping out the old stuff might seem like the right approach, but it's a nightmare job. You have to pry out the ceiling drywall along the edges and pluck out all the old drywall screws. If you've ever torn out drywall, you know that without taking extreme measures, the dust goes all over the house. As if that weren't enough fun, the attic insulation will likely collapse into the room. That in itself can make

the decision easy. If the attic insulation contains vermiculite, there's no question. It contains asbestos, and if it is disturbed and becomes airborne, it can enter your lungs.

If you can live with a slightly lower ceiling height, you can save a lot of time by installing a new ceiling below the old one. Add furring strips on the trusses, as shown. To make the drywall easier to hang, use 1x3s rather than 1x2s. If your ceiling sags more than 3/4 in., use 2x2s. Screw the 1x3s to the truss framing with 2-1/2-in. drywall screws.

Next, install, tape and finish new 5/8-in. drywall. If you have ceiling fixtures, you'll have to extend all the boxes to make them flush with the new ceiling. It's OK to use standard 1/2-in. drywall on existing ceilings as long as it meets building code in your area. But a better option is to use USG UltraLight gypsum board. It's stronger and lighter, and it meets fire code.

Recaulk a Tub or Shower

Anybody can recaulk a tub or shower. All you need is a tube of caulk and a caulking gun. But if you don't prep the surfaces properly, the caulk won't last long. And if you're sloppy, the messy caulk job will ruin the look of even the most beautiful tile job.

We talked to a few experts to learn how they get such smooth, clean-looking caulk lines. We'll show you their technique and the best way to remove the old caulk and prep the surface to get a long-lasting caulk job. Finally, we'll give you a heads-up on how to avoid the most common caulking mistakes.

You can remove the old caulk, prep the surface, and recaulk a tub or shower in about four hours (including drying time). You'll need a razor scraper and single-edge razor blades, caulk remover, mineral spirits, paper towels, a utility knife, a caulk gun, and kitchen and bath caulk. An oscillating tool with a flexible scraper blade really speeds up the job of removing old caulk, but you can do the job without it.

BUY THE RIGHT CAULK AND USE A QUALITY CAULK GUN

Tubs and showers require a special caulk that contains mold and mildew prevention additives. The tubes are usually labeled "For kitchen and bath use." Most are 100% silicone, but you can also find some latex versions. Latex caulk is easier to tool and cleans up with soap and water.

If this is your first time applying caulk, latex may be your best option. Silicone is more challenging to tool and requires mineral spirits for

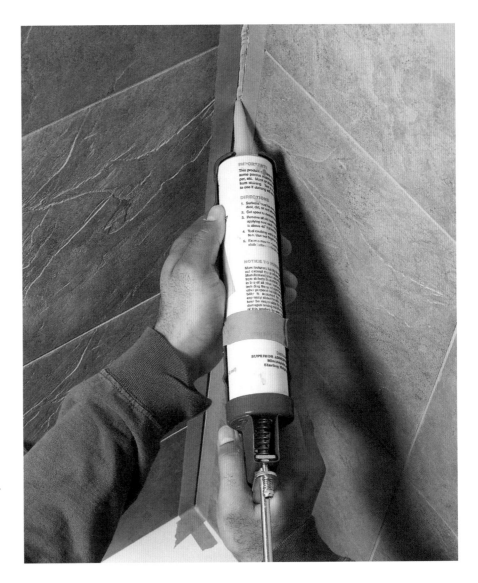

cleanup. However, silicone lasts longer than latex and stays flexible over its life. But it's harder to remove when it's time to recaulk. Both types can develop mold and mildew once the additives wear out.

Most home centers and hardware stores stock only three kitchen and bath caulk colors: white, almond and clear. However, ask a salesclerk whether you can special-order a custom color. And check out a paint or hardware store. Some can custom-mix colors right in the store.

A high-quality caulk gun can make a difference in your caulk job. It has a sturdier plunger mechanism to provide a smooth, even flow and a pressure release to stop the flow quickly.

High-quality caulk guns cost a bit more, but they're worth it. Economy guns usually have a ratchet action or a sloppy friction mechanism that pushes the caulk out in bursts so you end up applying too much in some areas and too little in others.

REMOVE THE OLD CAULK

You can't apply new caulk on top of the old and expect it to last, so the old caulk has to be removed. If the old caulk was silicone, you have to devote extra effort to remove all traces of it before applying new caulk. Start by slicing through the old caulk with a utility knife or an oscillating tool (Photo 1). Then scrape off as much old caulk as possible. Next, apply caulk remover (Goo Gone,

1 CUT AND PEEL THE OLD CAULK. Slice through the caulk along the walls with a utility knife or with an oscillating tool equipped with a flexible scraper blade. Then use your knife or tool to scrape along the tub or shower floor.

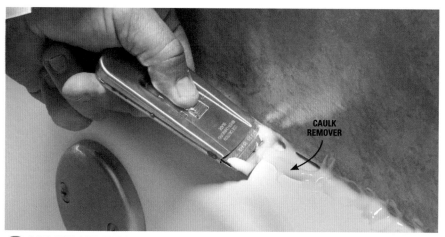

CAULK REMOVER

2 LOOSEN AND REMOVE THE REMAINING CAULK. Squirt caulk remover on all the remaining caulk and let it do the hard work. Then scrape off all the old caulk with a razor scraper. Wipe with a rag.

3 MASK THE GAP. Mask the wall corner gaps first. Then apply tape to the walls above the tub or the shower floor. Finish by applying tape to the tub or the shower floor.

DAP and Motsenbocker's all make caulk remover products) to break the adhesive bond and make the caulk easier to scrape off **(Photo 2)**.

Once the old caulk is gone, remove any loose grout between the walls and the tub or shower floor. Treat any mold in the grout along the wall/tub gap with a mold-killing product (one choice is ZEP Mold Stain & Mildew Stain Remover, sold at home centers). Scrub the grout, and then rinse off the mold killer with water and let it dry (use a hair dryer to speed the drying). Clean the surfaces one last time with mineral spirits. Let dry.

MASK THE GAP

Some pros scoff at the idea of using masking tape. But they caulk every day and can lay down a caulk bead with their eyes closed. For DIYers, we recommend masking the gap. It takes a bit more time, but you'll get much better results than caulking freehand. Start by finding the largest gap between the tub/shower and the walls. That gap dictates how far apart you must space the two rows of tape. Then apply the masking tape **(Photo 3)**. If you have a fiberglass or composite tub, fill it with water before you caulk.

APPLY THE CAULK BEAD

There are two schools of thought when it comes to tip angle and whether to pull or push the caulk. Our experts prefer cutting the caulk tube nozzle at a blunt 20-degree angle instead of 45 degrees. And they hold the gun at a 90-degree angle to the gap while pushing a small bead ahead of the tip **(Photo 4)**. That way, they can complete the entire bead in one pass. Plus, the gun pressure forces the caulk deeper into the gap for better holding power and sealing.

If you cut the tip at a 45-degree angle and pull the gun away from the starting corner, your gun will always run into the opposite corner, forcing you to flip it 180 degrees and start the bead again. That creates a blob where the two beads meet, making tooling more difficult. Plus, pulling the gun tends to apply a surface bead that doesn't penetrate as far into the gap.

Whichever tip angle you choose, always cut the tip with a sharp utility knife rather than the cheesy guillotine mechanism built into some caulk guns. Remove any burrs with a utility knife or sandpaper before caulking—the burrs will create grooves in the caulk lines.

SHAPE THE BEAD AND REMOVE THE TAPE

You can find all kinds of caulk-shaping tools at home centers. But if you take our advice and tape off the wall, you won't need any shaping tools. Just use your index finger to tool the caulk **(Photo 5)**. After tooling, remove the masking tape while the caulk is still wet **(Photo 6)**. Let the caulk cure for the recommended time before using the tub or shower.

Avoid These Caulking Mistakes

- Buying the wrong caulk. Always use kitchen and bath caulk in a tub or shower. It contains mold and mildew inhibitors that are not present in other types of caulk.
- Caulking on top of old caulk. New caulk doesn't bond well to old caulk, especially if the old caulk contains silicone. Just as with painting, better surface preparation provides better results.
- Not removing mold on grout near the caulk areas. Grout is porous, and any mold present in the grout above the caulk line will eventually spread down into the new caulk area and destroy the bond.
- Cutting the nozzle larger than the gap you're filling. A larger opening applies too much product, making it harder to tool and clean up.

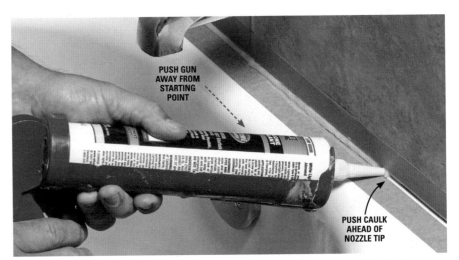

PUSH GUN AWAY FROM STARTING POINT

PUSH CAULK AHEAD OF NOZZLE TIP

4 CUT, PUSH AND APPLY. Cut the nozzle tip to match the gap width. Hold the gun at a 90-degree angle to the gap and push a bead of caulk slightly ahead of the nozzle as you push the gun forward and continue applying pressure. Apply only enough caulk to fill the gap.

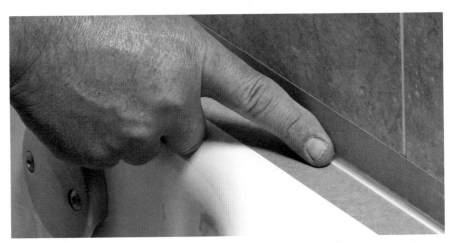

5 TOOL WITH YOUR FINGER. Wet your finger with water and start at an outer corner. Wipe your finger across the caulk to create a rounded bead and remove excess caulk from the gap.

6 PEEL OFF THE TAPE. Lift a corner of the tape along the tub and pull it off at a steep angle while the caulk is still wet. Then remove the tape along the wall. Remove the tape from the wall corners last.

The Best Way to Remove Grout

If you have grout that's stained or moldy, you may get lucky and discover that cleaning chemicals can handle the problem. Skip the traditional solutions like vinegar, bleach and baking soda though—they don't work nearly as well as a powdered oxygenated cleaner mixed into a paste (OxiClean is one brand). Or try commercial grout and mold elimination products from the home center. If chemicals work, great. If they don't, you'll have to remove a layer of the old grout and replace it with new.

After chemicals failed for us, we tried everything else: a grout removal attachment for a rotary tool, a grout removal blade in a reciprocating saw, a pulsating tool with a triangular carbide bit, and a tool that looks like an electric engraver with a chisel tip. All of them either destroyed tiles or were painfully slow. Plus, they all kicked up a gritty dust storm.

We finally figured out the easiest and fastest combination for the job—an oscillating tool fitted with a diamond blade. One source for diamond blades is fitzallblades.com.

You'll need at least two diamond blades, depending on the size of the job. You'll also need a scraper blade for your oscillating tool (such as the Dremel MM610 Multi-Max Flexible Scraper) to get at caulk inside corners **(Photo 1)**.

Next, it's worth fabricating a cooling system for the oscillating tool. We built ours out of inexpensive drip irrigation parts (see "Build a Cooling System"). Since you'll be working with water, plug the tool into the nearest GFCI-protected outlet. If you don't have one, buy a GFCI-protected extension cord. Don't do this project without GFCI protection.

Next, remove the grout (**Photo 2**). Your goal isn't to remove all the grout—only about 1/8 in. deep or so. Make several light passes until you reach the preferred depth. That will be deep enough to embed the new grout.

Once you're done grinding, clean the tile and let it dry before applying the new grout.

Build a Cooling System

Most home centers stock drip irrigation parts (but only during the growing season). If you can't find what you need, try a garden center or shop online (dripirrigation.com is one source).

Buy the components shown below. Then attach the pieces to the tubing and attach the tubing to the oscillating tool. Tape the waterline to the tool cord with electrical tape to keep it out of the way. You can also tape the tubing and sprayer nozzle to the tool body, but we used hook-and-loop tape instead—that way we could reposition the tubing and sprayer on the fly. Apply patches of hook tape to the tool. Then wrap loop tape around the tubing and press it onto the hook tape.

QUARTER-CIRCLE SPRAY NOZZLE

GARDEN HOSE ADAPTER

1/4" TUBING

VALVE

HOOK-AND-LOOP TAPE

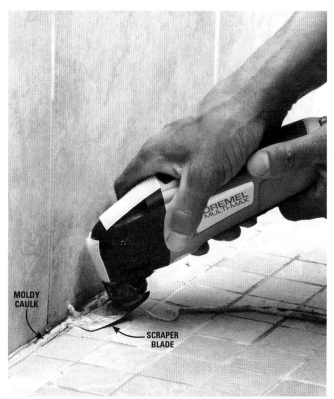

1 STRIP OFF THE OLD CAULK. Slice through the old caulk with an oscillating tool and a scraper blade. Then remove any remaining traces of caulk with a razor blade.

MOLDY CAULK

SCRAPER BLADE

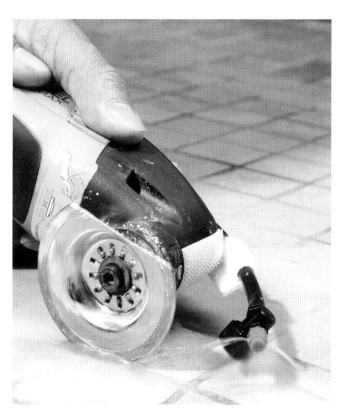

2 REMOVE THE GROUT. Turn on the water to get a light spray. Then center the oscillating tool blade in the middle of the grout line. Lower it into the grout and slowly push the blade forward.

Replace a Broken Ceramic Tile

You can remove a cracked ceramic tile by grinding out the surrounding grout and then smashing it to bits with a hammer. However, the brute force method can also break the bond between neighboring tiles and the tile backer board—then you have a real mess. Here's a better way.

Start by removing the surrounding grout (**Photo 1**). Next, drill holes in the tile with a 1/4-in. tungsten carbide bit (**Photo 2**). The holes loosen the tile's bond to the backer board. Then chisel out the tile (**Photo 3**). Scrape out any remaining thin-set material and install the replacement tile.

1 REMOVE GROUT. Grind out the grout with a hand scraper or an oscillating tool that's been fitted with a grout removal blade.

2 DRILL THE TILE. Drill multiple 3/8-in.-deep holes in the tile using a tile bit. (A hammer drill will really speed this up.) Wear safety glasses.

3 CHISEL OUT THE TILE PIECES. Tap a tile or cold chisel straight into the center of a crack. Then angle the chisel to 45 degrees and chisel toward the edges.

Hardwood Flooring Fix

Easy steps to replace that "one bad board."

Repairing tongue-and-groove hardwood floorboards is easy with the right tools and a little know-how. Many common problems can be fixed in a day to make your floor look like new again.

Over the years, we've seen our share of damaged hardwood floors. Sometimes the flaw can be repaired with wood putty and a quick touch-up—but other times surgery is required. Here are some tips to help you repair your own flooring trouble spots.

PRO TIP

Stain and Finish to Match

We prefer to do this first. Test some stain colors on new floorboards and apply some urethane. Once you find a good match to the existing floor, repeat that process for the actual repair.

Even when you use the same stain and finish, each piece of scrap floorboard may look slightly different. Stain and finish several pieces and use the best match.

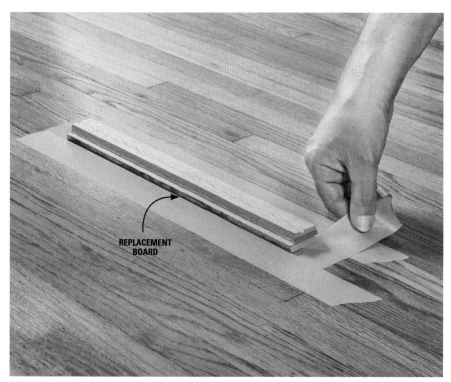

1 TAPE THE BOUNDARY. Inspect the damaged flooring plank and decide how much length to remove. Stagger the ends of the repair about 5 in. from the butt joints of the adjacent floorboards. Place masking tape to define the boundary, using the replacement board as a guide.

2 DRILL RELIEF HOLES. Drill three 1/2-in. holes close to each end of the board you're removing. Don't try to get the holes perfectly on the butt joint—about 1/8 in. away is fine.

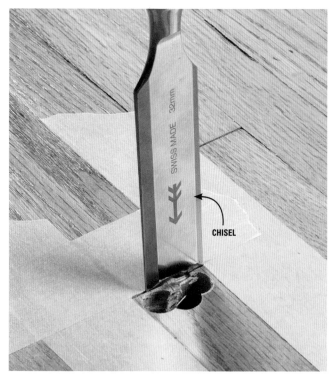

3 CHISEL THE BUTT JOINT. With a sharp chisel, clean up the space between the holes and the end of the repair. First, make a vertical cut to cleanly sever the wood fibers, then come in at a slight angle to remove waste. Repeat this process until you reach the subfloor.

4 MAKE RELIEF CUTS. Saw two parallel relief cuts an inch apart down the center of the floorboard to be removed. Use a blade with carbide teeth designed for demolition. To avoid cutting through the subfloor, set the saw blade no more than 1/16 in. deeper than the thickness of the flooring.

5 FINISH THE CUTS. You can get only so close to the ends of the repair with the circular saw. Finish the relief cuts using an oscillating multitool fitted with a narrow wood-cutting blade.

NARROW WOOD-CUTTING BLADE

6 REMOVE THE DAMAGED BOARD. With a small pry bar, remove the strip of flooring between the relief cuts. Next, pull out the tongue-and-groove edges of the damaged board. Completely clean out the open section of flooring with a shop vac.

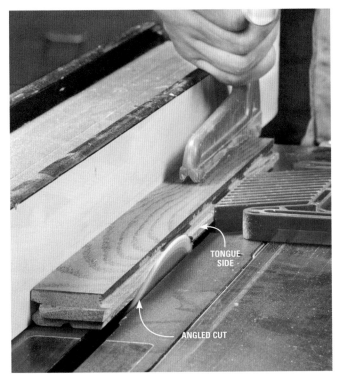

TONGUE-SIDE

ANGLED CUT

7 TRIM THE TONGUE. To make it easier for the tongue on the replacement board to slip into the existing floorboards, trim it at a slight angle. Angle the blade on the table saw to about 7 degrees, and set the fence so the blade just trims the tongue.

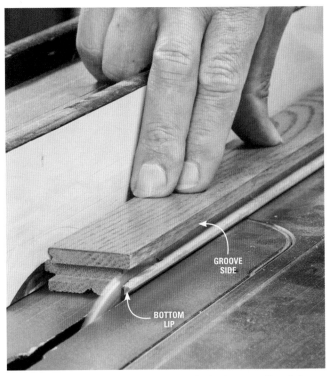

GROOVE SIDE

BOTTOM LIP

8 TRIM THE GROOVE SIDE. Cut off the bottom lip of the grooved edge of the replacement board. Be sure to set your blade depth so that it cuts off only the bottom lip and doesn't cut into the top lip.

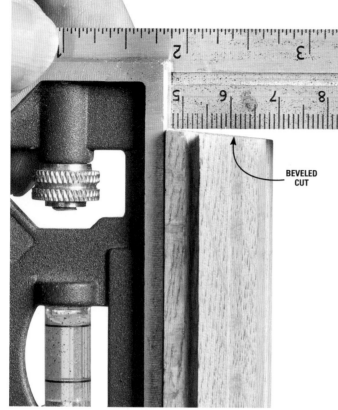

BEVELED CUT

9 CUT TO LENGTH. Cut the replacement piece to length using a miter saw. Make the cuts with a slight bevel so the piece will drop into place easier, creating a cleaner, tighter butt joint.

10 GLUE THE BOARDS. Spread glue on the tongues of both the replacement piece and the adjacent board. Any wood glue will work for this purpose.

11 INSTALL THE NEW REPLACEMENT BOARD. Tap the repair board into place with a rubber mallet. If you don't have a rubber mallet, a hammer will work, but use a piece of scrap wood to protect the repair. Wipe off any excess glue using a damp cloth.

23-GAUGE PINNER

12 SECURE THE REPAIR. After gluing in the replacement board, add 23-gauge pins for peace of mind. Angle the gun slightly, and drive in a pin every 4 in.

Repair and Reglue Sheet Vinyl Floors

Fix damaged or curling seams in vinyl floor with vinyl adhesive and a seam-sealing kit.

If you have an open seam in your vinyl floor, don't procrastinate making repairs. Foot traffic can wreck the vinyl's exposed edges, making a good-looking repair impossible. Worse, water can seep into the opening, leading to subfloor damage. We'll show you two ways to fix a loose seam. They're simple DIY repairs that you can do in just a few minutes. You can pick up the supplies you need at a home center or hardware store.

Start by inspecting the seam. Press the loose edges down to make sure they'll still join to form a tight seam.

If the seam closes neatly, you can make a nearly invisible repair using multipurpose vinyl adhesive and a seam-sealing kit. Vacuum out any grit under the vinyl—even a tiny grain of sand can create a pimple on the vinyl's surface. Curl the vinyl back as you vacuum, but be careful not to kink or crack it. If the vinyl is too stiff to bend, soften it with heat from a hair dryer. You can leave most of the old adhesive alone, but scrape away loose spots. A putty knife bent in a vise makes a good scraper. It's also a handy adhesive applicator **(Photo 1)**.

After you spread the adhesive, rub down the seam with a block of wood. Use a wet rag to wipe away any adhesive that squeezes out of the joint. Then lay wax paper over the seam, followed by a scrap of plywood. Weigh down the plywood with stacks of books or buckets of water. Leave the weights in place for at least 10 hours. Then apply the seam sealant **(Photo 2)**. Sealant is available in gloss and satin versions to match your floor's sheen.

If the edges are damaged or the seam won't close neatly, the best way to make a repair is to install a metal transition strip **(Photo 3)** that completely hides the seam. Transition strips are available at home centers and hardware stores in various styles, lengths and finishes.

1 **STICK ADHESIVE UNDER THE LOOSE FLOORING.** Protect the floor with masking tape and apply an even coat of adhesive. Then lay wax paper over the seam and press it down with a board and weights overnight.

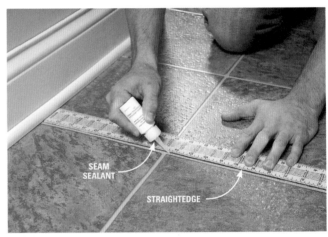

SEAM SEALANT

STRAIGHTEDGE

2 **SEAL THE SEAM WITH VINYL SEAM SEALER.** Apply a bead of seam sealant over the seam. Hold a straightedge about 1/4 in. away from the seam to guide the applicator nozzle, but don't get sealant on the straightedge.

TRANSITION STRIP

DAMAGED SEAM

3 **COVER THE SEAM WITH A TRANSITION STRIP.** Use a metal transition strip to cover a seam that has damaged edges. Cut the strip to length with a hacksaw, then nail or screw it into place.

Install a Basement Drain System

It's tough work that requires a lot of muscle, but the project is very doable. And you'll save considerable money by doing it yourself.

Do April showers bring a wet basement along with those May flowers? Then it might be time to consider installing a drain system. A wet basement not only prevents you from enjoying additional space in your house but also can turn into a giant petri dish perfect for growing unhealthy molds and fungi.

Installing a drain system is filthy, backbreaking work, but it's not complicated. With a little instruction, you can do a first-class job. And DIY pays off big in the money you can save compared to what you'd spend hiring a professional contractor to do the work.

BEFORE YOU GET STARTED

It's always best to stop water from entering your basement in the first place, so before you run to the rental center for your jackhammer, be sure to address the exterior issues. The grade next to the house should slope down away from the building by least 6 in. for the first 10 ft. Consider installing gutters, or make sure the existing gutters are working properly. And check that your irrigation system isn't adding to the problem by spraying water right up against the side of the house.

If your basement is finished, with stud walls and insulation covering the foundation walls, you can still install a drain system. When you break out the concrete, leave small sections of floor intact so the wall doesn't drop down. A 4 x 4-in. section every 6 ft. is enough to support the wall. If there are obstacles, like a furnace, plan to tunnel under them.

You'll find most of the materials you'll need at a home center. Order the rock from a landscape supplier. You'll also need a pickup to haul the dirt to the landfill.

Always check with your local building official. Explain your project, and see if any permits or inspections are required in your area. Sometimes a building official who has been around for a while may have information on how your house was built or what issues you may run into in your area.

CONTROL THE DUST

Busting up concrete is a dirty job. Shut down your furnace or central air conditioning while you're working, and cover all return air vents until you're finished cleaning up. Instead of covering furnishings with plastic, move everything out of the area and drape plastic from the ceiling to create an isolated work space **(Photo 1)**. If you have an unfinished ceiling, be sure you run the plastic up into every joist space. Set a fan in the window to exhaust the heavy dust while you run the jackhammer. And wear a dust mask and hearing protection.

> **RADON**
> A drain tile system creates a perfect pathway for dangerous radon gas to escape. If you've never tested for radon, it's smart to do so before you install a drain system. That way, you can plan for a radon mitigation system as well. To learn more, search for "radon" at familyhandyman.com.

1 GET READY FOR DUST. Instead of just covering your stuff with sheets of plastic, isolate your work area with a wall of plastic sheeting. Make sure to fill in the spaces between joists.

2 BUST UP THE FLOOR. Remove 16 to 18 in. of concrete along the wall with a rented electric jackhammer. Start by chipping in a straight line along the entire length of the wall, then come back and bust it into manageable chunks.

16" TO 18"

RUBBER FEED BUCKET

3 DIG A TRENCH ALONG THE WALL. Dig the trench as deep as the bottom of the footing. Instead of lugging pails of soil up the stairs, buy buckets that will fit through your basement windows.

BUST UP THE FLOOR

Professional contractors use electric jackhammers because the air that runs pneumatic jackhammers kicks up a lot more dust. You can get an electric one from a rental center. Start by hammering a line about 16 to 18 in. away from the wall **(Photo 2)**.

Once the perimeter is done, come back and break the row of concrete into manageable chunks. Each section will break free more easily if it has room to pull away, so remove the sections as you go. If you're working alone, make the most of your rental time; just set the chunks aside until you're done with the hammer. Don't forget to bust up a larger area for your sump basin.

DIG THE TRENCH

Once the concrete is removed, dig down to the bottom of the footing but not below. If you compromise the soil under the footing, you could end up with cracks in your wall, or worse.

Five-gallon buckets are OK for hauling out debris, but the pros we spoke to use rubber feed buckets (typically used for farm animals) because they fit through small basement windows and are less likely to bang up trim **(Photo 3)**. You can get them at farm supply retailers. And when it's time to haul the debris away, you may find that the landfill considers it to be "clean fill," which means you may be able to dump the debris for free!

INSTALL THE BASIN

It's best to locate the basin in an unfinished area of the basement so you can have easy access to the sump pump. If you never plan on finishing the basement, you can locate the basin in the same area where you want the water to drain out of the house so you don't have as much plastic pipe to install. Dig the hole so the top of the basin will sit flush with the finished concrete.

Many basins come with flat "knockout" areas meant to make cutting the hole easier. Don't assume the location of these knockouts will work for your system. Because the pipe will be slightly sloped down toward the basin, the longer the drain is, the lower the pipe will be when it reaches the basin. You never want standing water in your drainpipes, so make sure to choose a model that is deep enough. Our experts typically use 30-in.-deep basins. They use 36-in.-deep models for systems longer than 120 ft., and they install two basins if the drain is longer than 180 ft.

Set the basin in place, and then mark the locations for the holes where the pipes will meet the basin. Keep in mind there will be a thin layer of rock (one layer thick) under the pipe near the basin. Cut the holes using a reciprocating saw, jigsaw or hole saw. The holes don't have to be perfect.

Don't haul out all the dirt right away; you'll need some to fill in around the basin. Once it's permanently in place, fill

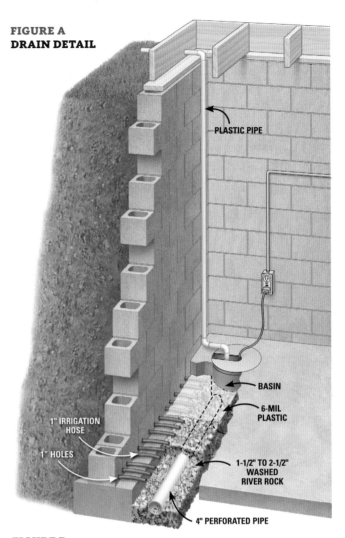

FIGURE A
DRAIN DETAIL

PLASTIC PIPE

BASIN

6-MIL PLASTIC

1" IRRIGATION HOSE

1" HOLES

1-1/2" TO 2-1/2" WASHED RIVER ROCK

4" PERFORATED PIPE

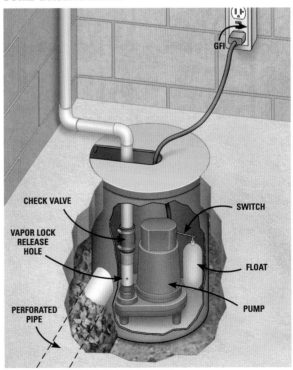

FIGURE B
SUMP BASIN DETAIL

GFI

CHECK VALVE

VAPOR LOCK RELEASE HOLE

PERFORATED PIPE

SWITCH

FLOAT

PUMP

4 LAY IN THE PIPE. Lay the pipe with the holes face down. Add or remove rock to slope the pipe so water flows to the sump basin. There's no need to cement the pipe connections.

RIVER ROCK

in around it, tamping the dirt with a 2x4 as you go. Caution: Never drill holes in the bottom of the basin! If you have a high water table, water could come up from the bottom and your pump will run nonstop, attempting to dry out the neighborhood.

DRILL HOLES IN BLOCK

If your basement walls are made from concrete block, drill 1-in. holes into each block core and mortar joint (**see Figure A**) to allow the water that collects in the cores and between the blocks to flow into the drain. Drill the holes as close to the footings as you can. You may find that the bottom blocks are filled with concrete. In that case, you'll have to remove any existing walls and install foundation wrap (see "If You Have a Solid Concrete Foundation"). Cut down on dust by laying a shop vacuum hose next to the hole as you drill.

INSTALL THE PIPE

Before you lay the pipe in the trench, shovel in a bottom layer of 1-1/2 to 2-in. washed river rock (a layer of smaller rock can become clogged with minerals and sediments). The pipe should slope toward the basin at least 1/4 in. for every 10 ft. Rake the rock around to achieve this pitch.

Lay your irrigation pipe on top of the rock. Don't use ordinary flexible drainpipe because it clogs easily. The pros

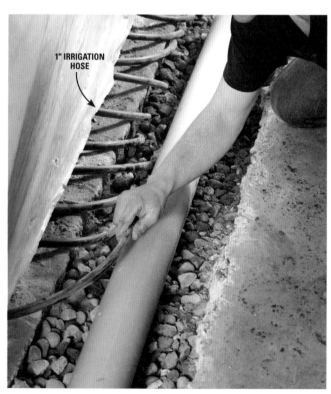

1" IRRIGATION HOSE

5 INSTALL HOSE IN THE BLOCK WALLS. Drill 1-in. holes in each block core and each mortar joint. Then insert sections of 1-in. irrigation hose from the holes into the gravel to carry away the water.

6-MIL PLASTIC

HAND FLOAT

6 CAP OFF THE TRENCH WITH CONCRETE. Lay plastic over the rock and cover it with concrete. Smooth out the concrete with a float. Wait 20 minutes, and work it smooth with a steel trowel.

prefer to lay down a 4-in.-dia. Schedule 10 perforated pipe. Buy the kind of pipe with rows of 1/2-in. perforation holes only on one side, not all around the pipe.

Lay the pipe with the holes facing down **(Photo 4)**, so the minerals and sediment in the water can flow down around the pipe and settle into the ground. This way, the water that does rise up into the pipes from underneath will be relatively clean. Clean water will add years to the life of the whole system. Start at the basin, and push the male end of the pipe into the basin about 4 in. Use PVC or ABS elbows at the corners. It's not necessary to cement the sections together.

DIVERT THE WATER INTO THE DRAIN

Once your pipe is installed, it's time to install the 1-in. irrigation hose that will carry the water from the blocks to the trench **(Photo 5)**. Softer hose, like garden hose, can get crushed flat by the new concrete, so stick with irrigation hose. Cut the hose with a hacksaw or reciprocating saw. Make sure each section of hose runs several inches past the footing.

COVER IT BACK UP

Once the hoses are in or the foundation wrap is in place, it's time to cover it up. Fill in the trench with river rock up to the bottom of the existing slab, and then cover the rock with at least a 6-mil thickness of plastic for a vapor barrier **(Photo 6)**.

To cut down on dust, mix your concrete outside. Bagged concrete mix for slabs and sidewalks works just fine. Slide a 3-ft. section of 2x4 along the floor to "screed" the new concrete flush with the floor, and then smooth it out with a hand float. Wait 20 minutes, then smooth it with a finishing trowel. Use the float to completely fill the gap under any existing walls.

HOOK UP THE PUMP

Pros prefer submersible pumps that have a vertical float switch on them because they're more reliable than pedestal or float switch pumps. Install a 6 to 8-in. section of pipe on the pump, then a check valve. Make sure the check valve doesn't interfere with the pump switch. Above the check valve, attach another section of pipe long enough to reach above the top of the basin.

Drill a 1/4 to 3/8-in. vapor lock release hole in the section of pipe that's just below the check valve **(see Figure B)**. This allows the pump to get up to speed before trying to force open the check valve, which may have many gallons of water pressing down on it. Angle the hole so water sprays down while the pump is working. It's best if you have a dedicated outlet for your pump. Extension cords get unplugged, and other appliances hooked up to the same circuit could trip a breaker.

The pipe that exits the basement needs to be located in an area that slopes away from the house. If that means running a pipe back across the basement, consider burying the waste pipe in the trench and having it come back up where you want it. If your pipe is going to discharge above grade and you live in a cold climate, run the pipe no more than 8 in. past the siding. This will keep it from freezing up in the cold winter months.

With few exceptions, basement drain water cannot be dumped into city sewer systems. Most systems can be drained into storm sewers as long as they're above grade when they do. Check with your local building official to determine what the rules are for your area.

If You Have a Solid Concrete Foundation

If you have poured concrete walls rather than block, you'll need to install a foundation wrap to let the water into the drain as shown below. Foundation wrap is made from tough plastic and consists of rows of dimples that allow water to flow behind it. Platon by CertainTeed is one example. Home centers can order it if they don't stock it.

Cut the sheets into strips with a utility knife. Bend them at 90 degrees and let the bottom half run past the footing. The length of the wrap that's up against the wall depends on your particular situation. At a bare minimum, run the wrap up 4 in. above the top of the concrete on a poured wall or up 4 in. past the holes you drilled in the block wall. If you're working along stud walls, try to tuck the wrap behind the bottom plate.

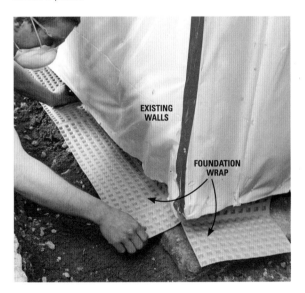

EXISTING WALLS

FOUNDATION WRAP

INSTALL FOUNDATION WRAP. Set foundation wrap over the footing and up the wall. If you have stud walls along the foundation, tuck the wrap up behind the studs if possible. On solid concrete walls, foundation wrap allows water to trickle down the wall surface and into the drain system.

How to Clean Carpet

Four cleaning strategies that can double the life of your carpet and save you a lot of money.

STRATEGY #1: BANISH DIRT

Dirt is like thousands of little blades that cut carpet fibers. When you walk across a dirty carpet, you grind sharp dirt particles against the yarn, making tiny nicks in the fibers. All that fuzz mixed in with the dirt in your vacuum cleaner bags is your beautiful carpet headed out the door one bag at a time. When dirt scratches the fibers, it dulls the sheen, which is why high-traffic areas appear duller than the rest of the carpet. Over time, grinding dirt wears away the fibers too, which mats them down and makes them stain more easily.

Follow these tips to keep your carpet as free of dirt as possible.

VACUUM OFTEN

To protect your carpet, vacuum entrance areas and high-traffic areas twice each week and the rest of the carpeting at least once each week. Oily soils attract oily soils, and frequent vacuuming will keep soil buildup in check.

VACUUM AT THE RIGHT SPEED

When it comes to vacuuming, speed matters. Vacuum slowly enough to get out as much dirt as possible. Make one quick pass over low-traffic areas and two slow passes over high-traffic areas. Two slow passes remove ground-in dirt much more effectively than if you were to vacuum a carpet in several fast passes.

USE WALK-OFF MATS

Use walk-off mats inside and outside entrances to keep dirt off the carpeting. Coarse-textured mats outside your doors remove soil and will make a future carpet-cleaning project much easier. Water-absorbent mats placed inside keep wet shoes off the carpeting.

Four Ways to Recognize Quality Pros

1 TRUCK-MOUNTED EQUIPMENT. Truck-mounted equipment is a better choice than portable steam-cleaning equipment because it exhausts the dirty air and humidity outside. Its stronger suction leaves carpets drier too.

2 EVERYTHING'S INCLUDED. Quality pros include furniture moving, vacuuming (some charge extra for this, so check), routine spot removal, preconditioning and deodorizing as part of a standard cleaning package.

3 HIGH-PRESSURE RINSE. To agitate the pile and neutralize the carpet's pH, pros force a hot, high-pressure rinse solution into the carpet and then extract it.

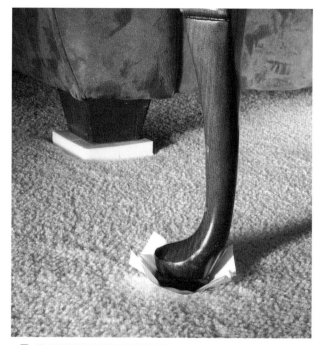

4 FURNITURE PROTECTION. After cleaning, quality pros set furniture on blocks or pads to prevent stains from transferring from furniture legs to the damp carpet.

SET THE VACUUM AT THE RIGHT HEIGHT

If your vacuum is set too low, you can damage the carpet as well as the vacuum's roller brush and drive belt. If it's set too high, you won't pick up any dirt. To set the vacuum's ideal height, raise it to its highest setting, turn it on and lower it until you can feel the vacuum trying to tug itself forward.

START WITH A CLEAN BAG OR FILTER

A dirty bag, dirt cup or filter can cut a vacuum's suction power in half. The main reason bagless vacuums stop working is that the filters aren't changed often enough. Replace or wash (if possible) the filters on bagless vacuums every three months. Replace vacuum bags when they're three-quarters full.

STRATEGY #2: USE A PRO WISELY

Most carpet manufacturers recommend professional hot water extraction as the primary cleaning method for synthetic carpets. Although it's often referred to as steam cleaning, there's no steam involved. The carpet is pretreated with a detergent solution, and then a very hot rinse solution under high pressure is forced into your carpet and vacuumed out. When done correctly, this process cleans deeply and doesn't leave behind a soap residue.

Quality pro cleaning isn't cheap, and you might be tempted to skip professional cleanings altogether and just rent a machine to clean the carpet yourself. Don't do that, or at least don't do only that.

A rented or purchased carpet-cleaning machine will remove the surface dirt. But deep cleaning to remove allergens, dust and greasy residues requires the specialized equipment and training of a pro.

The best strategy is to use our DIY carpet-cleaning tips most of the time and hire a professional every 12 to 18 months.

DON'T TAKE BIDS OVER THE PHONE

Quality pros will provide references, an in-home inspection and a written estimate based on the square footage, type and condition of the carpeting rather than the number of rooms cleaned. They'll also provide a written guarantee of the work.

BEWARE OF "DISCOUNT" CARPET CLEANERS

Discount pros depend on making volume sales rather than establishing ongoing client relationships. They typically spray soap on your carpet, suck up the water and are gone in 30 minutes. These services leave behind a soap residue that will actually attract dirt to your carpet. Those "three rooms for 50 bucks" offers also get them into your house so they can sell you high-priced add-ons like spot removal and deodorizers—services that quality pros include for free.

YOU GET WHAT YOU PAY FOR

Quality pros charge according to the type of carpeting, the services you need and the size of the job. The entire process can take one to three hours.

STRATEGY #3: DIY RIGHT

Carpet pros do a more thorough job than you can, but hiring a pro is expensive. So the next-best approach is to alternate between DIY and pro cleanings. DIY steam-cleaning machines can be effective if you understand how to use them and take the necessary time to clean your carpet carefully.

You can rent a steam cleaner from a grocery store or home center. If you pick up the machine late in the day, many stores will charge you a half-day rate and let you keep the machine until the next morning. The detergent cost is additional. Typically you should use a tablespoon or less per gallon of water.

If you prefer to buy a steam-cleaning machine, the pricier models have more powerful water jets and suction, and some even have a heating element to keep the water hot. The reviews on these machines are mixed, and some are prone to breakdowns. Do some online research (type "carpet-cleaning machines" into your browser) before you purchase one.

Most rental machines weigh more, hold more water and come with a wider wand than purchased models, making them useful for larger, high-traffic areas. Purchased models are usually smaller, more portable and easier to store. They're good for spot cleaning and are easier to drag up and down stairs. Whether you rent or buy, avoid damaging your carpets and make your cleaning last longer by following these tips.

CLEAN THE CARPET BEFORE IT BECOMES REALLY DIRTY

How often your carpet needs cleaning depends on the kind of carpet traffic you have (think kids and pets). Clean the carpet when the color starts looking dull. If you wait until the carpet is filthy, cleaning it will be much more difficult, take much longer and cost more.

VACUUM WELL BEFORE AND AFTER CLEANING

Vacuum beforehand to remove large particles of soil. Vacuum again after you clean and the carpet is completely dry to pick up soil that wicks to the surface during drying.

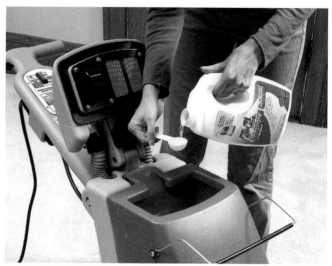

USE LESS SOAP THAN DIRECTED

The soap used in DIY machines foams a lot and leaves behind a lot of residue, which acts as a dirt magnet. Despite what the directions say, use a tablespoon or less of soap to 1 gallon of hot water to prevent soap residue.

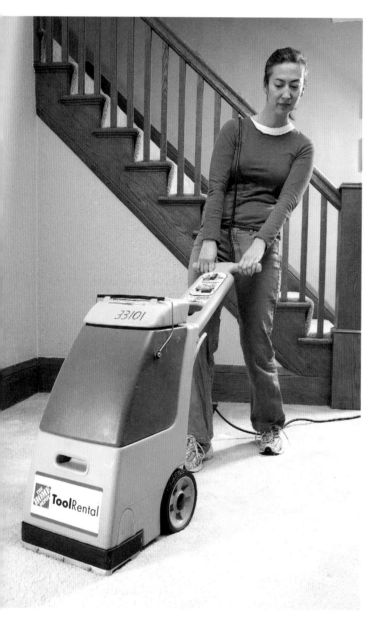

USE A MILD ACID RINSE TO NEUTRALIZE SOAP RESIDUE

DIY machines are often sold with a neutralizing rinse, or you can make your own using 1 cup white vinegar to 1 gallon hot water. Rinse after you make one pass with the detergent solution.

PRETREAT STAINS AND HIGH-TRAFFIC AREAS

Mix a drop of detergent with hot water in a spray bottle and lightly mist the dirtiest areas. Let sit 5 to 10 minutes before starting the general cleaning.

USE DIY MACHINES CAREFULLY

Hurrying through a cleaning will leave soap residue, a soaked carpet and a pad that can mold or mildew. Larger rental machines require you to pull them across the floor rather than push.

REMOVE OR ELEVATE FURNITURE

If your furniture is too heavy to move, put aluminum foil squares, wood blocks or plastic film under and around the legs of furniture to prevent rust from metal casters or stains from paint and finishes from transferring to damp carpet.

DON'T OVERWET THE CARPET

DIY machines put a lot of moisture into the carpet, and most don't have strong enough suction to extract it thoroughly. To avoid overwetting the carpet, just make one pass with the soap and water solution. Make one pass with the neutralizing rinse solution, and then make two or three drying passes with the water off.

LET IT DRY THOROUGHLY

Wet carpet is a perfect environment for mold and mildew. After you clean your carpets, open the windows, use fans and a dehumidifier, or put the A/C on a moderate setting (72 to 78 degrees) to remove excess moisture from the air. Don't replace the furniture or walk on the carpet until it's completely dry. This can take up to 12 hours, though six to eight hours is typical.

STRATEGY #4: CLEAN STAINS RIGHT— RIGHT AWAY

ACT QUICKLY

If you get to a stain immediately, there's a 99% chance you can remove it. The longer a stain reacts chemically with the carpeting, the harder it is to remove.

TRY WATER FIRST

About 80% of stains can be removed using plain tap water. To remove a stain, press a clean, dry, white cloth over the stain to absorb the spill. Repeat until the spill is absorbed. Then gently work water into the stain with a damp white towel and blot until the stain is gone. Change cloths when necessary. For a particularly stubborn spot, go to the online "CRI Spot Solver" resource at The Carpet and Rug Institute (the carpet manufacturers' trade organization, carpet-rug .org) to find your stain and a suggested solution for removing it. Use a fan to dry the area if it's very wet.

BLOT—DON'T RUB OR SCRUB

Scrubbing a stain will damage the fibers and create a fuzzy area. Always blot from the outer edge toward the center of the stain to avoid spreading the spot and creating a potentially larger problem.

ON TOUGH SPOTS, TRY VINEGAR OR CLUB SODA

If water alone doesn't remove a stain, try a white vinegar and water solution (equal amounts) or club soda before trying stronger commercial cleaning products.

BE PATIENT

Work water gently into the spill and then blot with a dry cloth. Repeat until the stain is gone and all the water has been absorbed. If you're patient, you'll almost always be able to remove the stain.

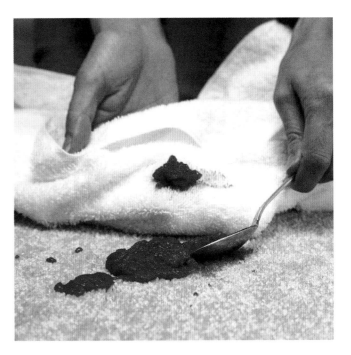

DON'T DIG OR SCOOP FOOD SPILLS

Digging or scooping can work the stain into the carpet. If there are solids on top of the stain, use a spoon or dull knife to carefully scrape the food toward the middle of the spill and into a white towel, and then treat the stain.

TEST COMMERCIAL PRODUCTS FIRST

Some products can cause carpet to get dirty faster or damage the carpet's color and texture. For a list of carpet manufacturer-approved spot and stain cleaners, go online to The Carpet and Rug Institute. Test carpet-cleaning products on an inconspicuous area before using.

USE A SHOP VACUUM ON WET SPILLS

Keep vacuuming until no more liquid can be removed. If the spill was a colored liquid, treat it as you would a stain, after vacuuming.

CHAPTER **EIGHT**

DOORS & WINDOWS

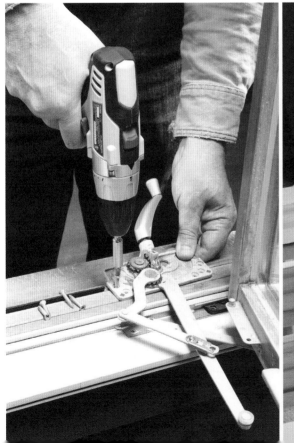

Steel Door Repair

Use auto body filler for an invisible door repair.

Make an invisible dent repair in a steel door using the same product you use to fill a dent on your car: auto body filler. It's an easy repair that requires just a little bit of time and some simple techniques. Follow these steps for a smooth result.

STEP 1: SAND THE DAMAGED AREA

You can do this with the door in place, but it will be much easier with the door lying flat on sawhorses. Remove an area of paint a couple of inches larger than the damaged spot **(Photo 1)**. You can sand away the paint with 60- or 80-grit paper, or use a small wire wheel in a drill.

Tip: If the damage is near the bottom of the door, you can skip the repair and cover it with a metal kick plate (sold at home centers and hardware stores). Kick plates are about 8 in. wide and come in lengths to match standard doors.

STEP 2: APPLY THE FILLER

Next, fill the wound with auto body filler (sold at hardware stores and home centers). To mix the filler, place a scoop of resin on a scrap of plywood or hardboard. Then add the hardener. Mix the two components thoroughly; unmixed resin won't harden and you'll be left with a sticky mess. A plastic putty knife makes a good mixing tool.

Apply the filler with a metal putty knife that's wider than the damaged spot **(Photo 2)**. The filler starts to harden in a couple of minutes, so work fast. Fill the repair flush with the surrounding surface. You want to avoid leaving humps or ridges, so make sure you don't overfill and don't try to smooth out imperfections after the filler begins to harden. It's much easier to add another coat of filler than it is to sand off humps or other imperfections.

STEP 3: SMOOTH AND PAINT

When the filler has hardened completely (about 30 minutes), sand it smooth with 100-grit paper **(Photo 3)**. Use a sanding block to ensure a flat surface. Prime the repair and paint the door. While you could paint over just the primed area, the newly applied paint won't perfectly match the older paint, so it's best to repaint the entire door.

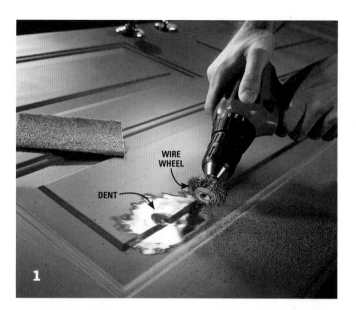

1 WIRE WHEEL / DENT

2 AUTO BODY FILLER

3 SANDING BLOCK

Repair a Broken-Out Hinge

1 **PREP THE DAMAGED AREA.** Chisel out the damaged wood and enlarge the area slightly to give the adhesive more area to grip. Remove all loose chips and blow off any remaining dust.

It doesn't take much of a blow to break hinge screws out of a particleboard door. If the screws just stripped and pulled out cleanly, you could fill the hole with toothpicks and wood glue, and then reinstall the screws. But if the surrounding particleboard has broken away, it's quicker to fill the void with gap-filling glue (Loctite Go2 Glue is one choice).

Start by removing the hinge and preparing the damaged area **(Photo 1)**. Apply petroleum jelly to the movable portions of the hinge to protect them from the glue. Then scuff the cup portion of the hinge with sandpaper where it will contact the adhesive. If you're using polyurethane adhesive, dampen the hinge with water to activate the glue. Apply glue to the damaged area and immediately install the hinge and screws **(Photo 2)**. Secure the hinge with weights or clamps until the glue dries. Then reinstall the door.

2 **FILL THE VOID WITH GLUE.** Squeeze in enough glue to fill the broken-out screw holes and coat the cup area. Then press the cup into the opening until the glue oozes out. Drop the screws into the hinge holes and tighten the ones that still have some wood to bite into.

Simple Fix for Stripped Screws

There are a bunch of good solutions for repairing stripped screws. But before you glue toothpicks into the hole or fill it with putty, try the simplest and quickest repair: Use a longer or fatter screw so that it will go into the framing. That will ensure a more secure anchor.

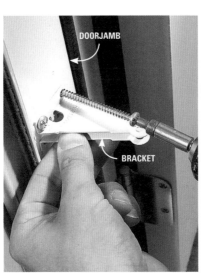

DOORJAMB

BRACKET

1 **TRY A LONGER SCREW.** The screws securing this storm door bracket had stripped. A longer screw—one long enough to penetrate the wall framing— solved the problem.

2 **TRY A FATTER SCREW.** A screw that's slightly thicker than the original one will grip firmly in a hole that's been enlarged by a stripped screw.

BENT CLOSER ROD

JAMB BRACKET

Repair a Screen Door

When a door is damaged at the jamb, grab your tools and some inexpensive supplies to make the repairs yourself.

All it takes is one big gust of wind to whip your screen door back so far that it rips the retaining bracket right out of the doorjamb. The damage looks pretty frightening, but the fix is actually fairly easy to make.

You can repair the jamb damage in about an hour. Then you'll need a half-hour to paint and to install a new closer

1 **PATCH THE JAMB.** Scoop up the filler with a disposable plastic spreader and force it deep into the cracks on the jamb. Then apply a second, thicker coat to cover the entire repair. Let it harden for about 45 minutes. Then sand until smooth, prime and paint.

PLASTIC SPREADER

and heavy-duty wind chain. After that you can call it a day.

To do the repair, you'll need two-part wood filler, a disposable plastic spreader or putty knife, a package of star-drive 3-in. screws, a star-drive bit and bit extension, sandpaper and a drill. Add a wind chain if your door doesn't already have one, and buy a new door closer if the rod on the old one got bent. Here are the repair steps.

PATCH AND PAINT THE JAMB

Start the project by yanking out any loose wood shards. Save the larger pieces and toss the smaller ones. Then mix up a small batch of wood filler, coat the backs of the larger pieces and press them back into place. Let the filler set up for about 10 minutes so the pieces don't move when you apply the final coat of filler. Then mix a larger batch and patch the entire damaged area (Photo 1).

MOUNT THE NEW CLOSER BRACKET

Position the new door closer bracket on the jamb according to the instructions. Level it and mark the hole locations. Then drill four pilot holes through the wood filler (to prevent it from cracking). Toss the mounting screws that came with the new door closer and mount the bracket using 3-in. screws (Photo 2).

INSTALL A HEAVY-DUTY WIND CHAIN AND CLOSER

A heavy-duty wind chain keeps the screen door from opening past the length of the door closer, so it prevents this type of accident from happening. Attach one end of the chain to the door and the other to the top jamb (Photo 3). Then connect the new closer to the bracket (Photo 4).

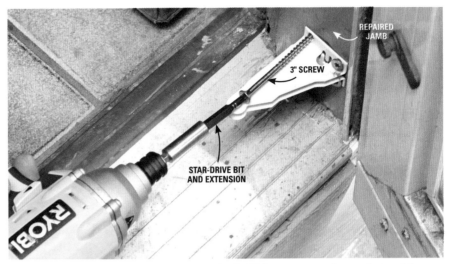

2 PREDRILL AND MOUNT THE BRACKET. Using an extension and star-drive bit, run two 3-in. screws into the upper holes first. Then install the two bottom screws.

3 MOUNT THE WIND CHAIN. Drive two 3-in. screws into the top jamb to secure the wind chain spring. Then attach the other end of the chain either to the upper door closer bracket or directly to the door itself. Finish by attaching the chain retracting spring.

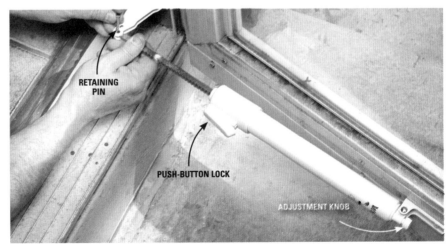

4 SECURE THE CLOSER AND ADJUST. Pull the rod out of the closer and install the retaining pin. Then turn the adjustment knob or screw to get the proper closing force.

Tips for Replacing Window and Door Screens

Sooner or later, most screens will need replacing. Follow these suggestions for avoiding pitfalls and making pro-quality repairs.

It's easy to replace the screen fabric in an aluminum frame. What's hard is figuring out which diameter spline to buy and how tight the fabric should be stretched. Here's how to conquer both of those issues.

Let's start with spline basics. Don't reuse the old spline unless it's fairly new. It's probably dried and brittle, so install new spline when you install new fabric. New spline is more pliable, will slip into the channel easier and will hold the fabric tighter. Besides, it's cheap.

There are nine different sizes of spline (yikes!), but most home centers carry only the four most common sizes. Forget about measuring the spline channel width. Just bring a small section of the old spline with you and visually match it to the new spline. If none of the options are dead-on, buy the two closest sizes. Then test-fit each one using a small patch of new screen. The spline should take just a bit of effort to snap into the frame. If you have to use a lot of muscle, the spline is too large.

You may be tempted to buy aluminum fabric. Don't. It is harder to install and is overkill for residential applications. Instead, take your old screen fabric with you to find new screen that matches the color and mesh size. That way it'll match your other screens. Then buy a concave spline roller and a roll of screen fabric.

Cut the fabric 1 in. larger than the opening. Then clip off a corner of the fabric and place that corner over a corner of the aluminum frame, squaring the fabric with the frame. Press the spline and fabric into the channel and continue rolling them into the long edge of the screen (**Photo 1**). Round the corner (don't cut the spline at the corners), and use the same technique along the second edge of the screen frame. Next, place a heavy object in the center of the screen fabric (**Photo 2**) and finish installing the screen. Note: Don't overstretch the screen trying to get it "banjo" tight. That'll bend the frame. Finish the job by trimming off the excess screen (**Photo 3**).

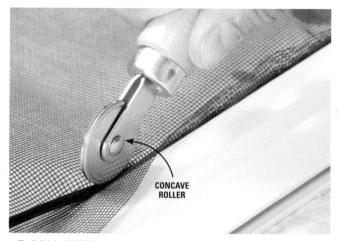

1 ROLL IN THE SCREEN AND SPLINE. Align the screen squarely to the frame along the longest edge. Lay the spline directly over the channel ahead of the roller. Lightly stretch the screen away from the starting corner as you roll the spline into place.

2 DEPRESS THE CENTER WITH A HEAVY OBJECT. Load a brick in the center of the screen to create the proper amount of slack. Then continue installing the fabric along the third and fourth sides of the screen frame. Remove the brick.

3 CUT OFF THE EXCESS SCREEN. Use a brand new utility blade and position the knife at a steep angle against the frame. Then trim off the excess screen.

Front Entry Face-Lift

Update your front door the easy way.

The usual way to replace a door is to tear out the old jamb and install a new "prehung" door. Often that's a good way to go. But in an older house, that would mean ordering a custom jamb width, fussing with tricky interior trim for hours and cutting back the hardwood flooring. So we chose to put a new door in the old jamb. This did require some extra work—we had to move hinges and strike plates for the latch and dead bolt. But we still think it was faster and easier.

You can skip those steps if you're lucky when you hang your new door and the new hardware locations match the old. But we'll show you how to change out a door slab and trim, and how to solve problems along the way.

BEFORE

To complete the new look, we replaced the dated light fixture, house numbers and mailbox with modern matte black options.

1 **REMOVE THE OLD DOOR.** Unscrew the hinges from both the new door and the existing door, then set the new door in place to find out if the strike plates and hinges line up with the old ones. If they do, screw the hinges into the jamb and consider yourself lucky—then skip to Photo 6. If the new hinges don't line up, draw a line from the bottom hinge to the top connecting the back edges of the old hinges. This will help you place the new hinges later.

DEAD
BOLT
PLUG

LATCH
PLUG

2 **PLUG THE HOLES.** Glue pine blocks into the latch and dead bolt holes. When the glue sets, cut the blocks flush with a chisel. Glue thin strips of pine into the hinge mortises.

LINE UP NEW HINGES HERE

MORTISE PLUG

3 FILL THE GAPS. Smooth over the plugs with auto body filler. The filler hardens fast—you can apply two coats if needed and sand it flat, all in about 30 minutes.

THRESHOLD BLOCK

4 MARK THE HINGE LOCATIONS. Cut two blocks of scrap wood to the height of the threshold plus 1/8 in. Set the door onto the blocks and move the door into position. Make sure the new hinges are aligned with the line you drew connecting the old hinges. Then temporarily attach the door with one screw in each hinge. Trace the hinges with a sharp pencil and remove the door.

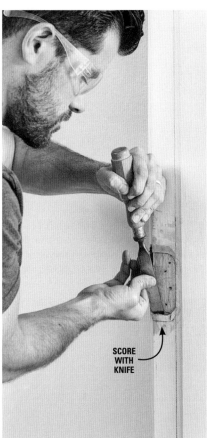

SCORE WITH KNIFE

5 CUT MORTISES. Follow the traced line with a utility blade, making this cut as deep as the hinge is thick. Then, with a chisel at the edge of the jamb, establish the depth of the mortise and work your way from the top down. Cut with the bevel of the chisel down to keep the blade from digging in. When you reach the knife line, the chips should fall away. Hinge-mortising router jigs make this job easy and fast, but if you have only one door to do, cut the mortises by hand.

6 INSTALL THE DOOR AND ADJUST THE THRESHOLD. Place the door back on the blocks, and predrill and screw the hinges in the new mortises. To make the fit airtight, turn the adjustment screws to move the threshold up or down. You want the door sweep to be pinched slightly when the door is closed.

ADJUSTMENT SCREWS

LOTS OF CHALK

7 LINE UP THE DEAD BOLT AND LATCH. Use chalk or lipstick to coat the ends of the dead bolt and door latch. Retract the dead bolt and latch as you close the door all the way, then turn the handles to let them contact the jamb. Use a 7/8-in. Forstner bit to drill holes where the latch and dead bolt touched the jamb. Place the strike plate over the holes, and trace and cut mortises as you did for the hinges.

8 REMOVE THE OLD TRIM. Cut any caulking between the trim and the siding with a utility knife. Otherwise, you might lift the siding as you pull off the trim. Take care not to dent the doorjamb as you pry away the trim.

Upgrade Your Trim

One advantage of putting a new door in an existing jamb is that you don't have to fuss with the trim. But we didn't think our old brickmold trim fit the sleek style of our new door. So we replaced the old trim with Boral TruExterior trim.

Four Things to Know Before You Buy a Door

Purchasing a door isn't an open-and-shut decision; there are many things to consider before opening your wallet. Here's how we break it down:

- Most doors are sold "pre-hung," which means they come attached to a doorjamb. The hinges are installed and the dead bolt/latch holes are bored. Because pre-hung doors are readily available, it might be easiest to buy one and scrap the jamb.
- Less common are slab-only doors. They require boring holes for hardware and cutting mortises for new hinges.
- Measure your existing door—height, width and thickness—and buy one to match.
- Door swing is important. Most doors swing inward. A left-hand inswing door has hinges on the left and opens to the left. A right-hand inswing door has hinges on the right and opens to the right.

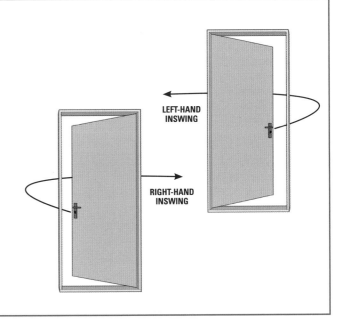

LEFT-HAND INSWING

RIGHT-HAND INSWING

9 CUT THE SIDING. If your new trim is wider than the old, you'll need to cut back the siding. We used 3-1/2-in.-wide trim and wanted a 1/4-in. reveal on the doorjamb, as well as some wiggle room for caulking, so we traced a line 3-7/8 in. in from the doorjamb. An oscillating tool worked well to cut the cedar shake siding.

3-7/8"

1/4" REVEAL

Z-FLASHING

1/4" JAMB EXTENSION, 1/8" FROM EDGE

10 INSTALL NEW TRIM. Cut a length of Z-flashing 1/4 in. wider than the top piece of trim. Tuck the flashing under the existing tar paper or house wrap. The sheathing on the house was about 1/4 in. proud of the jamb, so we cut a 1/4-in. jamb extension to let the trim sit flat. We tacked the extension 1/8 in. from the edge of the jamb.

11 FASTEN THE TRIM. Screw the trim to the sheathing and doorjamb with trim-head screws every 24 in. Since our trim is wider than the sill, we cut a notch around the sill. To finish up, caulk along the siding, fill the screw holes and paint.

NOTCH THE TRIM

SILL

DRY LUBRICANT

Lube a Sticking Vinyl Window or Door

When vinyl windows and doors don't operate smoothly, it's usually because gunk has built up in the channels. But sometimes even clean windows and doors can bind.

To help make them less resistant, try spraying dry lubricant on the contact points and wiping it off with a rag. Don't use oil lubricants; they can attract dirt, and some can damage the vinyl. Try DuPont Dry Film Lubricant, which contains Teflon. This quick fix could solve the problem.

How to Repaint Windows

Use these tips when it's time to freshen up windows with a new coat of paint.

Windows present a few unique challenges when it's time to repaint them. There's the glass, which you want to avoid slopping on, as well as all sorts of hardware and weatherstripping to work around. Window paint is often subjected to large temperature fluctuations and moisture from condensation. And, of course, windows have to move freely when you're all done painting.

That's a tall order, but one that's easy to accomplish with the right tips and techniques. We'll show you how to get the best paint job with the least amount of time and effort.

WET
GLASS

1 CLEAN AND SCRAPE BEFORE YOU PAINT. It seems counterintuitive to clean the windows first. But it's a good idea for two reasons. First, your paint job will last longer if the intersection of the glass and wood sash is sealed with paint—you can't get a good seal if the glass is dirty. And second, you'll get a neater paint job if you scrape off previous layers of paint and other crud that may be on the glass.

Use any window washing solution you prefer and a new single-edge blade to clean old paint and gunk from the glass. Apply the solution and then scrape, to avoid scraping on dry glass. You should never scrape dry glass. Grit pushed by the razor can scratch the window.

2 REMOVE THE SASH. It's quicker and easier to paint a sash if you take it out of the window frame and rest it on sawhorses or a workbench. The sashes in most modern double-hung, sliding and casement windows are removable. The photos show removing a casement sash. Most newer double-hung window sashes are removable by pivoting them in and twisting them to release. Old double-hung windows that are held in by wooden stops are more difficult to remove. These may not be worth the effort unless you're a perfectionist.

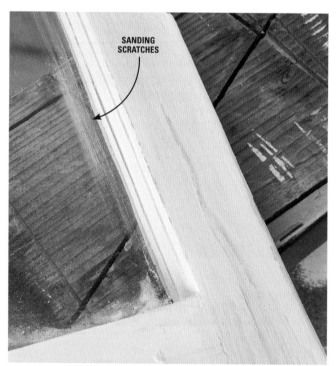

SANDING
SCRATCHES

3 SAND CAREFULLY. Sandpaper can scratch glass. And it's really easy to accidentally sand the glass where it meets the wood parts of the sash. You can either be extra careful when sanding along the glass, or you can protect the glass with masking tape. Avoid using a power sander along the edge of the glass because you'd be even more likely to scratch the glass.

4 REMOVE ALL THE HARDWARE. This may seem obvious, but if you look around, you'll notice that a lot of painters skip this step. Remove latches and handles from double-hung windows. On casement windows, it's much easier to get a neat-looking paint job if you remove the operating hardware from the sash. Just be sure to keep track of the screws and other pieces. Take photos with your phone so you'll know how to reinstall the parts.

5 START EARLY IN THE DAY. Unless you live in an area free of bugs and criminals, you'll probably want to reinstall your window sashes and be able to close your windows for the night. And you can't really do that with fresh paint. So plan your paint job to allow time for the paint on the sashes to dry before nightfall.

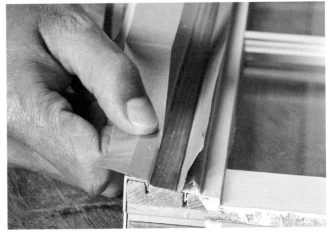

6 USE A 1-1/2-IN. ANGLED SASH BRUSH. Most of the areas you'll paint on a window aren't very wide, so a narrow brush will work fine and be easier to control than a wider flat one. And the angled bristles of a sash brush are specifically designed to neatly apply paint in all of the tight corners and small spaces on a window. Of course, we always recommend spending a little more money for a top-quality brush, and then taking care to clean and store it properly.

7 AVOID PAINTING THE TRACKS OR THE WEATHERSTRIPPING. Your window tracks and weatherstrips won't work correctly if they're covered with paint. In some cases, the easiest way to avoid painting these parts is to cover them with masking tape. If there's space, you can also slip a wide putty knife between the wood frame and the track to keep the paint off. If you do slop paint onto these areas, wipe it off right away with a damp rag.

9 MOVE THE SASH BEFORE THE PAINT DRIES. This tip isn't as important if you've removed the sash from the window and waited until it's completely dry to reinstall it. But if you paint your sash in place, avoid a stuck window by opening and closing the window a few times before the paint dries completely. Return to the window about an hour after you've painted it and open and close it to break any paint seal that may have formed. You may even need to do this again the following day just to be sure everything is unstuck.

10 PAINT OLD WINDOWS WITH A BENDABLE PAD. The upper sash in many old double-hung windows is painted shut, making it difficult to paint the lower rail. You could take time to free up the window, but this can be a big project. Another solution is to buy a window sash painter tool that's bendable (Hyde is one brand). Bend the metal to an angle that will allow you to apply paint. Then use a brush to spread some paint on the pad and carefully apply paint to the upper sash. It's a tedious process but one that's necessary if you don't want to look at ugly drips every time you open your lower sash.

8 DON'T BOTHER TO MASK THE GLASS. Covering window glass with masking tape is so time-consuming that it's usually quicker to simply paint neatly along the glass with your brush. If you get a little paint on the glass, it's easy to scrape off later with a razor blade. If you'd rather mask the glass, use masking tape that has edge-seal technology to prevent paint from creeping under the tape.

Repair a Cranky Window

When a casement window doesn't function properly, take these steps to track down the problem (it might surprise you!) and make repairs.

When a casement (crank-out) window is hard to open or close, people blame the operator (crank mechanism). It may have gone bad, but an operator usually doesn't fail on its own. Operator gears strip out when you crank too hard while trying to open or close a binding or stuck sash. If you just replace the operator without fixing the root cause of the binding, you'll be replacing it again—and soon. We'll show you how to get to the bottom of most casement window

problems and explain how to fix each one. The parts are fairly inexpensive. But, as with many other home repair projects, you'll spend more time searching for the right parts than you will making the repairs.

FIRST, THE USUAL SUSPECTS

A sash can sag and bind in the frame from worn, dirty or corroded hinges; loose or stripped screws; or settling. Loose or stripped screws are the easiest to fix, and they're usually the most common cause of binding, so start there. If you have interior hinges (hinges located in the head and sill area and covered by the sash), open the sash all the way to expose the screws. Tighten each one. If the screw holes are stripped, you'll have to remove the sash first to fix them **(Photo 1)**. Next, remove the hinge, enlarge the holes, and refill them with toothpicks and epoxy filler **(Photo 2)**. Then reinstall the hinge screws and sash, and see if that solves the problem.

Next, check the condition of the hinges. It's much easier to spot wear if a hinge is clean and lubricated. So clean away dirt and grease buildup with household cleaner and then lubricate the hinges **(Photo 3)**. Open and close the window and examine the hinge pivots (top and bottom) as they move. If you see "slop," replace the hinge. Exterior mounted hinges (common on windows from the '50s) are especially prone to corrosion and binding since they're constantly exposed to the elements. You can try lubricating them, but if the binding recurs, you'll have to replace them (see "Find Parts for Old Windows"). Remove the old screws **(Photo 4)**. Then, following the hinge profile, slice through the old paint with a utility knife. Pry off the old hinge and install the new one.

If the hinges are in good shape, or you've replaced them and the sash still binds, the window frame has probably settled and is out of square. Resquaring the window frame is a big job. But you can try to fix the problem by relocating the hinges. To learn how to move a hinge, go to familyhandyman.com and search for "repair old windows."

FINISH BY CHECKING THE OPERATOR

Now that the sash is opening and closing smoothly, turn your attention to the condition of the operator. First remove the sill operator cover trim. Then loosen the crank handle setscrew, and remove the handle and operator cover **(Photo 5)**. Reinstall the crank handle and rotate it while checking the condition of the gears. Look for gray dust or for rough, chipped or missing teeth. Those are all signs the operator needs to be replaced. However, if the operator looks clean and moves smoothly, just tighten the screws, apply a dab of lithium grease to the gears and reassemble all the trim. Now your window should be in tip-top shape.

FIND PARTS FOR OLD WINDOWS

You won't find these 1950s-era hinges (or other window parts) at many hardware stores, but they're available online. The new parts may not be an exact match for your old hardware, but they'll do the job and put your window back in the swing of things.

Just measure the old parts, shoot digital photos of the top and bottom pieces (they may be different), and email the info to an online window parts seller (blainewindow.com is one very reputable source).

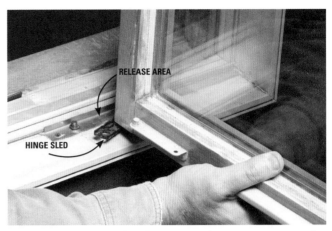

1 REMOVE THE SASH. Disconnect the operator arm and hinge arm locks from the sash while holding the window firmly. Then slide plastic hinge sleds toward the release area and lift the sash out of the frame. Tilt the sash sideways and bring it into the room.

RELEASE AREA

HINGE SLED

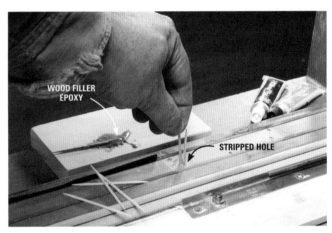

2 FILL THE STRIPPED HOLES. Mix a small batch of two-part epoxy wood filler and use a toothpick to spread it inside the enlarged hole. Then dip each of the toothpicks into the filler and jam them into the hole. Slice off the extended portions with a utility knife once the filler sets.

WOOD FILLER EPOXY

STRIPPED HOLE

3 LUBRICATE THE HINGES. Saturate each hinge with silicone or dry Teflon spray lube. Wipe up the excess. Then work in the lube by opening and closing the window several times.

4 CHIP OUT THE PAINT. Tilt a flat-blade screwdriver at a 45-degree angle and hammer it along the slotted head to chip out the paint. Then slice through any remaining paint with a utility knife.

PAINT-FILLED SCREW HEAD

5 REMOVE THE OPERATOR TRIM. Slide a flat bar under the sill operator trim piece and gently pry it up slightly on one end. Then move the flat bar to the opposite side and pry that up (see photo, p. 204). Next, remove the operator screws and the operator.

Clean Window Weep Holes

Many sliding windows and vinyl replacement windows have weep holes on the exterior bottom of the frame. These holes are designed to drain away rainwater that can collect in the frame's bottom channel. Weep holes can get plugged with bugs and debris, and if that happens, water could fill up the channel and spill over into your house.

To see if your weep system is working, simply pour a glass of water into the track or spray the outside of the window with a garden hose. If you don't see a steady stream of clean water exiting the weep hole, poke a wire hanger into the hole or spray it out with compressed air, and wet it down again. If the little flapper (designed to keep out driving wind) is stuck shut, it can be removed with a putty knife and replaced.

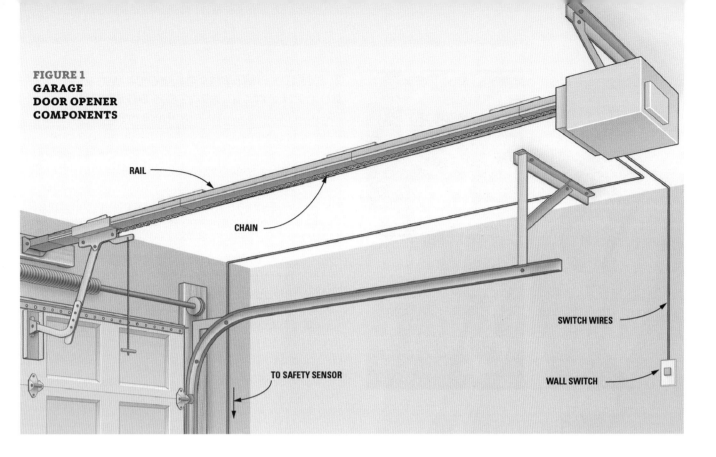

FIGURE 1
GARAGE
DOOR OPENER
COMPONENTS

RAIL

CHAIN

SWITCH WIRES

TO SAFETY SENSOR

WALL SWITCH

How to Repair a Garage Door Opener

Garage door not opening all the way? Garage door not opening with a remote? Garage door just not working? With a little troubleshooting, you can usually avoid a costly service call and get your garage door opener working again in no time.

1. CHECK YOUR DOOR FIRST

With the door closed, pull the emergency release cord and lift the door to see if it opens and closes smoothly. If it doesn't, the problem is with your tracks, rollers or springs rather than your opener. For more information, search for "garage door repair" at familyhandyman.com.

2. PLAY IT SAFE

Work with the door down. If your garage door opener trouble is a broken door spring and you pull the emergency release cord while the door is in the raised position, the door

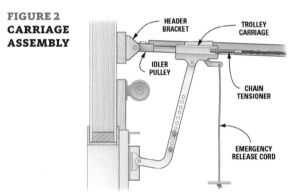

FIGURE 2
CARRIAGE
ASSEMBLY

HEADER BRACKET

TROLLEY CARRIAGE

IDLER PULLEY

CHAIN TENSIONER

EMERGENCY RELEASE CORD

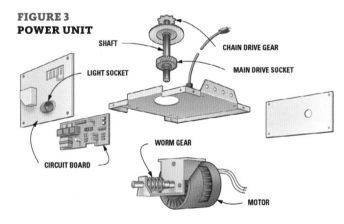

FIGURE 3
POWER UNIT

SHAFT

CHAIN DRIVE GEAR

LIGHT SOCKET

MAIN DRIVE SOCKET

CIRCUIT BOARD

WORM GEAR

MOTOR

could come crashing down, damaging it or anyone in its path.

Caution: Unplug the opener. That way you won't lose a finger if your unsuspecting housemate hits the remote button while you're working on the door. And you'll prevent the possibility of being electrocuted.

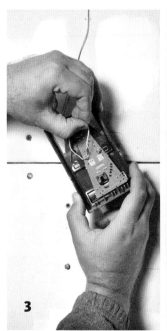
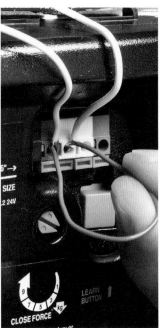

3. SYMPTOM: THE REMOTE WORKS BUT THE WALL SWITCH DOESN'T

FIX: REPLACE THE WALL SWITCH AND WIRES.
If the remote works but the wall switch doesn't, you may need to replace either the wall switch or the switch wires. To determine whether the switch or the wires are bad, first unscrew the switch from the wall and touch the two wires together (don't worry, the wires are low voltage and won't shock you). If the opener runs, you have a bad switch.

If you have an older-model opener, a cheap doorbell button might work. If you have a newer opener that has a light and a locking option on the switch, buy the one designed for your model. A new one is inexpensive.

If the opener doesn't run when you touch the wires, use a small wire and jump those same two wires at the opener terminal. If the opener runs, the wire that connects the opener to the switch is bad. Sometimes the staples that hold the wire to the wall pinch the wire and cause a short. To prevent it from happening in the future, install 18- to 22-gauge wire as part of the garage door repair.

4. SYMPTOM: THE WALL SWITCH WORKS BUT THE REMOTE DOESN'T

FIX: REPLACE BATTERIES OR BUY A NEW REMOTE OR RECEIVER.
If the wall switch works but one of the remotes doesn't, check the batteries first. Still nothing? You may need a new remote. Home centers carry a few models, and you can find a wide selection online.

If you can't find one for your garage door opener model, you can try a universal remote or you can install a new receiver. A receiver replaces the radio frequency the opener uses with its own. An added bonus of a new receiver is that it will automatically update older openers to the new rolling code technology, which stops the bad guys from stealing your code. Just plug the new receiver into an outlet close to the opener, and run the two wires provided to the same terminals where the wall switch is connected.

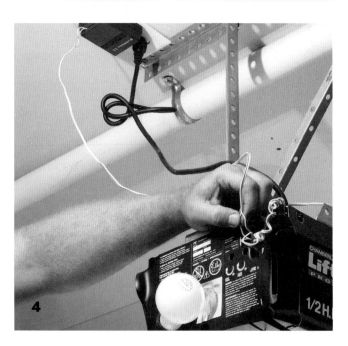

5. SYMPTOM: THE DOOR GOES UP, BUT IT ONLY GOES DOWN WHEN YOU HOLD DOWN THE WALL SWITCH

FIX: ALIGN OR REPLACE THE SAFETY SENSOR.
If the door goes up but goes down only when you hold down the wall switch, check to see that the safety sensors are in alignment. The small light on each sensor should be lit up when nothing is between them.

Door sensors do go bad, so if no light is showing at all, you may need to replace them. You can save yourself some time by using the existing wires with the new sensors. Also keep in mind that direct sunlight shining on sensor eyes can make them misbehave.

6. SYMPTOM: YOU HAVE POWER TO THE OUTLET, BUT THERE'S NO SOUND OR NO LIGHTS WHEN YOU PUSH THE WALL SWITCH AND REMOTES

FIX: REPLACE THE CIRCUIT BOARD.

If the outlet has power, but there's no sound or no lights when you push the wall switch and remotes, you probably have a bad circuit board. Lightning strikes are the most frequent reason for the demise of a circuit board. The circuit board consists of the entire plastic housing that holds the lightbulb and wire terminals. The part number should be on the board itself. Replacing a circuit board sounds like a scary garage door repair, but it's really quite easy. It will take 10 minutes tops and requires only a 1/4-in. nut driver. Just follow these steps: Remove the light cover, take out the lightbulb, disconnect the switch and safety sensor wires, remove a few screws, unplug the board and you're done. A circuit board isn't cheap, so make sure you protect your new one with a surge protector. You can buy an individual outlet surge protector at a home center.

7. SYMPTOM: EVERYTHING WORKS FINE EXCEPT THE LIGHTS

FIX: REPLACE THE LIGHT SOCKET.

If the bulbs are OK but don't light up, you probably have a bad light socket. To replace the socket, you'll need to remove the circuit board to get at it. Use the same steps as in "Replace the Circuit Board" (above) to accomplish this step.

Once the circuit board is removed, pop out the old socket by depressing the clip that holds it in place. Remove the two wire connections and install the new socket. Replacement sockets are inexpensive.

Be sure to use a bulb of the correct wattage. Using lightbulbs with a higher wattage than the socket is rated will cause a socket to fail. Not only is this

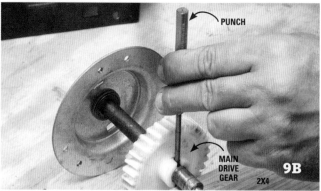

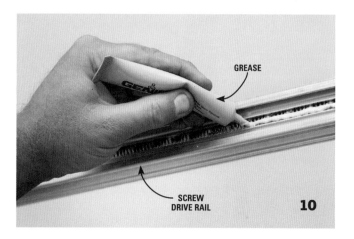

bad for the socket, but it can also be a fire hazard. If your light cover has turned yellow from heat, you're probably using too strong a bulb.

8. SYMPTOM: THE TROLLEY CARRIAGE MOVES BUT GARAGE DOOR DOESN'T OPEN

FIX: REPLACE THE TROLLEY CARRIAGE.

If the trolley carriage moves but the door doesn't open, the culprit is probably a broken trolley carriage. Before you pull the old one off to begin the garage door repair, clamp down the chain to the rail. This will help maintain the location of the chain on the sprocket and speed up reassembly. Once the chain is secure, separate it from both sides of the trolley. Disconnect the rail from the header bracket and move the rail off to one side. Slide off the old trolley, and slide on the new one. Reattach the chain and adjust the chain tension. Replacing the trolley on a belt drive and replacing it on a screw drive are similar procedures.

9. SYMPTOM: THE OPENER MAKES A GRINDING NOISE BUT THE DOOR DOESN'T MOVE

FIX: REPLACE THE MAIN DRIVE GEAR.

If the garage door opener makes a grinding noise but the door doesn't move, your main drive gear is probably toast. The main drive gear is the plastic gear that comes in direct contact with the worm drive gear on the motor. The main drive gear is the most common component to fail on most openers. Replacing it is a bit more complicated than the other repairs in this article but still well within the wheelhouse of the average DIYer.

Several components need to be removed before getting at the gear. Get a detailed description of how to rebuild a garage door opener. Once you get the gear out, you can remove it from the shaft with a punch, or you can buy a kit that comes with a new shaft. Make sure you lube it all up when you're done.

10. SYMPTOM: GARAGE DOOR DOESN'T OPEN

FIX: LUBE THE RAIL.

No matter what type of garage door opener you have, you should always lube the rail where it comes in contact with the trolley carriage. Use a lubricant that doesn't attract dirt. Silicone spray is a good choice.

If you have a screw-drive opener, you'll need to grease several spots along the rail gear at least once or twice a year. In colder climates, use lithium grease, which won't harden when the temperature drops. Many home centers sell specifically formulated products near the openers. And don't use too much or it could drip on your car.

11. SYMPTOM: GARAGE DOOR WON'T OPEN ALL THE WAY

FIX: CHECK THE CHAIN TENSION.

Most chain-drive openers suggest that you tighten the chain so there's about 1/4 to 1/2 in. of slack from the rail to the chain (check your manual). Overtightening the chain will put excess wear and tear on the shaft and gears. Too little tension could cause the chain to skip off the sprocket and fall down on your car.

12. SYMPTOM: GARAGE DOOR WON'T CLOSE

FIX: ADJUST THE TRAVEL OF THE DOOR.

Two knobs on the opener control how far the door travels up and down. Your door should press snugly against the garage floor so the weatherstripping seals the gap. If the door travels too far down, it will cause the rail to bow upward. This also causes excess wear and tear on the shaft and gears. Your door should travel up far enough so that the bottom of the door is just about the same height as the doorjamb. A door stop prevents the carriage trolley from crashing into the opener. Make sure the trolley stops before hitting this bolt.

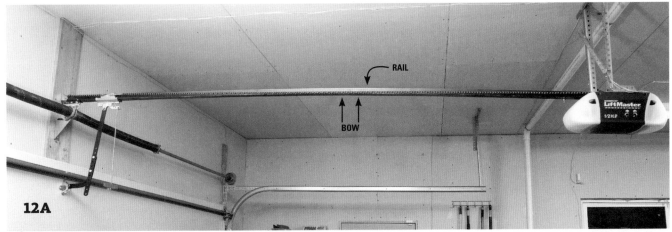

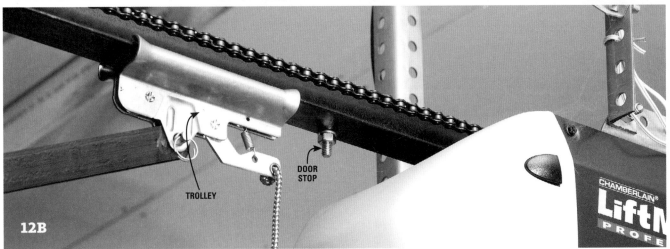

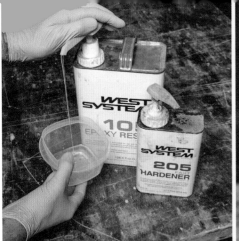

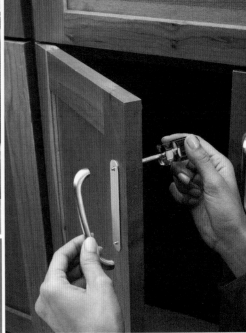

CHAPTER NINE

FURNITURE, CABINETS & COUNTERTOPS

Refinish Furniture Without Stripping

Less time, less effort, less mess. Better results!

Stripping furniture is a messy, time-consuming process. And sometimes the results aren't as great as you had hoped. Fortunately, you don't always have to strip furniture to restore it to its original luster.

To show an easier alternative, we'll give you tips from a pro for cleaning, repairing and restoring finishes without having to use all the messy chemical strippers and doing the tedious sanding. You'll save tons of time. And since you'll preserve the patina and character of the original finish, your furniture will retain the beauty of an antique. One word of caution, though: If you think your piece of furniture is a valuable antique, consult an expert before you do anything. Altering the finish could affect its value.

1. ASSESS THE FINISH WITH MINERAL SPIRITS

Before you start any repairs or touch-ups, wipe on mineral spirits to help you decide what your next steps should be. The mineral spirits temporarily saturate the finish to reveal how the piece of furniture will look with nothing more than a coat of wipe-on clear finish. Don't worry; this won't harm the finish. If it looks good, all you have to do is clean the surface and apply an oil-based wipe-on finish. If the surface looks bad even when wetted with mineral spirits, you'll have to take other measures to restore the finish. We show some of these in the following steps.

2. CLEAN IT UP

Removing decades of dirt and grime often restores much of the original luster. It's hard to believe, but it's perfectly OK to wash furniture with soap and water.

Use liquid Ivory dish soap mixed with water. Mix in the same proportion you would to wash dishes. Dip a sponge into the solution, wring it out and use it to gently scrub the surface. A paintbrush works great for cleaning carvings and moldings. When you're done scrubbing with the soapy water, rinse the surface with a wrung-out sponge and clear water. Then dry it with a clean towel.

3. REPLACE MISSING WOOD WITH EPOXY

If you discover missing veneer, chipped wood or damaged molding, you can fix it easily with epoxy putty. The resulting repair is so realistic that it's hard to spot. When it's hardened, the epoxy is light-colored and about the density of wood. You can shape, sand and stain it like wood too, so it blends right in. QuikWood and KwikWood are two brands of this Tootsie Roll–shaped epoxy. Look for them at home centers and specialty woodworking stores.

To use this type of epoxy, slice off a piece with a razor blade or utility knife and knead it in your gloved hand. When the two parts are completely blended to a consistent color and the epoxy putty starts to get sticky, it's ready to use. You'll have 5 to 10 minutes to apply the epoxy to the repair before it starts to harden. That's why you should slice off only as much as you can use quickly.

Photo 1 shows how to replace missing veneer. Here are a few things you can do before the putty starts to harden to reduce the amount of sanding and shaping later. First, smooth and shape the epoxy with your finger **(Photo 2)**. Wet it with water first to prevent the epoxy from sticking. Then use the edge of a straightedge razor to scrape the surface almost level with the surrounding veneer. If you're repairing wood with an open grain, like oak, add grain details by making little slices with a razor while the epoxy is soft **(Photo 3)**.

After the epoxy hardens completely, which usually takes a few hours, you can sand and stain the repair. Try sticking self-adhesive sandpaper to tongue depressors or craft sticks to make precision sanding blocks **(Photo 4)**. You can also use spray adhesive or even plain wood glue to attach the sandpaper.

Blend the repair into the surrounding veneer by painting on gel stain to match the color and pattern of the existing grain. You could use stain touch-up markers, but we prefer gel stain because it's thick enough to act like paint, and it can be wiped off with a rag dampened in mineral spirits if you goof up or want to start over.

Choose two colors of stain that match the light and dark areas of the wood. Put a dab of both colors on a scrap of wood and create a range of colors by blending a bit of each . Now you can use an artist's brush to create the grain **(Photo 5)**.

If the sheen of the patch doesn't match the rest of the wood when the stain dries, you can recoat the entire surface with wipe-on finish to even it out.

1 FILL THE DAMAGE WITH EPOXY. When the epoxy putty is thoroughly mixed, press it into the area to be repaired.

2 SMOOTH THE PUTTY. Use your wetted finger to smooth the putty. Press the putty until it's level with the surrounding veneer.

3 ADD WOOD GRAIN. On open-grain wood, like this oak, use a razor blade to add grain marks so that the repair will blend in.

4 SAND THE EPOXY. Sand carefully to avoid removing the surrounding finish. Make a detail sander by gluing sandpaper to a thin strip of wood.

5 STAIN THE EPOXY TO MATCH. Stain the patch with gel stain to match the color and pattern of the grain. Match the stain color to the light and dark areas of the wood.

4. FIX WHITE RINGS

White rings can be easy to get rid of, or they can be a real nightmare. First, slather the ring with petroleum jelly and let it sit overnight. The oil from the petroleum jelly will often penetrate the finish and remove the ring or at least make it less visible.

If that doesn't work, you can try a product such as Homax White Ring Remover or Liberon Ring Remover. These kinds of products often work but they may change the sheen. If these fixes don't get rid of the ring, consult a professional to see what other options you can consider trying.

5. SCRAPE PAINT WITHOUT DAMAGING THE FINISH

Paint spatters are common on old furniture, and most of the time you can remove them easily without damaging the finish. Here's a trick we learned to turn an ordinary straightedge razor into a delicate paint scraper.

First, wrap a layer of masking tape around each end of the blade, and then bend the blade slightly so it's curved. The masking tape holds the blade slightly off the surface so you can knock off paint spatters without the blade even touching the wood.

Hold the blade perpendicular to the surface. The tape also keeps you from accidentally gouging the wood with a sharp corner of the blade. The curved blade allows you to adjust the depth of the scraper. If you tilt the blade a little, the curved center section will come closer to the surface to allow for removing really thin layers of paint.

6. FILL SMALL CRACKS

If you find nail holes or tiny cracks after applying the final finish, fill them with colored wax fill sticks, wax repair sticks or fill pencils, sold at home centers and paint stores.

The directions typically tell you to rub the stick over the defect. But we recommend breaking off a chunk and warming it up in your hands. Then shape it to fit the flaw and press it in with a smooth tool. A 3/8-in. dowel with an angle on the end works well. For cracks, make a thin wafer, slide it into the crack and work the wax in both directions to fill the crack. Then buff it with a soft cloth.

7. GET RID OF DENTS

You can often get rid of small dents by wetting them. The moisture swells the crushed wood fibers back to their original shape. (You can't fix cuts or gouges this way, though.)

Moisture must penetrate the wood for this to work. Finishes prevent water from penetrating, so we suggest making a bunch of tiny slits with a razor blade to allow the water to penetrate. Use the corner of the blade, and keep the blade parallel to the grain direction. Next, fill the dent with water and wait until it dries. If the dent is less deep but

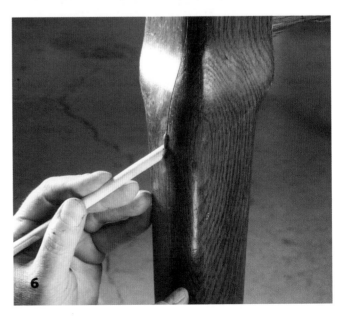

7A

7B

still visible, you can repeat the process. As with most of the repairs we talk about here, the repaired surface may need a coat of wipe-on finish to look its best.

8. RESTORE THE COLOR WITH GEL STAIN

It's amazing what a coat of gel stain can do to restore a tired-looking piece of furniture. The cool part is that you don't need to strip the old finish for this to work.

The finish on this round oak table was worn and faded. We loaded a soft cloth with dark gel stain and worked it into the surface. Then we wiped if off with a clean cloth. It was a surprising transformation. Of course, gel stain won't eliminate dark water stains or cover bad defects, but it will hide fine scratches and color in areas where the finish has worn away.

There are other products, but we prefer gel stain because we find it easier to control the color and it can leave a thicker coat if necessary. Also, since it doesn't soak in quite as readily as thinner stains, gel stain is somewhat reversible. Before it dries, you can remove it with mineral spirits if you don't like the results. Gel stains offer some protection, but for a more durable finish or to even out the sheen, let the stain dry overnight and then apply a coat of wipe-on finish as shown in the next tip.

9. RENEW THE LUSTER WITH WIPE-ON FINISH

The final step in your restoration project is to wipe on a coat of finish. After you clean your furniture piece and do any necessary repairs and stain touch-up, wiping on a coat of finish will restore the sheen and protect the surface.

Any wipe-on finish will work—Minwax Wipe-On Poly is one common brand. But we prefer a gel finish like General Finishes Gel Topcoat. It's more expensive, but it's thick so it's easy to put on with a rag (you can also apply it with a brush if you prefer). One coat is usually all you need to rejuvenate an existing finish. To find a retail store near you that sells General Finishes Gel Topcoat, visit generalfinishes.com and click on "Where to Buy."

To apply a wipe-on finish, first put some on a clean rag. Apply it to the surface using a swirling motion, as you would apply car wax. Then wipe off any excess finish product, going in the direction of the grain.

Let the finish dry overnight, and you'll be ready to proudly display your furniture restoration project.

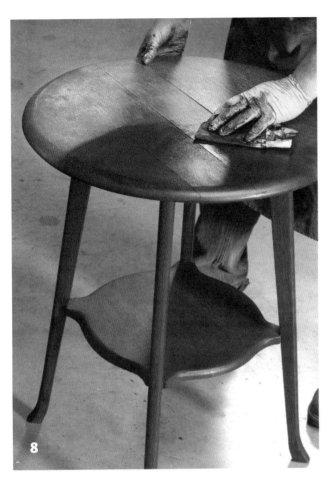

8

9

How to Repair Melamine Chips

SeamFil plastic filler paste comes in a tube and is commonly used by pros who work with plastic laminate to repair chips. And since the surface of melamine panels and shelves is also a type of plastic laminate, the repairs blend in well.

To use the SeamFil paste, first clean the area with the SeamFil solvent (typically sold with the filler paste). Then spread a small amount of the paste on a scrap of wood or plastic laminate. Work the paste around with a polished putty knife until some of the solvent starts to evaporate and the paste starts to thicken. Then press the thickened paste into the area to be repaired and smooth it with the putty knife. It may take a few coats to get a flush surface. Clean off excess paste using a rag that's been dampened with the solvent.

SeamFil paste is sold online or where plastic laminate (used for countertops) is sold. It's available in 20 standard colors that can be mixed to create custom colors.

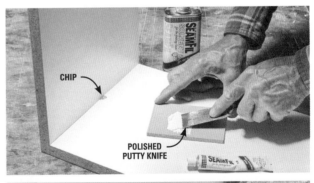

CHIP

POLISHED PUTTY KNIFE

Reinforce a Sagging Drawer Bottom

With some plywood, glue and a few basic tools, you can make a lasting repair quickly and inexpensively.

You don't have to replace a sagging drawer bottom. A typical drawer has a cavity beneath it that's just deep enough to allow you to strengthen the bottom with a piece of plywood. First make sure the drawer box is square by using a large framing square or taking diagonal corner-to-corner measurements (equal diagonal measurements means the box is square). If the box isn't square, square it up, clamp it and drive brad nails through the bottom **(Photo 1)**. Two brads placed near the middle of each side usually provide enough strength to hold the box square.

The back of the drawer shown here was bulging, so we used the clamps to draw it in while we drove in the brads.

Stiffen the old drawer bottom with any 1/4-in. plywood. You can buy a full sheet, but many home centers also sell half or quarter sheets. Measure between the drawer sides, front and back, and cut the plywood 1/4 in. smaller than the opening (1/8 in. less on each side).

Glue the plywood panel to the underside of the drawer bottom and place weights, such as a stack of books, on it until the glue sets **(Photo 2)**. If the underside is unfinished, use wood glue. If it has a finish, you can sand it or use construction adhesive. Wood glue forms a strong bond in about 15 minutes. If you use construction adhesive, leave the weights in place overnight.

NAIL SET

5/8"
BRAD

1 Square the drawer box and drive 5/8-in. brad nails at an angle through the drawer bottom and into the sides.

1/4"
PLYWOOD

2 Glue a plywood panel to the underside of the drawer bottom and place weights on it until the glue sets.

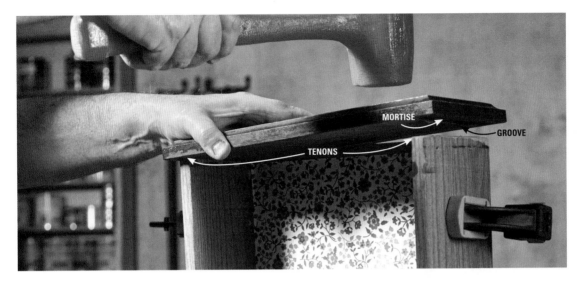

1 REINSTALL THE DRAWER FRONT. Remove the drawer pull and screws. Then line up the mortise-and-tenons and the drawer bottom with the groove, and tap the drawer front back onto the box.

2 REINFORCE THE DRAWER FRONT. Drill four 1/8-in. pilot holes through the newly installed box front. Then drive coarse-thread drywall screws through the new box front and into the old drawer front.

Repair a Broken Drawer Front

Round up some tools and a few supplies, and take these steps to fix your drawer permanently.

High-quality cabinet drawers are built with a sturdy box and a separate decorative drawer front. But the drawer fronts on economy cabinets are part of the box itself. They're attached to the sides and bottom with a mortise-and-tenon joint and held with glue and staples. Repeated openings and closings break the joint, and the drawer front falls off. You can try regluing the joint, but it won't last. Here's how to fix the problem permanently.

Cut a 3/4-in.-thick piece of wood to match the width and height of the drawer box. Then remove the staples from the tenons and clean up the rough edges so you can reinstall the drawer front **(Photo 1)**.

Glue the new wood block directly behind the drawer front (use polyurethane glue if the box sides and bottom have been varnished). Secure it with nails or screws. Then attach the old drawer front to the new wood block using coarse-thread drywall screws **(Photo 2)**.

Using the old drawer pull holes as a guide, drill through the new wood block. Buy longer No. 8-32 x 1-3/4-in. machine screws and remount the drawer pull.

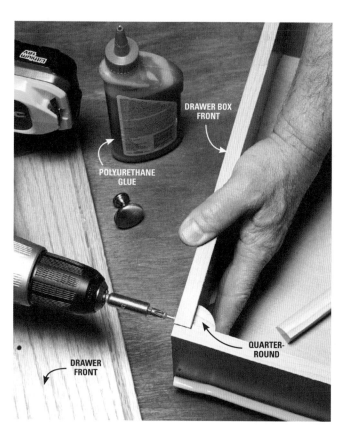

Reinforce a Drawer Front

A recent quick fix we made was to a drawer front that a child pulled off. To make the repair, we cut a couple of lengths of quarter-round the same height as the drawer sides. We held them in place while we drilled a couple of holes through the sides and front of the drawer box. Then we dabbed some polyurethane glue (wood glue doesn't stick well to finished surfaces) on the pieces of quarter-round before screwing them into place.

Tighten a Wobbly Chair

Got a chair with a wobbly leg? This usually happens because the glue holding the legs and stretchers together no longer holds. The best fix is to take the chair apart and glue it back together, but that's a lot of work.

If it's an old chair and there's nothing particularly special about it, you can fix it with trim-head screws. Just drill pilot holes and toe-screw into the loose joints. Be sure to drive the screws in from the bottom so you won't see them when the chair is upright. If a joint is really loose, you might need to force some epoxy into it to fill the gaps and make the joint stronger and the repair last.

Repair an Office Chair

When the casters freeze up, take these steps to diagnose the problem. Then repair them or replace them.

When casters roll around long enough in dust, dirt and hair, they stop rolling and start skidding. And that's how your floors get scratched or your carpet gets wear tracks. Sometimes you can bring casters back from the dead by cleaning and lubricating them. So try that first. Just spray household degreaser/cleaner right onto the roller axles. Then spin the wheels to loosen them up. If that helps, rinse off the cleaner, blow them dry with compressed air and then lubricate them. If cleaning doesn't help, you'll have to replace them. Here's how.

Most office chairs use a twin-wheel grip-ring style caster. The grip ring compresses and snaps into a groove in the socket. The easiest way to remove a grip-ring caster is with a flat bar **(Photo 1)**. Before you buy replacements, measure the width and height of the stem. The most common widths are 3/8 in. and 7/16 in. There's only a 1/16-in. difference between the two, so measure carefully! If you try to fit a 7/16-in. stem into a 3/8-in. socket, you'll crack the socket.

Next, measure the wheel diameter. If you want the chair to push back easier or roll over small items on the floor rather than get stuck, buy a caster with a larger wheel. Buy a urethane tread caster for wood (and composite), tile or vinyl floors. But if the chair will roll on carpet, buy a hard rubber or nylon tread caster.

To install the caster, tilt it into the socket to compress the grip ring **(Photo 2)**. If you can't get it started, apply a drop of oil to the ring. If the caster goes in only halfway, tap it with a mallet **(Photo 3)**.

2 **START THE NEW CASTER AT AN ANGLE. Rotate the open end of the grip ring so it's facing up. Then tilt the caster stem into the socket until the ring gap starts to close. Straighten it up and push it home.**

OPEN END OF GRIP RING

3 **TAP IT IN. Position a small block of wood directly over the caster stem. Then tap the wood with a mallet until the stem pops all the way into the socket.**

1 **POP OUT THE OLD CASTER. Slip the angled end of a flat bar under the caster and pop the caster out of its socket in one quick motion. If it doesn't come out all the way, grab it again and pry it the rest of the way.**

Freshen Up an Old Finish

If your old furniture or woodwork looks dull and lifeless, try renewing it with a few coats of wipe-on finish. Wash it first with dish soap and water, then lightly sand the old finish with 220-grit sandpaper. Vacuum off the dust, then apply the finish as usual. You'll need to apply at least two coats to achieve an even sheen.

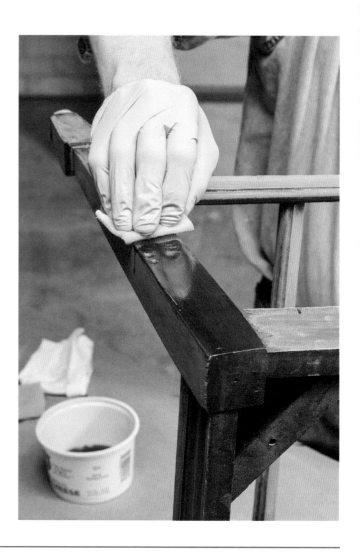

WET/DRY
SANDPAPER

Correct Bad Brushwork

When brush-on poly goes wrong—dust nubs, sags, brush marks—you can correct the problem. After the finish has fully dried, wet-sand with soapy water or mineral spirits and 400-grit wet/dry paper. After you've sanded the finish flat and smooth, a couple of light coats of wipe-on poly will give you a perfect surface.

Make Repairs with Epoxy

This versatile product can make a wide variety of household repairs, just use these tips.

Boat builders, surfboard makers and fabricators of all kinds use epoxy to form strong, waterproof, lightweight structures. And you can take advantage of this versatile product around the home. Epoxy for household use is available in liquid, gel and putty and in container sizes ranging from a mere half ounce to gallons.

Unlike many other adhesives and fillers that require drying time, epoxies require two parts that, when mixed together, begin a chemical reaction that causes the liquid or putty to harden. The amount of time you have to work with the epoxy before it sets up is determined by the chemistry of the hardener. For tiny jobs, you can choose one-minute epoxy, but epoxy that takes longer to set forms a stronger bond and gives you more working time.

Epoxy has several advantages. It can fill gaps and still retain strength, it's waterproof, and it sticks well to most surfaces. Choose an epoxy that matches the repair you're attempting.

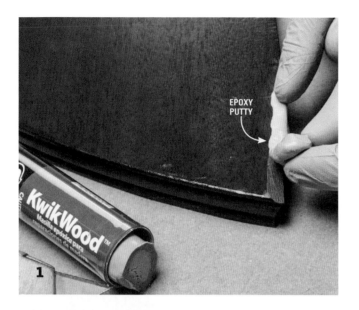

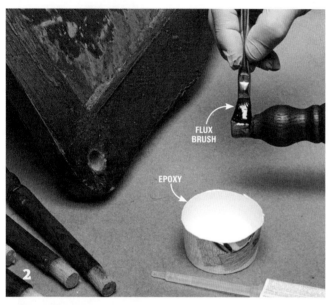

1. REPAIR CHIPPED FURNITURE

When it would be difficult or impossible to replace missing veneer or chipped furniture parts with real wood, epoxy putty makes a great substitute. Two-part putty in a Tootsie Roll shape is convenient to use and makes a strong repair. Just slice off a section and knead the chunk until the two parts are blended and the color is consistent. Then form the putty into approximately the right shape and press it into the damaged area. Use a wet putty knife to smooth and shape the putty. When the epoxy has hardened to about the consistency of bar soap, carve or scrape off most of the excess. When it hardens completely, you can sand it just like wood.

2. FIX LOOSE JOINTS WITH EPOXY RESIN

Epoxy is one of the few adhesives that can fill gaps without losing strength. That's why it's perfect for repairing loose-fitting joints in furniture. If you have only one or two repairs to make, buy a small quantity of epoxy in a double syringe at a home center or hardware store. Read the instructions on the label and make sure the epoxy is formulated specifically for wood repairs.

Brush a layer of epoxy onto both parts to be joined. Assemble and clamp the parts if necessary. Then wait the specified time for the epoxy to set up. Read the instructions to determine how long the epoxy should cure before you use the furniture. Even five-minute epoxy may take an hour or more to reach full strength. If you're repairing a valuable antique, you may want to avoid epoxy repairs because the result is irreversible.

3. MIX IT UP IN A CAN BOTTOM

If you need only a bit of epoxy for a small repair, you can't beat the bottom of an aluminum can as a mixing container. Just squeeze two-part epoxy into the concave can bottom and mix it up.

4. BUY SOME EPOXY PUMPS

The pumps shown are calibrated so that one pump from each, the resin and the hardener, gives you exactly the right proportion. No more measuring cups or guesswork. And with this setup, it's super convenient to mix a batch of epoxy whenever you need it. The cost of a quart of resin, a pint of hardener and the pumps is a little steep, but the epoxy will last for years, and a fresh batch of epoxy is just a few pumps away. Make sure to buy pumps that are calibrated for the epoxy you're using.

5. COLOR EPOXY REPAIRS WITH STAIN MARKERS

Epoxy putty is a handy material for repairing chipped wood or a bit of missing veneer, but if the wood is stained rather than painted, you'll have to blend the repair to make it match. Stain pens work great as a quick way to color an epoxy repair. Start with a lighter base color to match the background. Then add darker colors over the top if needed. Stain markers are available at home centers, hardware stores and paint stores. For an even more realistic repair, simulate wood grain by making tiny slits in the epoxy with a razor blade before it's fully hardened.

6. PREFILL WITH WOOD

Epoxy putty is expensive, so when you have deep holes or large areas to fill, start by filling most of the repair with wood. Cut a piece that's small enough to allow a layer of epoxy over the top. Then adhere it by pressing it into a bed of epoxy putty. You don't have to wait for this epoxy to set; finish the repair with more epoxy putty right away.

7. REPLACE ROTTED WOOD WITH EPOXY PUTTY

For small repairs, you can use the kind of epoxy putty that comes in a two-part roll (see Tip 1). But there's a better choice for repairing larger areas of rotted or damaged wood. Abatron WoodEpox and J-B Weld Wood Restore (sold online or at home centers and hardware stores) are two-part epoxy wood repair putty products. Mixing parts A and B according to the instructions results in a soft, easily formed putty that you can use to rebuild rotted or damaged wood. For a strong repair, first soak the wood fibers with liquid epoxy to consolidate and firm up loose fibers and to create a primer for the putty.

8. SPEED IT UP WITH HEAT

When you're working with epoxy in lower temps and need to speed things up, use a hair dryer. Warm up the two parts of the epoxy before mixing or the epoxy after it's applied. You can even warm up the surface where you're applying the epoxy. The heat speeds up the reaction for a quicker cure.

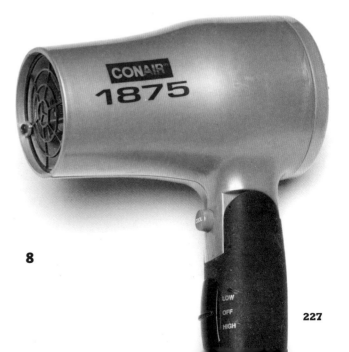

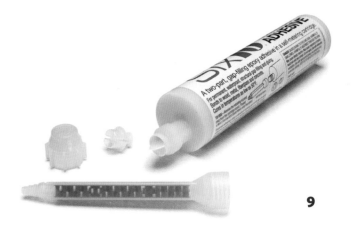

9. TRY EPOXY IN A TUBE FOR NO-MIX, NO-SAG REPAIRS

This tube of epoxy is divided down the middle to separate the resin and hardener. To use it, you install the special tip and put the tube in a caulk gun. The two parts mix in the tip as you dispense the epoxy. The thickened epoxy doesn't sag or run so it's great for working on vertical surfaces. It's also easy to smooth with a putty knife, which makes it handy for repairing things like cracked siding boards. This West System Six10 Epoxy Adhesive is available online or where boat repair supplies are sold. Remember to buy extra mixing tips if you don't think you'll use the entire tube within about 30 minutes.

10. SPREAD IT OUT TO SLOW IT DOWN

Epoxy heats up as the two parts react after mixing. The heat speeds up the reaction, giving you less time to work. To avoid this problem, spread your epoxy thin after mixing it. This tip works with liquid epoxy too. Wide, shallow mixing vessels are preferable to deep, narrow vessels to greatly slow down the hardening reaction. Shallow vessels work because the epoxy then has more surface area exposed to release heat.

BACK PLATE

Hide Cabinet Damage with Back Plates

New cabinet hardware that includes back plates can hide the wear that occurs around cabinet knobs and pulls. You'll find a small hardware selection at home centers and an endless selection online.

BACK PLATE

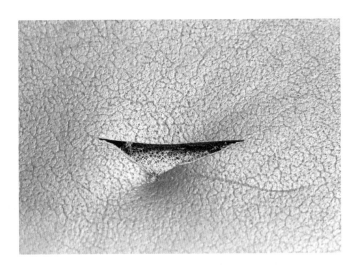

Patch a Hole in Leather or Vinyl

Pick up a repair kit and patch it yourself. It won't be perfect, but it will prevent further tearing.

Do you walk around with tools in your pockets? Don't be surprised if one day you tear a hole in your car seat, sofa or easy chair.

If a perfect repair is important, call a pro to fix it. But if you just want to prevent further tearing, you can fix it yourself with a leather/vinyl repair kit. These kits are inexpensive, and the repair takes only an hour. You'll still see the tear, and you probably won't get a perfect color match. But this fix will prevent the tear from getting larger and it will look a whole lot better than a gaping hole.

You can buy a kit at a hardware store, home center or auto parts store. One kit is the 3M 08579 Leather and Vinyl Repair Kit. Follow the cleaning instructions in the kit and trim the damaged area to remove any frayed edges. Then cut the reinforcement fabric so it extends under the tear by at least 1/2 in. Glue it in place (**Photo 1**) and let it dry for the recommended time.

Next, mix the heat-set colored filler. This is the hardest and most frustrating part of the repair. So take your time and get as close to the color as you can. Apply just enough colorant to fill in the tear.

Then cover it with the textured mat and apply heat (**Photo 2**). Let it cool and remove the mat (**Photo 3**) to inspect the patch. It won't be perfect, but it will provide a smooth surface and will make the tear less noticeable.

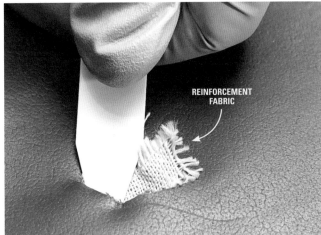

1 GLUE IN THE REINFORCEMENT FABRIC. Tuck the backing under the damaged area to form a patch. Then apply adhesive around the edges and the middle. Let it dry before adding colorant.

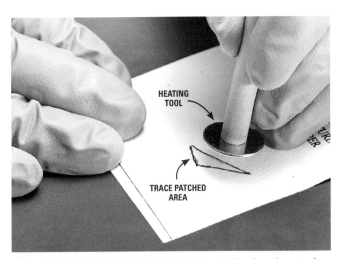

2 CURE THE PATCH WITH HEAT. Touch the heating tool (included with the kit) to the face of a hot clothes iron until it heats up. Then press the hot tool onto the textured mat and hold it in place.

3 CHECK OUT THE RESULTS. The patch won't be perfect. But it sure beats the look of a tear or burn.

Repair Stone Countertops

You may not get an invisible repair, but filling chips or gouges in stone countertops with super glue hides the flaw and can help prevent further damage. For this edge chip, we cut a small rectangle of polypropylene plastic from a plastic container lid and taped it to the side to form a dam. Fill any recess in layers until the super glue is slightly proud of the surface. After the super glue hardens, use a single-edge razor blade held at about an 80-degree angle to scrape the glue until it's level with the surface. On soft stone like marble, use masking tape to protect the surrounding surface from scratches.

You can make the patch blend in somewhat by adding stone powder or plastic pigment to the super glue. But if you do add pigment, work fast because the pigment can accelerate the hardening process.

PLASTIC DAM

Hide Scratches with Wax

To revive a finish on woood, rub colored paste wax over the entire surface and buff. This isn't a perfect fix; heavy scratches or dents will still be visible. But light scratches and wear will almost disappear.

For the best camouflage, pick a color that's slightly darker than the finish. You can find Minwax or Briwax colored paste wax at some paint stores or home centers, or you can order it from online retailers.

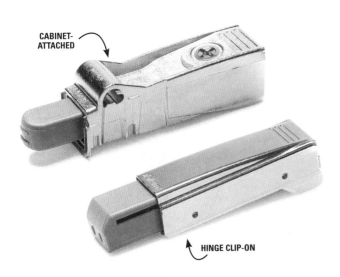

CABINET-ATTACHED

HINGE CLIP-ON

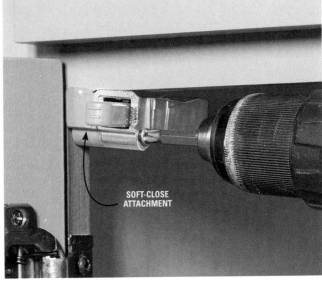

SOFT-CLOSE ATTACHMENT

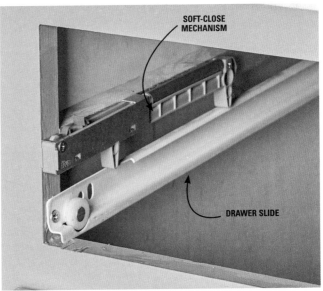

SOFT-CLOSE MECHANISM

DRAWER SLIDE

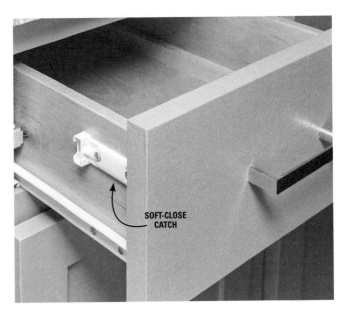

SOFT-CLOSE CATCH

Add Soft-Close to Cabinets

You don't have to buy new cabinets to get soft, quiet-closing doors and drawers. Soft-close doors and drawers not only keep the kitchen quiet but also help reduce wear and tear on your cabinetry.

FOR THE DOORS

One thing you never need to hear again is a kitchen cabinet door slamming shut. Luckily, soft-close attachments are an easy add-on for doors with any type of hinge. Many hinge manufacturers offer soft-close hinges, but clip-on varieties are also available for retrofitting Euro-style hinges. There are many options for traditional face frame cabinetry with barrel hinges too. You'll also find a wide variety of soft-close adapters for doors. They're typically sold at specialty hardware stores or online.

FOR THE DRAWERS

Drawers can also be updated with soft-close mechanisms. Often the best solution is to swap out the existing drawer slides with soft-close slides. However, there are a few situations that allow for aftermarket soft-close add-ons. The Soft-Close Device from Rockler is designed for epoxy-coated roller slides.

CHAPTER **TEN**

PESTS

Get Rid of Yard Pests

Here are 12 proven solutions to deal with unwelcome guests.

There are hundreds of ways to deal with yard pests. But what works and what doesn't? Sometimes small deterrents are enough. If you make food or shelter just a little harder to find, critters will often move to friendlier areas. But if animals are especially hungry or stubborn, you may have to try several solutions. Here are some strategies that might work for you.

1. LOCK DOWN YOUR TRASH
Raccoons are especially good at opening trash cans, but a bungee cord is usually enough to foil them. Also deal with trash odor. Garbage may smell bad to you, but to many pests it smells like dinner. Put trash in plastic bags and seal them. If your trash can is dirty, wash it out with soap and water.

2. PICK UP NUTS AND FRUIT
Lots of animals love nuts and fruit. Removing these treats while they're on the tree usually isn't practical. But gathering fallen apples or raking up nuts is an effective way to send critters elsewhere for dinner.

3. ELIMINATE HIDING PLACES
Small animals seek out hiding places. So trim the shrubs around your foundation. Also check around your property for any other hiding spots, like wood piles, and move them away from your house.

4. LET YOUR DOGS OUT
Animals are less likely to come near your yard if they know a predator is around. Your dog may show you where the invaders are hiding out—and leave scents that ward off unwanted visitors.

5. KILL OFF CLOVER

Clover isn't the worst weed in most lawns, but it's one of the most attractive to rabbits and deer. There are a few ways to eliminate clover, but the best defense is to cultivate healthy grass so clover has no room to grow.

6. CONTAIN COMPOST

Uncovered grass or leaves are fine, but any compost that contains food scraps needs a pest-proof container or cover. Otherwise, you're inviting animals to a feast.

7. REMOVE SQUIRREL NESTS

Squirrels can be a yard nuisance, but it gets worse: Eventually they'll look for ways to get into your house, seeking nesting sites in your attic or eaves. To make them feel unwelcome, it's best to knock down their nests. Sometimes you can do that with a long pole. In other situations it's easier to cut off a tree branch to bring down the nest. Either way, removing squirrel homes is a great incentive for them to seek friendlier yards.

8. INSTALL A CHIMNEY CAP

Various animals will occasionally find their way down a chimney, but raccoons especially like chimneys as nesting sites. Chimney caps, sold at home centers and online, are inexpensive and keep out critters.

9. INSTALL PLASTIC PREDATORS

Plastic owls often scare off rodents. The key is to mount them up high, usually on the roof or in a tree—that's where animals expect to see predatory birds. You can get a plastic owl at a home center or online.

10. WIPE OUT GRUBS

Grubs living in soil are yummy to some rodents. Little cone-shaped holes in your yard are usually evidence that raccoons or skunks are digging for grubs. Moles and voles also go where the grubs are. Eliminate your grub problem with grub killer, sold at hardware stores and home centers.

9

8

10

11. SPRAY THEM AWAY

Motion-activated sprinklers often discourage deer, rabbits and raccoons. Just keep in mind that animals may get used to the sound and spray and eventually ignore them. Motion-activated sprinklers are available at home centers and online.

12. CATCH AND RELEASE—FAR AWAY

Live trapping can work, but homeowners often make mistakes using this technique. Here are a few tips for success:

- When handling the trap with an animal inside, wear Kevlar gloves.
- Choose a trap with a metal plate under the handle to protect your hand from teeth and claws.
- Call a wildlife preserve to get permission to release an animal there.
- Release animals at least 10 miles from your home; their ability to find their way back is incredible.
- When finished, clean the trap with a bleach solution to eliminate scents that may scare off the next critter you want to trap.

MOTION SENSOR

11

Fence Out Rabbits

Keeping rabbits out of gardens with chicken wire is an old idea that works, but patience is the key to their departure. It may take months for the bunnies to give up and move to other feeding grounds.

12

Got Carpenter Ants?

They can do a lot of damage, so use these tips to get rid of them and stop a future invasion.

Carpenter ants can damage your home, but they can also warn you of serious trouble. They're attracted to damp, rotting wood. If you see them, there's a good chance moisture is entering your walls or ceilings, causing structural damage that could cost thousands to repair. For some help identifying carpenter ants, see the website listed in the last paragraph below

FIND THE NEST

To get rid of the ants, you have to find the nest. "Worker" carpenter ants are black or red and black. Look for them when they're most active–generally between sunset and midnight during the spring and summer months. Try setting out honey or tuna packed in water to attract them, then follow them back to their nest. Use a flashlight with red Mylar film over the lens (they can't see red light) so you can see them in the dark (you can buy Mylar film at art supply stores). Small piles of coarse sawdust are a sure sign that an active nest is nearby.

Once you locate the nest, figure out why the wood is getting wet and fix the problem. We have lots of advice about that at familyhandyman.com—just search for "water leak."

KILL THE ANTS

After you fix the water leak, it's time to fix the ant problem. Spray an aerosol insecticide into the nest. Reduce the risk of future infestations by not leaving food or sweet drinks out in the open, and by keeping pet food in a tightly sealed container. Also trim any bushes or tree branches that contact the house, and never store firewood against the building. Call an exterminator if none of these strategies work.

The University of Minnesota Extension has lots more helpful information about dealing with carpenter ants. Go to extension. umn.edu/garden/insects/find/carpenter-ants/.

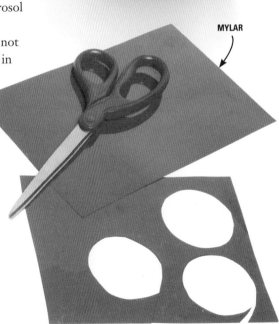

MYLAR

Tips for Trapping Mice

1

Here's how to deal with the little varmints!

After dealing with a serious infestation of mice, we learned to appreciate the effectiveness of the good old-fashioned spring trap. And our research on what attracts mice taught us the best ways to bait and trap them.

However, our preferred trapping method might not be everyone's cup of tea. It can be downright grizzly and entails some dirty work from time to time. If trapping isn't for you, learn about alternatives by searching familyhandyman.com for "humane rodent control."

1. BUY AND SET LOTS OF TRAPS

Anywhere you see mouse droppings is a primo place to set traps. The more traps you set, the more mice you'll catch—period. So don't think you'll place a few traps around the house and take care of your mouse problem. Concentrate on the worst room—the kitchen—and set six traps or so. We used ordinary Victor traps and baited them with peanut butter, then waited. Mice typically come out only at night.

2

2. PET FOOD IS A PROBLEM—AND AN OPPORTUNITY

If you have pets, you might be surprised to discover the mice have been stealing their food. Set several traps next to the cat or dog dish. Cats might choose to ignore the traps, but dogs love peanut butter just as much as mice do. So if you don't want Rex (or a curious cat) to get his tongue caught in a trap, let him sleep in your bedroom and keep the door closed.

3. LOOK FOR THE PATHWAYS

A mouse is like Tarzan when it comes to climbing. In fact, a mouse can jump up to 8 in. and climb up electrical cords to get to other places. So if you find droppings in high places, look low and put your traps there.

3

4

4. PLACE TRAPS NEXT TO VERTICAL SURFACES

Mice are prey after all, so they're born scared. That means they're terrified to be out in the open and prefer traveling close to walls. Once again, the more traps the better, especially in areas where you know mice are hanging out (usually where there's food).

5. LOOK FOR WALL PENETRATIONS

Mice love to live inside walls where they're safe and warm. Look around to see where plumbing or anything else penetrates drywall or plaster and put traps just below these areas. That's where they'll come in at night to feed.

6. LOOK FOR FEEDING AREAS

Just as around pet dishes, there are other potential sources of food for mice besides the main kitchen. Do you have a mini kitchen in your shop or basement? Do you store snacks in the family room? Where there's food, there could be mice, so put some traps there.

7. UNDER CABINETS

The spaces under cabinets are like a freeway for mice. Pull out the bottom drawers and look for droppings. Put traps on the floor, replace the drawers and check them every morning.

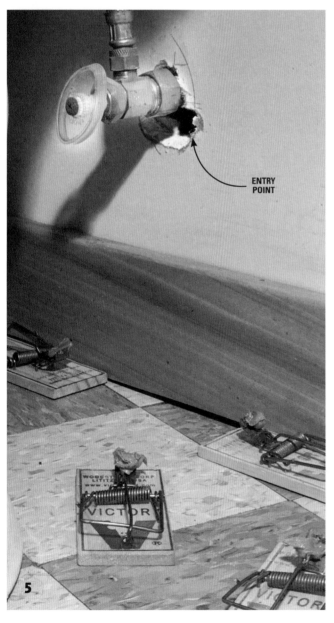

ENTRY POINT

5

Our Mouse-Trapping Philosophy

We know most people don't relish killing animals—even mice—but for us, it was the best choice. Here's our take on some other options:

1. Live traps. Mice, by nature, build nests and store food. So you trap them this fall and let them go outside where they'll start their lives anew, right? Well, that's not how it works. They have no food stored away and no nest to live in, so they'll most likely die of starvation and/or exposure.
2. Poison. Most poisons are ingested and cause severe dehydration or blood coagulation. It's not a painless death.
3. Live with the disease-carrying creatures. But as they run around your floors, countertops, plates with leftovers and your pet's food dishes, they're leaving a trail of waste behind them.
4. Sticky mouse traps. So then what? The mice are not dead and you have to either kill them with your shoe or throw them into the trash can where they'll die a slow, miserable death from thirst.

All this mouse-killing business isn't for the faint of heart. Sometimes, but not too often, our method of dealing with mice means they don't get killed right away. And sometimes they suffer. But if you have a mouse problem and ignore it, you're putting your family's health at risk.

6

8. KEEP 'EM OUT!

When the temperature starts dropping, mice are looking for a warm, dry place with food and good nesting conditions. In other words, they want to live inside your house. They enter through the smallest imaginable holes and cracks. Young ones can worm their way through a 1/4-in. opening. Take a very close look around the outside of your house, and then caulk, plug or do whatever it takes to close every entry point you can find.

Worn weatherstripping under doors can be a perfect, easy entry point for mice looking for a warm place to winter. Replacing it is usually as simple as taking the door off the hinges and slipping a new weatherstrip into the slots. Take the old weatherstripping to the home center to find a match.

7

8

Prevent Nighttime Visitors

If you have bird feeders and live in an area where you see elk, deer, coyotes, bears or other animals, you may get unwanted nighttime visits by these wildlife neighbors. To prevent the house calls, try putting out the feeders during the day but bringing them indoors at night.

How to Beat Bedbugs

Make your home free of bedbugs. Here's how to find them and exterminate them ... and avoid having an infestation in the first place!

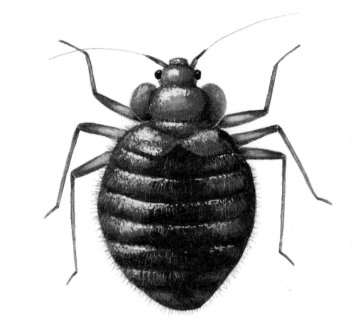

Bedbugs have been pestering humanity for thousands of years, but in the 1950s they finally met their match: the pesticide DDT. Then DDT was banned, but for most of the years since then, bedbugs have not been a major problem. Now, however, these blood-sucking vermin are back. That's the bad news.

The good news is that, unlike mosquitoes and ticks, bedbugs don't spread disease, and there are practical steps you can take to prevent an infestation. And if you do get bedbugs, you can get rid of them yourself. We'll show you what to look for, how to kill bedbugs if you find them and how to keep them out!

BEDBUG DETECTION

Pest control pros tell us that almost half the bedbug calls they get turn out to be false alarms. So before you take action, make sure you actually have them. Here are four key ways to detect them.

1. CHECK YOUR MATTRESS

Bedbugs don't like being jostled, so they avoid hanging out in your hair or clothes, but they do like to stay close to their food source, namely, you. Your mattress is the first place you should inspect. Bedbugs love to hang out in cracks and crevices. They can fit into any gap the thickness of a business card. One of their favorite spots is the piping along the edge of a mattress. Look for the bugs themselves, their dark droppings, your dried blood, eggs and gold-colored shells that have been left behind after molting.

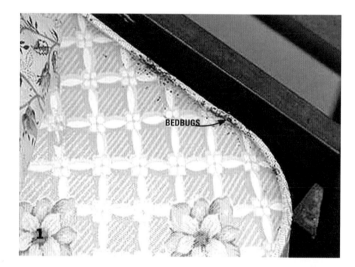

Perform a quick inspection of the upper piping every time you change your sheets. Make a more thorough examination by folding the piping over and closely inspecting both sides all the way around, top and bottom. Do this a couple of times a year or every time you flip or rotate your mattress.

2. LOOK FOR BITE MARKS

Bedbugs love fast food. They like to feed and then scurry back to their hiding places. They try to avoid crawling all over their food for fear of waking it (us). They usually bite the bare skin they find closest to the mattress. That's why it's common to see two or three bite marks in a line along the skin that was in contact with the mattress or pillow.

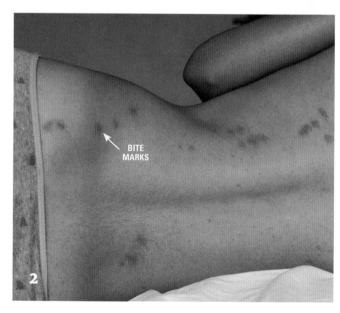

Everyone reacts differently to a bedbug bite. Some will develop small itchy bumps like mosquito bites; others will suffer from large, puffy red lesions the size of a quarter. A lucky few will have no reaction at all. Other signs of bedbugs are bloodstains on your sheets, pillows and blankets. Are you scratching yet?

3. KNOW WHAT THEY LOOK LIKE

A fully fed adult bedbug is about the size and shape of an apple seed. An unfed bedbug is more round and flat like a tick. Newly hatched bedbugs are the size of a poppy seed and are golden in color. Their eggs look like small grains of white rice, about 1 mm in length.

If you find what you think may be a bedbug, take it to the entomology department of the nearest university or to a pest control company for official identification.

4. SET TRAPS

Traps aren't an effective way to wipe out a bedbug infestation, but they're an excellent way to determine whether you have them. Set traps in areas where they may hide or travel, like near baseboard trim or under nightstands. If they aren't living in your mattress or other parts of your bed, that means they need to travel up the legs of the bed frame to get to you, so place traps there as well.

If you confirm you have bedbugs in one bedroom of the house, you'll have to treat that entire room, but you won't necessarily need to treat the entire house. Set up traps to monitor other bedrooms and living areas to make sure they stay bug free. The Hot Shot traps shown below are available at home centers and hardware stores.

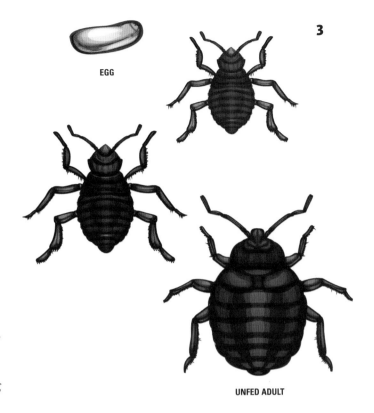

EGG

UNFED ADULT

Bedbugs in Apartments

Your bedbugs may be migrating from your neighbor's place. Call your property management company. Insist they inspect the apartments on either side, above and below.

TRAP

TRAP

4

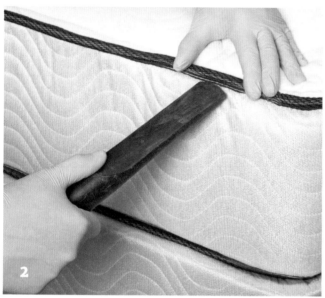

TIGHT
KNOT

INSECT
INTERCEPTOR

DIY EXTERMINATION

Hiring a pro to wipe out bedbugs isn't cheap. You'll likely need a few chemical treatments. Professional heat treatments cost even more (see "Use Heat Instead of Chemicals"). And even if you hire a pro, you'll still have to do lots of work yourself (moving furniture, washing all clothes, etc.). So consider declaring a DIY war on bedbugs. If you're willing to do things right, your chances of success are excellent.

When working with chemicals, always read the directions. You should be able to stay in the room during the treatment process. Room treatments entail thorough cleaning and applying chemicals. The process needs to be repeated three times, two weeks apart.

1. BAG AND WASH CLOTHES AND BEDDING

The first thing to do after confirming an infestation is to bag up all your clothes, towels, bedding and curtains in plastic bags. Tie tight knots to seal the bags and keep them tied until they reach the washing machine. Wash with hot water and dry thoroughly. Temperatures over 120 degrees will kill bedbugs and any eggs they've left behind.

Store clean clothes in another room until you've finished treating the infested room. If you plan to take laundry to a professional cleaner or public laundromat, treat it chemically first to avoid spreading the bugs (see "Create a Kill Chamber").

2. CLEAN EVERYTHING

Now that all the stuff is out of the bedroom, it's time to treat the room itself. The first step is to vacuum every surface in the room, the baseboards, all the furniture, the mattress, the box spring, the bed frame—everything. Use a small wand to get into all the corners and crevices.

When you finish, throw out the vacuum bag to avoid spreading the bugs. If you use a shop vacuum or bagless vacuum, dump the contents you've collected into a bag, tie it up and throw it out. Then treat the filter and the inside of the canister with contact spray insecticide. Flat surfaces like walls and dresser tops can be wiped with alcohol. Wipe a small inconspicuous area first to see if the alcohol will damage the paint or finish.

3. ISOLATE THE BED

What's the best way to get rid of bedbugs? Stop feeding them. To prevent those unwanted dinner guests, isolate your mattress from the rest of the room. Start by pulling the bed away from the wall and away from other furniture such as nightstands and chairs. Remove box spring skirting that hangs down to the floor. Oversize blankets that drape to the floor can also act as a ladder for the little buggers.

Finally, place all the legs into insect interceptors like those shown made by ClimbUp. They allow bugs to climb into the outer pitfall area, but the slick plastic coated with talcum powder keeps them from climbing out or reaching the center well and climbing up your bed frame leg.

4. SPRAY BUG KILLER

Spray insecticide on all the areas where you've seen signs of the bugs or the bugs themselves. And spray all the areas where they're likely to hide, such as the furniture near the bed, the entire bed itself and the perimeter of the walls near the baseboard.

Most sprays are contact killers, which means they kill only the bugs and eggs they touch directly, so there's no reason to spray all the walls, the ceiling and the entire floor. Spray pesticides are available online, at home centers, and at hardware and discount stores. Many brands kill other insects, like fleas and roaches, as well.

5. BAG YOUR MATTRESS

Once you've vacuumed and chemically treated your mattress and box spring, enclose them in encasement bags. If the bedbugs found a way inside the mattress, the odds are that the spray chemicals did not kill them. Encasement bags have special zippers that trap the bedbugs and prevent them from escaping. Keep these bags on for at least a year because a fully fed bedbug can live more than 10 months between meals.

If the idea of sleeping on a tiny bedbug cemetery is too much to bear, the only alternative is to toss the mattress and box spring and buy new ones. Just be sure to wrap up the infested one before hauling it through your house, and don't buy a used mattress!

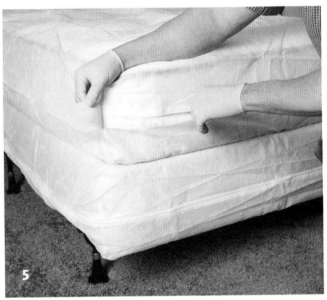

6. SPREAD A RESIDUAL POWDER

It's not likely that you'll kill all the bedbugs with a bedbug spray. That's where a residual powder insecticide comes into play. It kills any bugs that wander through the powder. Some powders can kill bugs for many years if left undisturbed. Skip the open areas and spray the powder in those places where you think they'll be traveling to and from, such as near bed legs and under baseboard trim.

If at all possible, pull up the carpet where it meets the wall and puff powder around the whole perimeter of the room. Inside outlet boxes is a great place to use powders because sprays and electricity don't mix. Bellow dusters work great for spreading residual insecticide powder. An old makeup brush is a good tool to spread the dust around on hard surfaces. Bedbug powders are available at the same places you'll find the spray pesticides.

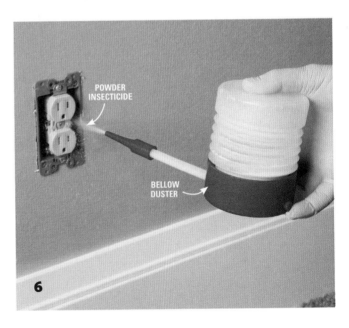

POWDER INSECTICIDE

BELLOW DUSTER

7. CREATE A KILL CHAMBER

OK, you've dealt with your room, clothes and bedding—now it's time to deal with your stuff. Everything in the bedroom needs to be treated: every book, shoe, lamp, photo, power strip, alarm clock, magazine—every knickknack and bric-a-brack ... everything! If you don't treat it, bag it, tie it up and throw it out.

Flat surfaces can be wiped with alcohol or sprayed with a bedbug–killing contact pesticide, but all items that have a small nook or cranny where bedbugs could hide (which is most stuff) need to be treated with penetrating fumes. Build yourself a kill chamber out of a large storage bin. Tape a pesticide strip to the side or lid of the bin, and seal your stuff inside for a couple of days or however long the manufacturer recommends. Seal the lid of the bin with duct tape.

You can treat all your belongings by reusing the same bins; just make sure to keep your other stuff that's waiting to be treated bagged up in the meantime. Always wear gloves when handling pesticides and be sure to follow all safety instructions. The pesticide strips shown here are Nuvan ProStrips.

8. USE HEAT INSTEAD OF CHEMICALS

Insecticides are an effective way to eradicate bedbugs, but not the only way. If you or someone in your house is highly sensitive to chemicals, or you're just not crazy about the idea of spraying chemicals where you sleep, kill the little blood suckers with heat. Temperatures above 120 degrees kill all stages of bedbugs. Steamers can be used to treat all the same areas where you would have sprayed contact killers. Steamers like the one shown are good for many other projects like removing wallpaper, cleaning tile, removing labels, cleaning engine parts and removing wrinkles from fabric.

Heat chambers can be used to heat personal belongings and kill any hidden bedbugs without chemicals. They come in various sizes. In the summer, you could let Mother Nature do the dirty work. Bag up your belongings and set them on the driveway. On a day when the temp tops 95 degrees, a bag placed in the sun should easily reach 120 degrees inside.

STEAMER

8A

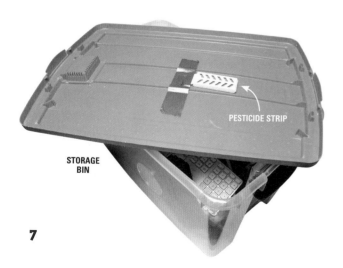

PESTICIDE STRIP

STORAGE BIN

7

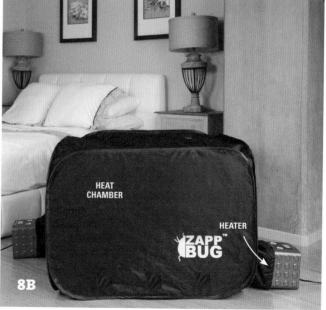

HEAT CHAMBER

HEATER

ZAPP BUG

8B

9. TURN UP THE HEAT

Professional heat treatment is one of the least invasive ways to get rid of bedbugs. Large heaters are used to heat entire rooms to more than 120 degrees for a few hours. Unfortunately, these large heaters are expensive, and whole-house treatments can cost thousands of dollars.

KEEP 'EM OUT!

1. HOUSEGUESTS AND BEDBUGS

Telling Aunt Harriet or Uncle Charlie not to come for a visit is probably not going to work, but you can still boss your kids around. Send your kids off to college with the information they need to inspect for bedbugs in their dorm room. And include as a parting gift a package of a few detection traps.

Instruct those returning scholars to bag up their mountains of dirty laundry and leave the bags in the garage until transporting them directly to the washing machine. Wash clothes in hot water and dry thoroughly.

2. DON'T PICK UP HOTEL BEDBUGS

Hotels are a common source of bedbugs, and even the best hotels can have infestations. Here's how to avoid bringing them home:

- Inspect mattresses when you arrive in your hotel room.
- Ask for a new room if you find them.
- Keep clothes and luggage off the bedspread and floor.
- Hang up clothes and keep other clothes in your suitcase, not dresser drawers.
- Keep suitcases in large bags tied off or in store-bought luggage bags.
- Bag up daily items like shoes and wallets.
- Bag up dirty clothes and transport them directly to the washing machine upon return.
- Wash clothes in hot water and dry thoroughly.
- Inspect luggage and store away from living/sleeping areas.
- Wipe down luggage with alcohol or spray with insecticide if you find bedbugs.

LUGGAGE BAG

1

Banish Bugs & Crack Down on Critters

Do you have bats in your attic or ants in your pantry? Are mosquitos, moles and wasps driving you nuts? Check out these great ideas from critter control experts and readers to get rid of your worst pests—both inside your house and out in the yard.

1. HOLY MOLE-Y!

Even experts don't agree on what works for moles, so we can't give you any magic bullets. But some of our readers have real-world success stories to tell.

"Get rid of the grubs that are their food source," suggests reader Jerry Young. "Use a good grub insecticide in the spring and again in July, and you'll starve out the moles."

"I tried all the typical mole products and remedies, and finally the Wire Tek Easy-Set Mole Eliminator Trap did the trick," says reader Ed Stawicki. "It traps the moles with a 'scissor-effect.' Very effective."

"The Mole Chaser worked for me," says reader Scott Craig. "It's a foot-long metal cylinder that vibrates underground intermittently and causes the moles to find a new home." Mole Chaser stakes are available in several models at home centers and online.

2. THE RIGHT BAIT IS THE KEY TO LIVE-TRAPPING

Reader Michael Finfrock has lots of experience live-trapping rodents and small mammals.

"In the past seven years, I have trapped well over 50 small animals." Finfrock says his success comes down to researching appropriate baits and trapping methods for each particular animal. Local extension services, the "learning center" on havahart.com, and your state's Department of Natural Resources are several places to check for detailed trapping and baiting information.

In many areas, it's illegal to relocate nuisance animals, so check with local authorities. Also, according to wildlife experts, more than 50% of relocated animals don't survive because they don't have an established shelter, food source or territory.

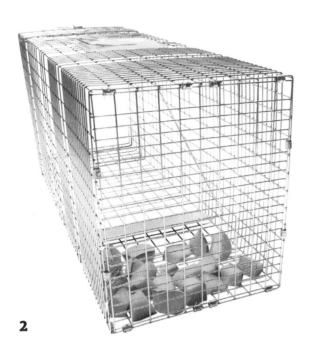

2

3

3. HEALTHY TURF FENDS OFF BURROWING WASPS

These large wasps live in all states east of the Rockies. Male cicada killer wasps are aggressive, but they don't have stingers. The females do, but they will sting only if they feel threatened. These wasps, which feed cicadas to their young, typically nest in disturbed, sandy areas and rarely infest healthy turf.

Adequate lime and fertilizer as well as frequent watering promote a thick growth of turf and can usually eliminate a cicada killer wasp infestation in one or two seasons. Mulch heavily around flower beds and shrubs to cover sandy soil. For severe infestations, call in an exterminator.

4

4. REPELLENTS WITH MINT

Discourage ants from entering your home by planting a mint barrier around your foundation, according to reader Wayne Piaskowski.

"Over the past three years I've tried ant bombs, spraying their nests out in the yard. I even physically dug up a stubborn colony near the street that was 3 feet deep and wide. The mint that I've planted around the house seems to be helping a lot."

5. LIGHTS AND SPRINKLERS DETER RACCOONS AND FOXES

If you have chickens in your backyard, you may have a problem with foxes and raccoons. Installing an electric fence may help, but a motion-activated light on the chicken coop along with a motion-activated sprinkler works even better.

6

6. BLEACH GETS RID OF DRAIN FLIES

Tiny drain flies are harmless but can gather in huge numbers in your house. They're sometimes mistaken for fruit flies, but they actually live on the gunky slime in your drainpipes. Reader Lindsay McLeod told us about a recent plague of drain flies in her basement.

"An exterminator would have charged a lot to come investigate plus the cost of exterminating. Instead, I poured a teaspoon of bleach down the basement drain and the flies started pouring out! Gross! So I poured a little more bleach in, blocked the drain hole, waited an hour and presto! No more drain flies!"

If the bleach doesn't work, experts suggest starving the flies by cleaning the gunky slime out of the drain with a long-handled brush.

7. BANISH BATS WITH A SPECIAL DOOR

When reader Chris Phelps counted 70 bats exiting his attic one evening, he knew he had a problem. He quickly discovered the solution—a bat exclusion door—which lets bats out but won't let them back in. One type of "exclusion door" is a piece of netting that hangs a foot below the bats' exit point. You tape the netting along the top and sides but leave the bottom free. The bats will slip out the open bottom but won't be able to fly back in.

"We installed the door," says Phelps, "and within a week the bats were gone. I sealed the hole to keep them out permanently. We also built a couple of bat houses since bats eat mosquitos."

7

8. A KINDER MOUSETRAP

Instead of using traps that kill, try this: Prop up an empty soda bottle at about a 20-degree angle and then bait it with peanut butter. When we tried this, a day later we had a very scared mouse trapped in the bottle. He was relocated to a field more suited to his skill set.

9. GEL ANT BAIT TARGETS TOUGH AREAS

Chemical ant baits are most effective for grease- and sweet-eating ant species. The key is to allow the ants to eat the bait and take it back to kill the entire colony, which may take several weeks. Gel ant baits let you apply bait in hard-to-reach areas such as behind appliances and in cracks and crevices (keep all chemical baits away from pets and kids).

8

10. CONTROL CRICKETS WITH DIY STICKY TRAPS

If you're concerned about chemicals in bug sprays, try this simple trap: duct tape. Set out a long strip of duct tape, sticky side up, where you're finding crickets (they like damp areas such as basements). After a few days, check the tape. When we tried this, we found it had about 15 to 20 bugs attached. Since then, we have set out tape several times with the same successful results.

Note: To permanently banish crickets, seal entrances by caulking around basement windows. Also set up a dehumidifier in your basement.

11. DIY CRITTER TRAP

To trap and relocate larger critters, use a big, empty 32-gallon plastic trash can and lay the can on its side. To the critter, it looks like a dark tunnel to hide in. Force the animal in with a stick, flip the can upright, put the lid on and transfer. Another way to use the can is to place it over the animal. Slide a flat board underneath, then flip the whole thing upright.

12. USE EXPANDING FOAM WITH A PEST REPELLENT

Expanding foam seals small holes and cracks. But be sure to choose one that's designed for use where you intend to use it (indoors or outdoors) and that contains a pest repellent (but not a pesticide). The repellent discourages insect pests and rodents from gnawing on the insulating foam (which they will do) to gain entry to your home.

10

11

9

12

WATER

SPECIAL SECTION

PREVENTIVE MEASURES

1A

INSULATED DUCT

Six Silent Signs Your House Is in Trouble

Learn to recognize the clues to potentially serious problems so you can make timely repairs.

We don't mean to scare you ... well, actually, we do. We sat down with a longtime home inspector, and he told some tales and shared some photos that were downright frightening. Much of the damage he's encountered could have been

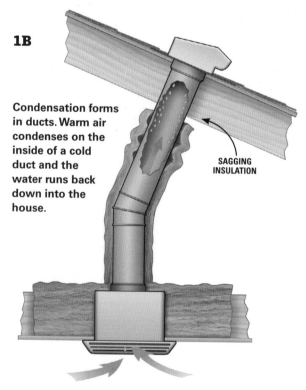

1B

Condensation forms in ducts. Warm air condenses on the inside of a cold duct and the water runs back down into the house.

SAGGING INSULATION

prevented if the homeowners had just heeded the silent signs that their house was in trouble.

1. SIGN: STAINS AROUND A BATH FAN

WHAT IT MEANS: CONDENSATION IS FORMING INSIDE THE DUCT The stain could be caused by a roof leak, but condensation inside the duct is the most likely cause. If you live in a cold climate, there's a good chance the warm, moist air from the bathroom is condensing inside the duct and the water is seeping back down into the fan housing **(Photo 1B)**. It's soaking the drywall around the fan, and it may be ruining your fan motor or even the framing components in your attic.

WHAT TO DO: INVESTIGATE, INSULATE AND RUN THE FAN LONGER Start by checking the damper inside the fan housing and the one on the vent outside. Vents are usually on walls or roofs, but sometimes they're in the soffits. A stuck damper can lead to heavy condensation.

A bath fan duct that's not insulated (or poorly insulated) gets really cold in the attic. A cold duct filled with warm moist air is a recipe for condensation. On exceptionally cold days, that condensed water freezes and then drips back down when the temperature rises.

Even insulated ducts get cold enough for condensation to form when the fan first starts up. If a fan is run long enough, the duct will warm up and dry out. Consider replacing the wall switch with a timer switch that will run the fan for a set period of time.

2. SIGN: BULGE IN THE WASHING MACHINE HOSE

WHAT IT MEANS: THE HOSE IS READY TO BURST A bulging washing machine hose is an emergency. It may burst next year, next week or right now. But it will fail, and it won't just leak—it will gush. In just a few minutes, it can do thousands of dollars in damage.

WHAT TO DO: REPLACE RUBBER HOSES WITH BRAIDED STAINLESS STEEL Immediately turn off the valves connected to the hoses. Before your next load of laundry, you'll need to replace the hoses. New hoses are inexpensive.

While you're at the home center picking up your new hoses, invest a little more money in a pressure gauge that hooks onto a spigot or laundry room faucet. Your rubber hoses may have bulged because your water pressure was too high. It shouldn't be more than 80 psi. If it is, install a pressure-reducing valve (PRV) before you damage other appliances and fixtures in your house. If you already have a PRV, it may be set too high or due for replacement.

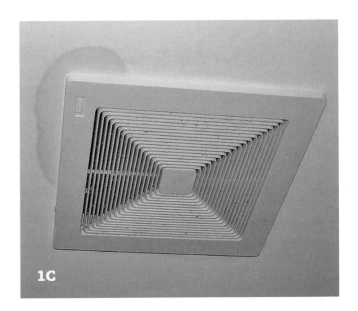

1C

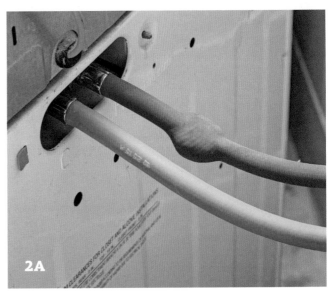

2A

2B

3A

3. SIGN: EFFLORESCENCE ON CHIMNEY BRICK

WHAT IT MEANS: TOO MUCH MOISTURE INSIDE THE CHIMNEY Efflorescence is the white material that appears on brick. It occurs when moisture moves through masonry, picking up minerals and leaving them behind in the form of tiny crystals. The minerals themselves do no harm, and a small amount of efflorescence is common. But heavy efflorescence on your chimney is a cause for concern. It's a sign of moisture inside the chimney—and when that moisture freezes, it can slowly wreck the chimney from the inside out.

Even more alarming, your flue liner could be cracked or broken, and deadly combustion gases from your furnace, fireplace or water heater may be leaking into your home.

WHAT TO DO: FIX THE CROWN OR CALL AN EXPERT Immediately have your chimney inspected by a licensed chimney sweep certified by the Chimney Safety Institute of America (CSIA). Small cracks in the crown can be sealed with an elastomeric masonry sealer, but a crumbling crown will have to be replaced. Smear on the sealant by hand, then smooth it with a brush. Search for "chimney" at familyhandyman.com for instructions on how to repair a crown and additional chimney maintenance tips.

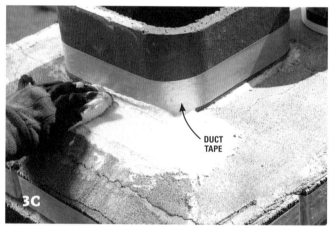

DUCT TAPE

3C

3B

3D

4. SIGN: MELTED GROMMETS ON WATER HEATER

WHAT IT MEANS: DEADLY GASES MAY BE ENTERING YOUR HOME Exhaust from a gas water heater is supposed to flow through a duct and out of the house. But sometimes exhaust doesn't flow up and out. Instead, it "backdrafts," spilling deadly carbon monoxide into the air you breathe. One sign of backdrafting is damaged plastic grommets on top of the water heater, melted by the hot exhaust. This shows that your water heater has backdrafted badly on at least one occasion—and you must take action

WHAT TO DO: TEST AND GET CARBON MONOXIDE ALARMS Test for proper drafting: Close all the windows and doors and turn on all the bath and kitchen fans to create a worst-case scenario for backdrafting. Run some hot water and light an incense stick to see if the smoke is drawn up the vent.

Sometimes the cause of backdrafting is obvious: A vent pipe may be disconnected from a vent hood, for example, or a vent may slope downward **(Photo 4C)**. Water heater vents need to slope upward at least 1/4 in. per foot. But even a properly installed vent might occasionally backdraft because of high winds or other unusual circumstances. The surest way to protect your family is to install carbon monoxide (CO) alarms. If you don't have CO alarms in your house, go get them today.

Install one on every level, outside sleeping areas and within 5 to 20 ft. of any sources of CO, such as water heaters, furnaces and fireplaces. If an alarm ever goes off, get out of the house immediately and call the HVAC repair service to correct the problem. The symptoms of CO poisoning are dizziness, headaches and vomiting. If anyone in the house is experiencing these symptoms, leave the house and call the fire department.

MELTED PLASTIC GROMMET

4A

INCENSE STICK

4B

4C

4D

Kidde

CARBON MONOXIDE ALARM

5A

ROTTEN SHEATHING

NO FLASHING

DAMAGED SIDING

5B

COMPLETELY ROTTED RIM JOIST

5C

5. SIGN: DECKING DIRECTLY UNDER THE DOOR

WHAT IT MEANS: ROT COULD BE WRECKING YOUR HOUSE

Decks that are built right up to the bottom of a door often mean trouble. Rainwater splashes off the deck up onto the door. That much water is hard to keep out. Even if the flashing holds up, water may eventually find its way through the door components. This can ruin the siding, door and interior flooring or, worse, destroy the rim joist and other framing components both inside and outside your home.

WHAT TO DO: DIVERT THE WATER AWAY

Diverting the water with gutters will help. However, the bottom line is that as long as the deck boards are up tight under the door, there's a chance of water infiltration. If you plan to build a deck, install it about 4 in. below the door threshold. And never let snow pile up against the door.

6. SIGN: THE WATER METER NEVER STOPS

WHAT IT MEANS: YOU'VE GOT A LEAK

If all the faucets and plumbing fixtures in your house are turned off and the low-flow indicator on your water meter continues to measure running water, you're wasting water and money.

WHAT TO DO: LOOK FOR THE LEAK

Indoor leaks usually create obvious signs. Look for water stains on walls or ceilings or a puddle on the floor. Also listen to toilets—a worn-out flapper on the flush valve creates a hiss and is a common cause of slow, constant water flow.

Outdoor leaks usually seep into the ground and can go on for years without being noticed. If your water meter is outside the house (warm climates only), the first step is to check the waterline between the house and the meter. Shut off the main water valve at the house and check the meter. If it's still registering water flow, you know there's a leak between the meter and the house. Fixing this problem will likely require some excavation.

A leaking water spigot may go unnoticed if a hose is attached that runs out into the yard or garden. If you find a spigot that keeps dribbling water, a new valve seat washer is probably the solution. If the spigot leaks at the top near the handle, replace the packing nut washer. To see how, search for "faucet repair" at familyhandyman.com.

Irrigation systems are another cause of hidden leaks. Check for irrigation leaks by shutting off the valve in the house that feeds the irrigation system. If the meter stops spinning, you've found the problem. Narrow the search even more by looking for wet spots in the yard or for areas of grass that are especially green. A malfunctioning zone valve is usually the cause of the problem.

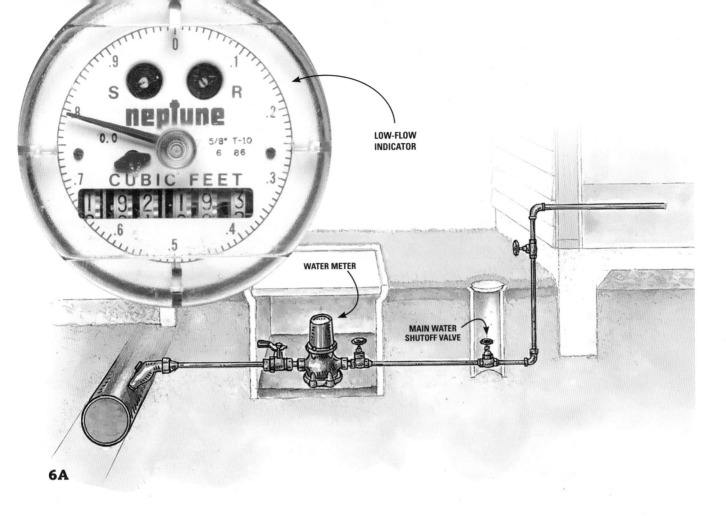

LOW-FLOW
INDICATOR

WATER METER

MAIN WATER
SHUTOFF VALVE

6A

6B

6C

Sharpening Knives and Tools

Use these tips to get the proper edge on your tools so that your chores in the kitchen and in the shop are safer and accomplished more efficiently.

If sharpening your dull kitchen knives or blunt chisels sounds like drudgery, we can help. We'll show you some cool sharpening tips and tools that'll motivate you to tune up the edges on all the dull tools and knives in your shop as well as in your kitchen.

We don't have space here to teach every sharpening step, but we've collected tips to help you get started on the most common sharpening tasks. For more detailed sharpening information, go to familyhandyman.com and search for the topic you're interested in.

1. FLATTEN THE BACKS OF CHISELS AND PLANE BLADES

It's impossible to get a sharp edge on a chisel or a plane if the back of the blade isn't flat. If you're using the glass and sandpaper method of sharpening (tip 9), press the back side of the blade against the sandpaper and move the blade back and forth, being careful to hold it perfectly flat. Sand the back of each blade until it's uniformly shiny along the cutting edge. Do this with each grit as you move through the progression from coarse to fine. Use the same technique with natural or diamond sharpening stones.

2. KEEP A HAND-HELD SHARPENER IN YOUR KITCHEN DRAWER

Most of the time you don't need a power tool or an expensive knife-sharpening system to keep a workable edge on your kitchen knives. Regular use of a handheld sharpener will be fine. The Wusthof sharpener we're using works great. Other brands may work equally well, but we haven't tried them. The sharpener has carbide steel rods to shape the blade, and diamond rods to finish the edge. Follow the instructions to quickly sharpen kitchen knives that have standard beveled edges. You'll have to use another sharpening tool if your knives have unusual or asymmetrical angles.

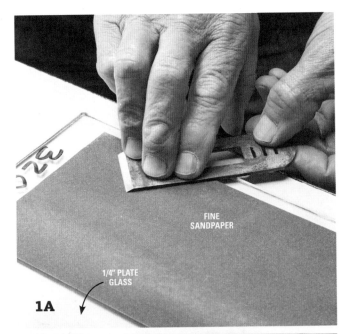

FINE SANDPAPER

1/4" PLATE GLASS

1A

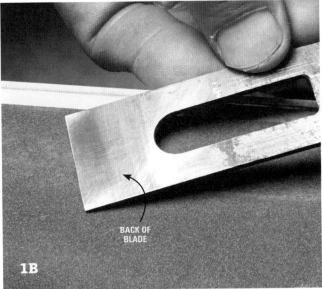

BACK OF BLADE

1B

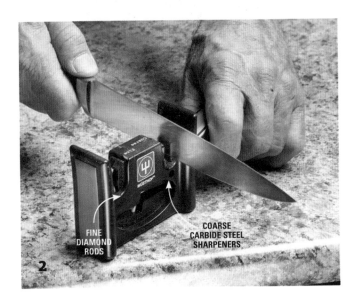

FINE DIAMOND RODS

COARSE CARBIDE STEEL SHARPENERS

2

DIAMOND STEEL SHARPENING ROD

3. SHARPEN SERRATED BREAD KNIVES WITH A DIAMOND STEEL SHARPENER

The only hard part of this tip is finding the right size diamond steel. The curve of the steel has to fit the scallops on your serrated knife. Take your knife to a cookware store and find a diamond-coated steel that matches the scallop size on your knife. If you're shopping online, you can find the diameter you need by holding drill bits against the scallops. Then use this dimension to order the right diameter sharpener. Another option is to buy a tapered, pocket-size diamond steel that is able to accommodate a variety of different scallop sizes.

You'll notice that one side of the knife blade is flat and the other is tapered. Sharpen only the tapered side. Starting at one end, sharpen each scallop with two or three strokes, matching the original angle. When you're done, run the knife through corrugated cardboard to remove metal filings.

4. SHARPEN HATCHETS AND AXES WITH A FILE

You don't need a power tool to sharpen hatchets or axes, just a sharp mill bastard file with a handle. Buy a good-quality American-made file brand like Nicholson. And pick up a file brush while you're at it. You'll use the file brush to clean the metal filings from the file's teeth to keep it cutting well.

Clamp your hatchet to your bench or in a vise. Then file the edges, following the original angle. The file cuts only on the push stroke, so don't go back and forth with a sawing motion. Start your stroke on one end of the blade and push the file up and across, applying a little pressure. Make three or four passes on one side, then do the same on the other side. Keep the number of passes equal for both sides. File until the edge is uniformly sharp. Look directly at the sharp edge with a strong overhead light. Dull spots will show up as bright reflections.

File hatchets or axes used for cutting or felling wood at about a 25- to 30-degree angle on each side. Splitting axes work better with a blunter angle, so for them you should increase the angle to about 35 to 40 degrees. Filing will get your hatchet or ax blade back in good shape, but if you want it really sharp, you'll have to follow up with a stone or diamond hone.

MILL BASTARD FILE

5. TOUCH UP YOUR KNIVES WITH A HONING STEEL

You've probably seen a chef on a cooking show brandishing a knife and a steel like a samurai and thought it was just for pros. But a honing steel isn't hard to use and is perfect for restoring a sharp cutting edge to your knives. You can't fully restore a dull blade with a steel, but you'll be surprised how quickly you can take a slightly dulled edge to almost razor sharpness with just a few strokes.

The safest method for using a steel is to rest the tip on a surface that's not too slippery, like a wooden cutting board. Then pull the knife down and across, alternating sides. Keep the knife at about a 25-degree angle so you're just tuning up the edge. The steel doesn't actually sharpen. It simply straightens out the wavy edge so the knife slices through material better. Eventually you'll have to resharpen the knife. But for between-sharpening tune-ups, you can't beat a steel. You can buy a steel wherever good knives are sold.

6. TUNE UP CARBIDE ROUTER BITS WITH A DIAMOND PADDLE

Chipped or severely dulled carbide router bits require professional sharpening, but you can restore a slightly dulled edge with a diamond paddle. The paddle shown here is relatively inexpensive and is available online and at sporting goods and woodworking stores.

To avoid changing the cutting profile of the bit, sharpen the backs of the cutters only. A handy method is to clamp the diamond paddle to your workbench and move the bit back and forth over the diamond-impregnated surface. Start with the coarser-grit side of the paddle. Then switch to the fine side. The sharpened carbide should have a consistent shiny band along the cutting edge.

HONING STEEL

5

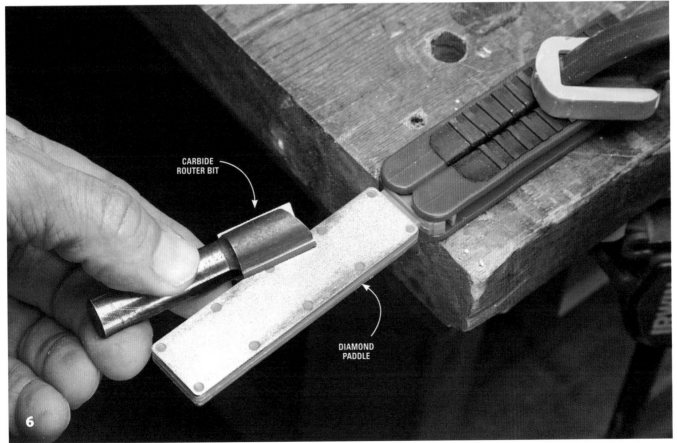

CARBIDE ROUTER BIT

DIAMOND PADDLE

6

7. A 1-IN. BELT SANDER IS A VERSATILE SHARPENING TOOL

Most carpenters know that a belt sander is a good ad hoc tool for getting a reasonably acceptable edge on a dull chisel. And knife-makers and professional sharpeners often use special belt grinders to shape and sharpen blades. You can get many of the benefits of a professional belt grinder for a fraction of the cost with a 1 x 30-in. benchtop belt sander. The one shown here is from Grizzly Industrial. Buy 180- and 240-grit belts and you'll be set for serious knife sharpening. Plus, you can use the belt sander to grind other tools like axes and chisels and to sand small woodworking projects.

For really dull knives, start with a 180-grit belt and finish with a 240-grit belt. Practice on an inexpensive knife until you get the feel of holding a knife at the correct angle as you move it across the belt. Try to maintain the angle that's on your knife. This is usually about 20 degrees. For a razor-sharp edge, buy a leather belt along with honing compound and mount it on your sander for the final sharpening step.

8. DON'T THROW AWAY THOSE OLD DRILL BITS

If you've ever tried to sharpen a drill bit on a grinder, you know what a hit-and-miss proposition it is. It's hard to maintain the correct angle, keep the chisel point centered and avoid burning the bit.

Drill Doctor offers several versions of a special tool that makes drill-bit sharpening almost foolproof. The least expensive tool is perfect for the home shop. You simply follow the instructions for chucking the drill bit into the tool and then rotate the bit on the grinding wheel to sharpen. Go to drilldoctor.com to compare features of the different models and to get tons of great information on techniques for sharpening drill bits.

9. FOOLPROOF CHISEL AND PLANE SHARPENING

There's nothing like working with a razor-sharp plane or chisel, and nothing more frustrating than trying to use dull options. Arkansas or Japanese stones are the traditional sharpening tools, but they're expensive to buy and take practice and skill to use. An easy and inexpensive way to get great results without stones or much practice does exist. The key to success is a honing guide, which ensures a consistent bevel. The guide shown (sold at woodworking stores) works for both chisel and plane blades. You'll also need a 12-in. square of 1/4-in. plate glass to provide a perfectly flat honing surface. You can order one at any hardware store, but be sure to have the sharp edges sanded smooth. You'll glue sandpaper to the glass and use it like a sharpening stone.

Use spray adhesive to attach half sheets of silicone carbide sandpaper to the glass. Cover one side with 220- and 320-grit

1" FINE SANDING BELT

7

paper and the other with 400- and 600-grit. The sharpening
angle is determined by how far you extend the blade before
clamping it to the guide. Dimensions on the side of the guide
show where to set chisels and planes to maintain 25- and
30-degree angles.

Clamp the blade in the guide and roll it back and forth on
the coarsest paper until the edge is uniformly shiny. It should
take only 15 to 20 seconds. Repeat this process with each
progressively finer grit.

10. IT'S EASY TO KEEP YOUR SPADE BITS SHARP

Most of us grab a spade bit instead of our expensive Forstner
bits when it's rough material that needs drilling. But this
abuse takes a toll. Luckily, a spade bit doesn't have to be
sharpened with precision to work better. A few strokes along
the bottom with a file and you're back in business.

Clamp the bit in a vise and file the cutting edges, making
sure to maintain the existing angle. A tapered triangular file
works well for many sizes of spade bit.

8

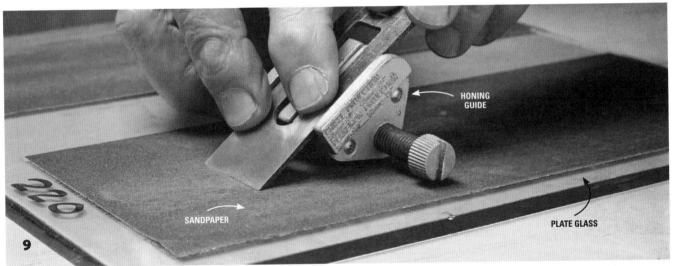

HONING GUIDE

SANDPAPER

PLATE GLASS

9

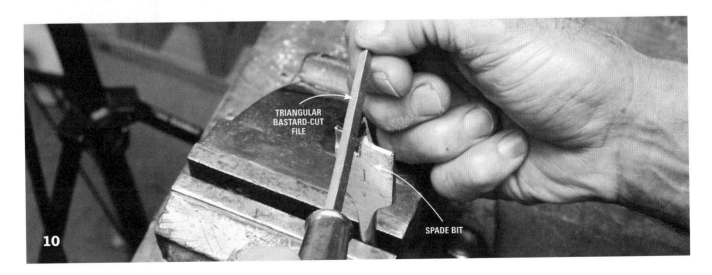

TRIANGULAR BASTARD-CUT FILE

SPADE BIT

10

BOOT TRAY

1

Eight Ways to Pet-Proof Your House

Even the best-trained pet can have a bad day. But you can keep the damage to a minimum with these hints and tips.

1. AVOID FLOOR DAMAGE

This Australian shepherd puppy loves water. He even plays in his water bowl. But an inexpensive plastic boot tray placed under the water bowl catches the water and protects the floor. Pick up a boot tray at a home center or hardware store.

2. CAT-PROOF POTTED PLANTS

If you were a cat and you saw a potted plant, you might have an epiphany: "Why go all the way to the litter box when this potted plant is so much closer?" And then you would use it. But you're the parent and the solution is simple. Cover the soil around each plant with decorative rock. Thwarted by the rocks, your cat will rediscover the litter box. You can buy small bags of decorative rock at a craft store.

2

3

4

5

3. PET-PROOF SCREEN

If your dog or cat destroys window screen, replace regular screen with pet screen. It's available at home centers and at most places that do screen replacements. You can buy the pet screen and install it yourself, or take the screen and frame in and have it done for you. Pet screen is much stronger than regular window screen so it resists tearing and other damage. And it's inexpensive.

4. AUTOMATIC ACCIDENT CLEANUP

If you have a dog with some gastrointestinal issues, consider investing in the Bissell SpotBot. After you scoop up the big stuff, you just plug in the SpotBot, put it over the spot, push the button and walk away. After it shuts off, you simply empty and rinse the reservoir. You can buy a SpotBot at home centers and online retailers.

5. KEEP YOUR CAT OFF THE COUNTERTOP

"Sssssscat!!" You can yell at a cat to get off a countertop, and that might work for a while, but the clever feline will likely be back on the counter as soon as you leave the kitchen. For a better and more permanent solution, try the PetSafe Ssscat motion-activated spray (sold online).

Basically, an electronic head sits on top of an aerosol can. The head—which requires four AAA batteries—has a built-in motion sensor and sprays a short blast of an odorless gas anytime kitty walks in front of it. The spray won't hurt, but your cat will sure think twice about jumping on the counter again. Be sure to buy extra refill cans if your cat is particularly stubborn.

7A

CHICKEN WIRE

7B

6. ENTRYWAY TOWEL

Hang a dog-dedicated towel near your entry doors for when the mutt comes in with wet or muddy paws. Wipe those paws right there in the entryway before Fido steps inside and your floors will stay much cleaner.

7. STOP THE DIGGING

Some dogs love to dig in the dirt, especially around shrubs. You can throw the soil back into the hole, but the dog will likely return to dig it up again. To permanently solve the problem, rake back the mulch and lay chicken wire over the ground. We used U-shape landscape fabric staples to hold the mesh in place. Then we covered the mesh with the mulch. It worked great! No more filling holes under the shrubs.

8. OUT OF SIGHT, OUT OF MIND

Does your dog jump on the windowsills to bark at dogs he sees outside? This can scratch the finish and even break a window. To solve the problem, put privacy film on the lower sashes of all the windows facing the street. The film is sold at home centers. It lets in sunlight, but the dog can't see those canine trespassers anymore. Life will be much quieter!

WINDOW FILM

WATER

8

Portable-Tool Battery Smarts

Lithium ion (Li-ion) batteries are expensive. So get with the program and follow these care tips to get the longest life and best performance out of them.

- Li-ion batteries can handle only 800 to 1,000 charges. Don't recharge a battery if you've used it for just a few minutes.
- Don't leave them in the car—either in the cabin or in the trunk. Heat (above 140 degrees) and subzero cold can reduce battery life by 15%.
- Storing a battery in direct sunlight can really heat it up, so shield it from the sun.
- Don't store a discharged battery that has less than one-half charge. Give it a full charge and then store it.
- If your tool was sold with two batteries and you're a part-time user, stick the extra battery in the refrigerator. It'll last for years and you'll have a new one to use when the first one dies.

Prevent Clamp Stains with Wax Paper

Moisture in glue triggers a reaction between iron and chemicals in wood (called tannins). The result is black stains on the wood, especially with tannin-rich woods like oak or walnut. A strip of wax paper acts as a barrier between the clamp and the wood. You can also use wax paper to keep glue off your cauls.